DON'T FORGET TO WRITE

The true story of an evacuee and her family.

In June 1940, ten-year-old Pam Hobbs took the long journey from her council home in Leigh-on-Sea to faraway rural Derbyshire. In some foster homes Pam found a second family, with babies to look after, car rides and picnics, but other billets took a more sinister turn, as the adults found it easy to exploit the children in their care. Returning home, the war was far from over. Making do with rations, dodging bombs and helping with the war effort, it was a time that was full of overwhelming hardship and devastation; yet also of kindness and humour, resilience and courage.

DON'T FORGET TO WRITE

DON'T FORGET TO WRITE

by

Pam Hobbs

Magna Large Print Books
Long Preston, North Yorkshire,
BD23 4ND, England.

British Library Cataloguing in Publication Data.

Hobbs, Pam
    Don't forget to write.

    A catalogue record of this book is
    available from the British Library

    ISBN   978-0-7505-3349-2

First published in Great Britain in 2009 by Ebury Press
an imprint of Ebury Publishing
A Random House Group Company

Copyright © Pam Hobbs 2009

Cover illustration © mirrorpix

Pam Hobbs has asserted her right to be identified as the author
of this work in accordance with the Copyright, Designs and
Patents Act, 1988

Published in Large Print 2011 by arrangement with
Ebury Publishing
one of the publishers in the Random House Group

Magna Large Print is an imprint of Library Magna Books Ltd.

Printed and bound in Great Britain by
T.J. (International) Ltd., Cornwall, PL28 8RW

For Michael, whose love and encouragement make all things possible

Contents

Prologue

In June 1940, on a Friday afternoon, my sister Iris came home with a letter that changed my life. It informed us that schools on our part of England's southeast coast would be closed, and their pupils evacuated to safer areas. Ten months earlier, at the outset of war between Britain and Germany, some one and a half million children from major cities had been evacuated. Now it was our turn, because we lived just sixty miles from German-occupied France, and an enemy invasion appeared imminent. Iris was eleven; I was ten.

On the following Sunday morning, the letter said, children were to assemble in their classes, wearing name tags, and carrying a small case apiece containing a change of clothes. Few families on our council estate owned suitcases, so most had brown paper carrier bags or pillowcases. We, and some others from Kent Avenue, put our worldly belongings in burlap sandbags provided by my father, who had been using them to reinforce buildings along the seafront.

I wanted my mother to come with us to the school, but she said it would be too hard.

Instead, we kissed goodbye at the garden gate, and my father walked with us. Joined by neighbours along the way, ours was a small army of children – some as young as five years – with sandbags slung over our shoulders. At the school, Dad told us to be sure to stick together. Then, hurriedly wiping his eyes, he turned and was lost in the crowd. It was two eventful years before I saw him again.

I don't know of a parent today who would send their child to live with strangers, selected not for their suitability but because they had a spare bed. But, this was seventy years ago. Urged on by posters and pamphlets, our parents were convinced they were sending us out of harm's way.

Buses shuttled us between our school and the nearest major railway station, where we boarded trains heading north. Then, from various stops in Derbyshire, coaches took us in small groups to outlying communities. In a village called Charbury, fifteen or twenty of us lined up in its one-room school for prospective foster parents to pick us over, much as they would select fruit at the market. Pretty little girls and strong boys were the first to be chosen. Iris and I were neither.

During my two years as an evacuee, I stayed in four different homes, throughout central England. Some of my 'pretend parents' loved me as if I was their own. One couple showed me what it was like to feel unwanted, to live with hostility and complete indifference to my welfare, and to be hungry.

With the threat of invasion over, in June 1942 I returned home to Essex. But the battle was far from over. As the rest of our family worked towards winning the war, it was left to my mother and me to keep things going on the home front. This meant queues, queues and more queues. Critical food shortages had us experimenting with nettle tea, and meatless stews. And let's not forget the ubiquitous Spam, which we disguised in more ways than I'd have thought possible. Night after night we slept in our garden shelter. We endured regular bombs and incendiaries, and ack-ack guns outside our house. And then, just when we thought it was all over, we were introduced to 'doodlebugs' and V2 rockets.

The pealing of church bells on 7 May 1945 heralded Victory in Europe; Japan surrendered three months later. In England we had little to show for it. Serious shortages of food, coal and housing continued for years. And with peace came the unwelcome realisation that our lives would never be the same again. For my part I had grown strong and independent. I developed a deep appreciation for the English countryside and a passion for writing that stemmed from the long descriptive letters I sent home. Once I was home I experienced an inherent rest-lessness that couldn't be stilled, and itchy feet that have taken me far.

This is the story of one child's war. My war, as I remember it.

Note: Some names have been changed.

PART I

Evacuation

CHAPTER ONE

No Peace in Our Time

Just as all of us know where we were on 9/11, and when John F Kennedy was assassinated, so everyone who was in Britain on 3 September 1939 can remember exactly what they were doing on that fateful day when the Second World War was declared. We were a family of nine: seven girls and our parents, Ede and Jack Hobbs, living on England's south-east coast.

Located on the Thames Estuary, bordered with thick black Essex mud, Leigh-on-Sea was a tiny fishing village when my mother moved there with her two young daughters during the First World War. Soon the village was to expand up the hill and inland, where post-war council housing estates grew on former orchards and dairy farms to provide rental homes for working-class tenants.

Streets on our particular estate were fancifully named after English counties, to give the impression of meadows and open spaces and wild flowers growing in abundance. We had Sussex and Surrey, Norfolk and Suffolk, whose houses in truth resembled

17

dreary army barracks in orderly straight lines. On Kent Avenue, at number 19, this Sunday morning saw seven of us, and our cat Clarabelle, huddled around the wireless in our tiny front room. Nine years old at the time, I was the youngest. My eldest sister, Edie, in her early twenties, was married and living at Stanford-Le-Hope, Essex. Another sister, Kath, was with her husband in their London home.

Although I didn't appreciate the full impact of this broadcast scheduled for eleven o'clock, I understood its seriousness. As we did when the King spoke on Christmas Day, now we sat in respectful silence. Dad had come in from the garden, leaving his wellies on the back porch – shirt sleeves rolled to his elbows because it was a hot day, his tweed trousers held up by both belt and braces, and his worn chequered cap clenched between soiled hands. Mum, short and comfortably plump, her face flushed from the heat of the kitchen where she had already started on our roast beef lunch, sat with hands crossed above her lap. There, Clarabelle, her jet-black cat with cabbage-green eyes, tried to relax, but sensing the tension kept turning in circles – a precarious feat in so limited a space.

Prime Minister Neville Chamberlain began his momentous speech, his voice tinny as it percolated through our cheap wireless.

'This morning,' he said, 'the British Am-

18

bassador in Berlin handed the German Government a final note stating that unless we heard from them by eleven o'clock that they were prepared at once to withdraw their troops from Poland, a state of war would exist between us.'

As one, we turned our eyes to the walnut clock ticking loudly on the mantelpiece, although we knew full well that eleven o'clock had come and gone.

'I have to tell you now,' Chamberlain continued, 'that no such undertaking has been received, and that consequently this country is at war with Germany.'

It was expected, had been for months, but this didn't lessen the shock of hearing our nation's prime minister put it into words. In silence, my father slowly retrieved a hand-rolled cigarette from behind his ear, took a match from its yellow Swan Vestas box and, on the third try, with trembling hands he lit his smoke. My mother wiped her perspiring face with her apron, holding it there for a few minutes while she composed herself.

'Poor Mrs Hardy,' she said at last, of our neighbour who had sons of call-up age. 'That's it, then,' she added briskly, puffing herself together. 'If this Hitler bloke comes our way, he'll have me to answer to.'

With no more to say on the subject, she marched off to deal with her roast beef and Yorkshire pud.

I don't think 'this Hitler bloke' was exactly quaking in his boots over Mum's threat, nor at the time did he have thoughts of coming our way. He was too busy gobbling up continental Europe. For Adolf Hitler, head of Germany's Nazi regime that had come into power six years earlier, it was take-back time.

Following their defeat in the First World War, Germany had been forced to give land to France. Now Hitler's armies were relentlessly on the march, reclaiming what he deemed to be rightfully parts of Germany. Already they had reoccupied their formerly owned Saar Valley and Rhineland, annexed German-speaking Austria and parts of Czechoslovakia.

The summer of 1939 brought the signing of a Nazi–Soviet pact. In England, army, navy and air force reservists were recalled. And in the early hours of 1 September 1939, as German troops invaded Poland, a government plan to evacuate hundreds of thousands of London children to the country was put into effect.

We didn't need modern-day mobiles or BlackBerries or even television sets to tell us all this. Our family didn't even own a telephone. But what we did have was the BBC, and the sombre voices of its newsreaders. Although they did not identify themselves by name until 1940, when the change from anonymity was made to prevent German propagandists from pirating the airwaves, we knew who they were. I doubt there was a person in Britain who wasn't familiar with the voices of Bruce Belfrage and Alvar Lidell, both of whom kept their emotions harnessed while reporting momentous happenings in Europe. It was Lidell who had informed us of Edward VIII's abdication in 1937, and introduced Chamberlain's declaration of war on 3 September. And Belfrage, who failed to keep excitement from his voice in July 1942, when telling us of the British victory at El Alamein.

Our two wireless sets, each the size of a small suitcase, stood importantly on their own shelves in our kitchen and front room. If they were on at the same time they crackled noisily, causing constant arguments and wall thumping and shouts of *turn that bloody thing off*.

Better still was the cinema news. For many an adult, the double feature films, shown continuously for the price of admission, were almost incidental. The real reason for a visit to the 'flicks' during those traumatic weeks leading to the Second World War was a few minutes of news, which at that time was largely devoted to Hitler's armies jackbooting their way across the continent.

It was courtesy of Pathé News, with the cockerel crowing to herald its opening shot, that we witnessed the prime minister returning from Munich a year previously. That's when he waved a written agreement before the cameras, while informing the world there would be 'peace in our time'. In the Odeon, on Southend High Street, this particular clip was met with jeers.

My father, Walter John Hobbs (known as Jack) was no stranger to war. Born a cockney in London's East End, he joined the Royal Navy during the First World War in 1914 aged seventeen. Willing and strong, he was an obvious candidate to become a stoker, firing the great coal furnaces that drove the fleet. Aboard HMS *Implacable* he had his first taste of battle at the Dardanelles. He wrote a fascinating diary of the famous battle from his viewpoint, recording exactly how much coal the *Implacable* took on, how many casualties were brought on board and vivid descriptions of their injuries. I have it still, with its faded writing on yellowing pages and the hard cover smudged, probably with coal dust.

As that war progressed, fuel oil replaced coal, forcing my father to learn new skills that saw him promoted to petty officer. He looked forward to a steady career in the navy, expecting to become an engineer officer. But things went horribly wrong. In 1919, a few months after war's end, the British Government ordered its navy's first cutbacks. More severe reductions came three years later, when completely serviceable ships were sent to the scrapyards, and their crews informed they were no longer needed. Jack was among them. Gone were the happy homecomings from the Far East with silks for his wife, and exotic toys for his daughters. Now he was penniless, without a pension or job prospects above that of a labourer.

Finding no work in Leigh, he travelled to London on an early-morning train to the great coking ovens of Beckton Gas Works near the docks. Here, former naval stokers – skilled, strong men who knew how to get the most heat from coal – transformed it into coke and gas for London households. The pay was reasonable, the work hard and hours long, often including weekends. Also, the train journey from Leigh proved expensive, in spite of so-called 'workmen's fares' available to anyone travelling in the early morning.

Somewhere around 1930, Southend Borough Council took advantage of the Labour Government's post-war subsidies to develop a housing estate north of Leigh's established community. One of my father's stepbrothers was an onsite foreman. He took one look at Dad's muscled arms, and gave him work as a hod carrier. Not exactly what he had dreamed of as a career move, it meant climbing ladders all day with a hod full of bricks on his shoulder. On the plus side, the estate could be reached by bike, and a regular pay packet earned locally was incentive enough now that his children numbered seven. A bricklayer by 1939, he no longer had shoulders blistered raw from carrying a fully loaded hod, but at forty-two he was a quiet, disillusioned man. He loved his family and his prolific vegetable garden, his favourite football teams and his local. And he was consumed with sadness that he was not with Britain's naval fleet in this his country's hour of need.

My mother too was a cockney, born Edith May Thurley in Camberwell Green, which wasn't green at all, but grey and dirty, its streets littered with toffee papers and squashed cigarette boxes, and newspapers greasy from the fish and chips they had kept warm earlier. She loved London, forever saying she was more of a Londoner than the lions in Trafalgar Square. She loved its bright lights at night and busy streets by day, and noisy markets where stall-owners showed off their inborn cockney humour. She loved its royal parks. As a young mother, she would take the first two of her seven daughters into these verdant oases to feed the ducks, and picnic on neat lawns alongside nannies pushing their charges in elegant bassinets.

Mum's move to Leigh was not planned. Living in Greenwich in 1917 she was awakened one sultry night by her baby's screams. According to the story retold over the years, her eyes went first to Rose's bleeding arm and then to a huge grey rat scuttling into a hole in the floor. A picture postcard from a friend on holiday at Southend stood on her mantelpiece. It depicted a bright, cheerful place, with a beach and the sea and nice clean air. Ede reasoned that if Elsie went there for day trips and weekends, it couldn't be too far from London. And whatever it was like there, surely it would be better for them than a rat-infested Greenwich.

By dawn the decision was made, her pram loaded with her infants' clothes, her own belongings stuffed into a bulging canvas bag. Three hours later she was on a train, steaming out of Liverpool Street station. Her ticket read Southend-on-Sea, but as the grime of London gave way to green fields and a high tide in the estuary, she decided to disembark at a quiet little fishing community with cockleshells piled up beside bright green sheds, and a huddle of cottages on each side of its main street.

This was foreign territory for my mother. Despite her brave and optimistic beginning, she hated her damp cottage across from the sheds, the constant smell of cockles, the clattering steam trains hissing past her front door on their way to her dear old London.

There was no greenery down there by the sea, only tiny row houses bent with old age, spilling on to a broken sidewalk. Whether they backed on to the sea or the railway line, all were smothered in soot from the trains.

This was the domain of fisher-families. On higher ground above the Old Town, houses were far more substantial, nestled in pretty gardens with inspired views of the estuary below. But Mum saw none of this. Her small world was the village itself, so inviting from the train window, and now closing in on her like a heavy dark cloud. Rain or shine she would walk the length of the tiny community twice a day – once to the dark little general shop, and once to watch the red-sailed cockle barges come home with their catch. Arriving in the Old Town along a man-made creek, the fishermen lowered planks from their decks to the squishy black mud, then ran ashore with buckets of cockles swinging from yokes across their shoulders. In their hip-boots, and heavy jerseys, they were doing exactly what their fathers and grand-fathers had done before them. The Met-calfes, the Osbornes, Attridges and Denches were Old Leigh families of several genera-tions, and wanted little to do with a young woman who wouldn't join them in their pubs for a friendly pint.

The war was won, Jack went to sea for months on end and Ede told herself she could no longer afford to waste time yearning for her beloved London. She had her future to plan. A third baby was due within weeks, and with the dampness of Leigh Old Town proving unhealthy for young Edie and Rose, she rented an old terrace house halfway up the bill. On this wickedly steep Church Hill, she was closer to the bright new shops on Leigh Broadway, yet enjoyed panoramic views of the sea from the front. She was within walking distance of the Old Town's railway station, as well as a bus service into the carnival atmosphere that was Southend. She bonded immediately with neighbours, former Londoners like herself, and found a new contentment in her expanded world.

When summer's heat in London became too much, her friend Elsie sometimes came for a weekend. She asked if a couple of her workmates could visit as paying guests. Ede enjoyed their company so much, she decided to look for more. And so, on a summer's morning with Kath, daughter number three, happily gurgling at passers-by from her pram in the front garden, she removed all traces of her personal life from the bedroom with its lovely view, and slipped a To Let sign in the window.

In winter, Ede spent her evenings happily bent over a second-hand treadle machine from Singers on the Broadway. At first she made little dresses with matching knickers and hair bands for her daughters. Soon, though, her sewing became a business, as she produced outfits for kiddies whose mothers stopped her to admire the children's clothes. When the fabric shop on Leigh Broadway displayed her creations alongside their latest patterns, she had strangers knocking at the door with material in hand saying Millie up at Singers thought she wouldn't mind.

My mother was a happy young woman. Her daughters were a joy. She missed her husband, but appreciated his love for the sea, and prospects of a naval career. What's more it enabled her to save for the future. Her dreams were not overly ambitious: she would own a large semi-detached house on the seafront in Westcliff – an upmarket community between Leigh and Southend – operate it as a Bed and Breakfast when Jack was away, yet still have a comfortable home for her growing family. Almost daily she stared at the mounting total in her post office savings book, and knew this was a possible dream.

Then, without warning, her lovely bubble burst. With Jack's involuntary departure from the Royal Navy and his resultant depression, there was no room for holidaymakers in the house. No time for sewing either, as more daughters were born. Her savings disappeared, along with her dreams. In the mid-

1930s she and Jack moved their few furnishings, and seven daughters, to the beginnings of the new council estate, which to Ede was in the middle of nowhere. With no friends nearby, and an infrequent bus service to the shops, she turned to creating a spectacular garden, discovering to her sheer disbelief that she had a green thumb.

Now in 1939, had you asked her how everything was, she would have truthfully told you she was 'Doing nicely, thanks.' Her family was in good health. Jack was steadily employed by a small builder, while Rose, Violet and Connie contributed towards their keep. A frequent bus service from the estate to Leigh Broadway made life much easier now. Of great importance, too, she had become a better than competent rose grower.

'Have you seen little Mrs Hobbs's front garden? Just like a park,' passers-by would say to their friends living two or three streets over. In summer evenings and at weekends, they would return with their neighbours to point it out. Many went home with cuttings to start their own rose bushes, few of which bloomed as well as Ede's, nurtured with such love.

While her front garden brought admirers from all over the estate to see her huge cross-bred blooms, the house's rear was a private haven drenched in the perfume of hundreds more roses, few of them smaller than your average cabbage. Climbers clung merrily to trellises and arbours, a giant elderberry tree draped itself over the coal shed to disguise its ugliness. A rockery halfway down the garden divided it in two. The back half belonged to Dad, who never seemed to stop in his planting and harvesting of vegetables. His tomatoes were so sweet and juicy we'd sit on the garden bench and eat them straight from the vine. His new potatoes, with home-made mint sauce, transformed even the cheapest cut of spring lamb into a delicacy.

At the end of the garden, beside the back gate, a pet cemetery had been established, with small wooden crosses indicating the graves of Tommy Tortoise, several birds and Horace Hedgehog, who was accidentally speared with a fork during his winter's hibernation. Another personal marker is probably there still, beneath the arbour at the foot of the crazy-paved path dissecting the garden. Before the cement dried, Dad used the upturned handle of a metal bucket to draw a sailboat with the name *JackEde* on its bow. It is the boat he had planned to build, when we were little and my parents still had dreams.

CHAPTER TWO

The Phoney War

In the years leading to that fateful September day, Mum had often counted her blessings. Her husband's lack of ambition was sometimes cause for frustration, but she'd learned to accept it. She had a comfortable home, with everything exactly as she wanted. Her garden was a treat. And her daughters were good girls, every one of them.

Ede was proud of the way they had turned out. The eldest, Edie, had made her a grandmother last year by giving birth to beautiful twin babies. Some shock that was, there being two and all. Sam, the proud young father, cycled all the way from Stanford-Le-Hope to tell us they had a son. Then, some hours later he was back to say there was a girl too. This made me an aunty at the ripe old age of eight, to Billy and Jean.

We didn't see much of them after that. Too busy, I suppose, and public transport from the country being erratic at best. Now, with the advent of war, Mum decided they would do okay in this war. Sam's job at Shell Oil's refinery would make him exempt from the forces, and they were comfortable in a nice little house on the village's outskirts. So, we shouldn't worry about Edie and Sam in these troubled times. They were good at looking after themselves.

After Edie was Rose, and why she wasn't going steady by then was a conundrum to our parents, who viewed her single status with disappointment. Both Rose and Edie had met Sam when his aunt invited them to tea for the sole purpose of an introduction. Twenty minutes later Rose returned home, saying the chocolate eclairs were lovely, and the aunt was a nice woman, but Edie was welcome to the young man. Her work as a dental receptionist afforded little opportunity to meet Mr Right. Doubtless her good looks and friendly disposition brought a few hopefuls her way, but nobody who was worth a second look.

Next down the line, Kath, had met her husband Wally at Southend's Kursaal. Wally was a Londoner and, like so many, escaped that city's grime for a day by the sea at weekends. The Kursaal, with its bumper cars and games of chance, was a magnet to young people. An added incentive for locals was free admission, if they bought a bag of peanuts.

A cabinet maker by trade, Wally was a kind and generous soul. As war clouds gathered overhead Kath moved to East Ham to be

closer to him, and worked at Plessey's, manufacturing wireless parts in their Ilford
factory. Most weekends they visited us at 19
Kent.

I loved those Sundays. Iris and I would run
down to Chalkwell Station to meet them, so
we could ride home in the luxury of their
taxi. As if that wasn't enough, along the way
we were given first choice of sweets and
chocolates they brought for the family.

A couple of weeks before Chamberlain
made his dramatic speech, Kath and Wally
were married in a Southend register office.
Years later, Rose remembered it well
because the dress she chose so carefully for
the event was worn by the bride – who had
left her own outfit in the train from London.

Violet and Connie had few cares before the
outbreak of war. At sixteen and fourteen
both of them worked in shops: Vi in a bakery
on Leigh Broadway and Connie at a Southend grocer's. I best recall Violet in those pre-
war months for her Mickey Mouse cakes
with chocolate ears. Day-old bread and
cakes at the bakery were offered at half price,
and anything left unsold at closing time was
given to the staff. Eccles cakes, iced currant
buns and sponge rolls gave us some lovely
teas while she worked there, but it was the
chocolate Mickeys that had me drooling.

As a child Vi had attended one of the area's
Open Air Schools, designed to give sickly

youngsters lots of fresh air in the classrooms. Now, as a young adult, she no longer suffered bouts of pneumonia, but remained a delicate-looking girl, her pale face framed by golden curls. Looks can be deceptive though, for when it came to dancing she had more energy than the rest of us put together.

Connie was our daredevil. She was the one who was forever cutting her knees and scraping her elbows – who climbed trees to their highest branches, and thought it funny to knock on some old lady's door then run away before the poor soul struggled to open it. Unlike Violet, Connie was robust from the day she entered the world. I should add that she was a born businesswoman. According to my mother, her fifth child's first words weren't the usual Mumma or Dadda, but 'How much?' – I can believe it.

In the summer of her sixth birthday Connie operated her first lemonade stand. Strategically located halfway up Church Hill, it catered to gasping travellers coming off the trains. By the time she was ten she was carrying suitcases up the hill for a penny a time. Her wild heather and lavender tied into sprigs sold well outside the station; Guy Fawkes Day saw her there again with me dressed as the guy stuffed into an old pram. Still, her most lucrative enterprise was her Christmas choir. Featuring her sisters and the neighbours' children, they always sang two full carols before knocking on doors in the exclusive Marine Parade district. Inevitably she was rewarded with a threepenny bit or a sixpence to share with her singers, and invited to return next year. Little wonder then that fourteen-year-old Connie was bored silly with selling cheese, and saw the outbreak of war as an opportunity for a more exciting life.

This left two children in our immediate family: bold Iris and timid me, each of us happy in her own way. Never at a loss for something to do, Iris only had to walk down the front path with her skipping rope or a piece of chalk, or a cloth bag of marbles, and she would be surrounded by neighbouring children who wanted to play. Whether I chose to watch from the porch, or join in the game, it was all right with her.

Even I, with my cautious nature, enjoyed our last summer of freedom. Led by Iris we caught tadpoles with home-made nets, and brought them home in jam jars for deposit in an old footbath where they lived until maturing to frogs and hopping away. We spent hours in fields behind the estate – usually five or six of us – hunting for specific wild flowers, or scrumping apples from an orchard and then squealing like pigs if an outraged farmer chased us. Sometimes we played hide-and-seek among the tall trees of Belfairs Woods, which held even more terror for me than threats from the irate farmer whose apples we filched.

On the day before the declaration of war, Iris and I had brand-new whips and tops, which spun giddily on the flat concrete square across from a nearby laundry. We played there for hours, just the two of us, spinning our tops faster than catherine wheels – colouring them with chalk for a more dazzling effect. From that day on our freedom would be curtailed by orders to run home fast if the siren sounded, and not to leave Kent Avenue without telling Mum where we'd be, and to carry our gas masks at all times.

At first, conscription didn't affect our family. A month into the war, men aged between twenty and twenty-three years of age had to register for service in one of the armed forces. As Mum had predicted, Sam's work at Shell Oil's refinery made him exempt, and we felt sure Wally was safe on account of his having only one lung. By 1941, single women aged between twenty and thirty were conscripted to work in factories and on farms, by which time we expected Rose to have been called up. When her papers eventually arrived they went straight into the dustbin. By this time she was already an air-raid warden, and confident she was doing her bit.

In the weeks leading up to the war we were one of the few families on our estate to own an air-raid shelter. Had good sense prevailed it would have been closer to the house, but because at first Mum refused to relinquish her rose gardens, the shelter was banished to the bottom of our lot – calling for a twenty-five-yard dash when the air-raid siren sounded. Dad, helped by Wally, dug a room-sized hole, topped it with wooden planks to form an inverted letter V, and fitted it inside with plank seating. Iris and I used it as our private hideaway, where we would read our comics by torchlight while snacking on chocolate and nuts from the emergency biscuit tin.

The only emergency we had that spring was a torrential rainstorm that caused the shelter's roof to collapse, leaving it as a blight on an otherwise neat garden until an Anderson shelter was delivered a year later.

The Andersons, named for Sir John Anderson who was the cabinet minister responsible for the Air Raid Precautions (or ARP), were free to families with an income of less than approximately £250 a year. Everyone else paid eight pounds. Delivered as galvanised corrugated steel panels, they were designed to accommodate up to six people, and equipped with a small drainage pump to collect rainwater. Topped by a regulation fifteen inches of soil on their roofs, many were planted with vegetables and flowers that were entered in competitions. My mother vowed she would never glorify such an eyesore with flowers. In any case, for added safety ours was packed with sandbags.

Boy scouts and other youthful volunteers erected most of the shelters on our street, but Dad and Wally chose to build ours over the existing hole. Customising its interior with shelves and bunk beds, they put sacking over the entrance and a Union Jack on the roof. In dry weather, by day at least, it was almost cosy.

Over the summer of '39 we received countless pamphlets telling us what we should know and do, in the event of war. One explained that children would be evacuated from London, and major industrial cities across the country. School-age youngsters were to go with their teachers and preschoolers with their mothers, but since Leigh had little by way of industry we felt safe on this score.

The most dramatic happening for us that summer was our trip to Iris's school to be fitted with gas masks by ARP wardens.

In 2006 at an exhibition in London's Imperial War Museum, I stood behind a man with his granddaughter in a typical house of the Second World War. On its hall table was a gas mask that the young girl described as 'cool'. Her grandfather told her that pupils who arrived at school without a mask were sent home to fetch it, so he forgot his often.

He also reckoned he used his as a football, and it became too battered to be of real use anyway.

I have to say I was less cavalier with mine, occasionally putting it on, tightening the straps and holding a piece of paper under the nozzle while breathing deeply – just to be sure it worked. In my nervous state, I fretted a lot about getting it on properly before being gassed, and during the early days insisted on always hooking it over my chair at mealtimes. How the gas would arrive, or when, I had no idea. It was simply another uncertainty to be concerned about.

The masks came in cardboard boxes with string attached so we could hang them on our shoulders. Older girls, including my sisters, often carried sandwiches or cosmetics in theirs, which would have made expedient retrieval of the masks during an emergency virtually impossible. Pre-schoolers were given red and blue Mickey Mouse masks, instead of the traditional black. Parents were encouraged to make a game of it all, by allowing their tots to wear them now and again. It wasn't uncommon to see a four-year-old at play, wearing her gruesome mask as if it covered some hideous facial disease or was part of a latest fashion. Babies were provided with body masks that covered them to their waists.

I shall never forget the horrible smell of

rubber against my face, and the panic I felt when the Perspex eye-piece fogged up to render me sightless. (We were urged to spit on the little window before wiping it clear, but this seemed too impolite to me.)

I am not allowed to forget the first air-raid warning either. It came during the night, soon after the declaration of war, when wardens were either jittery or simply unfamiliar with enemy aircraft. Either way, it turned out to be a false alarm. I had memorised the drill, which was to pick up the mask from the box with my name on it, and run as fast as I could to our new shelter. This I did.

Meanwhile, in the kitchen, the rest of my family assembled ready for the mad dash down the path. But first they tripped over each other searching for me, under the beds, in the bathroom, even in the outside toilet and a cupboard under the stairs. Then, deciding I must have found somewhere safe from the bombs, they picked up Clarabelle the cat and headed for the shelter's safety beneath brilliant searchlights etching dramatic patterns in the skies.

Violet was the first to lift the piece of ragged sacking from the Anderson's doorway, and peer into the gloom. Her screams caused Mum to arm herself with a gardening fork. (Dad had already gone into the streets to see what he could do to help.) For there I was, scrunched up in the far corner with an upturned saucepan on my head and gas mask covering my face. Over gales of laughter, my mother explained how I had no need to wear the mask until I heard a warning rattle, but it was thoughtful to wear the saucepan. Later she said that only my clown-patterned pyjamas saved me from being stabbed.

It took me years to live that one down. In fact, when discussing our war some decades later, at least two of my sisters said I must surely remember that night. One recalled quite graphically the saucepan's gooey contents dripping down my mask-covered face, but I swear it had been empty.

During the long hot summer of '39 my father was recruited to work on the seafront, sandbagging buildings taken over by soldiers, and any others deemed important in time of siege. He and his team also installed huge tank traps, which were in effect large cement blocks staggered along the seafront to halt anyone who thought they could bring a vehicle ashore and get further than the beach. Coils of barbed wire along the seafront provided a further deterrent.

Dad talked little of the war in front of his family. On the old garden seat though, with a pint of bitter in hand, he and his mate Bill would discuss it well into the night. There was an air of resignation about my father these days, and irritability at politicians or military commanders who in his mind made one huge mistake after another.

Towards the end of the year he came home for his lunch one day – always a cooked meal unless he took something to eat on the job – threw his bike against the garden hedge, and angrily told my mother the Jews were running faster than greyhounds at the track. He said he couldn't believe this was England. There they were, poor sods, leaving washing on the line, even kiddies' playthings in the front gardens, and fleeing for their lives.

Since the early 1920s Jewish families had moved into many of the splendid houses along Chalkwell and Westcliff seafronts. On weekdays they travelled to City offices, but on weekends they made the most of their lavish waterfront homes. In summer, especially, we would see them entertaining friends on their terraces, or working on pleasure boats resting lopsidedly on the mud – until the tide swept in to lift them off.

Now, unsettling news of their friends and relatives in occupied Europe was filtering across the channel. The distance between them and us was alarmingly small, which meant that invasion of this part of England's coast had become a genuine threat. And so, while the rest of us in the area were worried, and fed up with shortages, members of the Jewish community felt they had to run for their lives.

Those lovely homes were abandoned, or sold for a song; jewellery sewn into clothes to be redeemed later. Anyone with friends or relatives in North America, South Africa or Australia snapped up passages on ships sailing from Liverpool and Southampton. The rest scattered to the remotest regions of Britain.

Their exodus was a frightening thing to see. Lulled by what was generally called the Phoney War or Bore War until now, we at home decided it was time for us to sit up and take notice. When a newsreel showed Londoners planting vegetables in their beautiful parks and public gardens, Mum came home and dug up most of her roses. Necessity caused us to follow advice on placards telling us to Make Do and Mend. But when, to conserve water, we watched the King gravely examining a painted line at the five-inch level in his bath, we had a good laugh, because hot water at 19 Kent went cold long before it reached that height. As for the suggestion that we 'share a bath with a friend', well, we'd been doing that for years. If two of us wanted a bath within an hour of each other, the first person would hop out and a second nip in after adding a kettle of boiling water.

It took Dunkirk, in May 1940, to bring thoughts of invasion foremost to our minds. Immediately after then, War Secretary Anthony Eden announced the formation of the LDV (Local Defence Volunteers) and over a quarter of a million men came forward. By the end of June, we had one and a half million unpaid men and boys dedicated to defending their particular parts of Britain in the event of an invasion.

At this time, car owners received instructions on how to immobilise their vehicles if German troops landed on our shores. (Remove distributor head and leads, and empty the tank, then hide removed parts well away from the vehicle.) 'Do Not Give Any German Anything', the news reporter boomed down at us in our hard little seats at the Odeon. He continued with warnings to hide food, bicycles and maps, and to think always of our country before thinking of ourselves.

For those of us living on England's south coast, evacuation of children and pregnant women was hovering closer every day. Already, London had been emptied of more than a million of its children, following a plan hatched after the First World War when bombs dropped on London killed almost 500 citizens. Whitehall's thinkers decided that deaths from bombings in this present war would be in the tens of thousands, and guaranteed to cause pandemonium in major cities. To clear London of non-essentials, evacuation orders for this city's children were given three days before war broke out.

Most were from the East End's working-class and slum areas. So-called 'upper-' and many middle-class families made private arrangements to rent or borrow country accommodation, from which their women and children, elderly and infirm, continued to have a fairly pleasant life. It is estimated that between July and the beginning of September 1939, some three and a half million people moved from vulnerable areas to what were considered safer regions.

Hundreds of children whose parents could afford the passage were sent to friends or relatives in the USA, Canada, South Africa and Australia under a plan called the Children's Overseas Reception Board (CORB). This scheme was suspended after 17 September 1940 when the SS *City of Benares*, bound for Canada, was torpedoed. Loss of life was huge, including seventy-seven of the ninety child evacuees on board.

Meantime, on the morning of 31 August 1939, schoolchildren with their teachers were ordered to leave England's anticipated target zones for safer regions across the country. From London alone more than 350,000 children gathered at their schools as instructed, not knowing where they would be by the end of the day. Children as young as nine years old were told by parents to hang on to their smaller siblings. Many were inconsolably homesick, some were abused, others completely happy. Whatever their situation, almost all had returned home by Christmas of that same year.

Iris continued to bring home notices from school about our contribution to the war effort. I read them, as I did almost everything brought into the house. Still, the pamphlets didn't alarm me, perhaps because I hadn't received them with reinforced commentary from teachers. Their importance was diminished when I found them under the teapot on the kitchen table. I should perhaps explain, too, that I felt very removed from the school since I hadn't attended its classes for the past year.

My long holiday from school started in the early summer of 1938 when diphtheria crept into town as a silent killer, filling Southend's isolation hospital with young patients from local schools, mine included. One morning I woke up with a sore throat, which became so bothersome I didn't return to school after lunch. Next day I felt as if I had broken glass blocking my throat. Mum felt my forehead, declared me to be 'burning up', and sent Dad off on his bicycle to find Dr Nicholls. Our elderly family doctor didn't put council estate patients at the head of his list, but we knew he would come to our house eventually.

Late that night, he arrived, took my temperature, and wearily told my worried parents I was the fifth case of 'the dip' he had seen that day. Mum was urged to keep me comfortable overnight in the front room, away from the other girls, and to press cold flannels on my face. Had she explained that I was going into hospital next morning, I wouldn't have screamed bloody murder when a nurse arrived with a porter, who bundled me into a red blanket, as my mother stood silently by.

On our way to hospital I calmed down enough to ask if I was to have an operation, like my aunty who came home on a stretcher just two weeks before, without a tongue because of cancer.

Southend's fever hospital was very old, and at first very frightening. Visitors were not allowed inside, and no one under fourteen was supposed to be admitted to the grounds. Iris came anyway, along with my parents and as many other sisters as were free on Sunday afternoons. On weekdays Mum arrived on her own, by tram, lugging a footstool that allowed her to reach the window through which I could be seen. She looked so exhausted, I used to ask her to stay home. It worried me to see her perspiring face reaching up over the windowsill. One afternoon she disappeared suddenly, popping back up with blood streaming from her chin to say everything was okay.

Only new toys were allowed, so my family

brought me *Rupert* books and my favourite comics, and ribbons for my hair. All the girls in my ward collected ribbons. When we weren't wearing them they would be wound around our iron bed railings, and we'd swap with each other to get the colours we most wanted.

Several students from my school died during this diphtheria epidemic. All the others went home after six weeks. Except for me. My stay was longer because I couldn't walk when I eventually left my bed. Nobody seemed to know why. I practised walking daily, and eventually managed to wobble down to the bus stop with Mum and Iris for the journey home. Having been told that my inability to walk was psychological, that I liked the quiet calm of the hospital and constant attention, my mother took my reluctance to come home as a personal insult and was not as overjoyed as I expected to have me there.

By the time we reached Kent Avenue I was blinking furiously, and felt compelled to twist my face into unattractive contortions. Dr Nicholls gave me a tonic, as well as a certificate to stay off school for another month. This became two months, then three, and so long as I continued to squeeze my eyes tight, and stretch my mouth every few minutes while in his presence, another certificate for another month changed hands.

This strange illness was a terrible inconvenience to my parents. My father was largely unemployed through that winter; my mother cleaned offices and houses. If he did get work, I went with Mum and sat on the stairs of her employer's house, reading my books as she worked. When Dad was home, I got comfortable by the fire with my comic annuals while he filled out his football pools, read every inch of the *Daily Mirror,* and did his best to cook a decent dinner, which often contained ash I had seen fall from the end of his cigarette.

An unusually cold winter brought snow. Dad made me a sledge, and together we went around the streets, offering to clean paths and driveways. Some days we went to the yards for coal. Why, I don't know. Perhaps the harsh winter caused it to be scarce, or too expensive to buy by the hundredweight. In any event, we collected small chips and slivers to fill boxes tied to the sledge, instead of having the coalman deliver it in sacks to our own coal shed.

Winter eventually slipped off to make way for spring, and for the first time I took pleasure in our front garden bursting with daffodils and hyacinths, deep purple and gold primulas. Often it was warm enough to take my books on to the front porch from where I watched Mum mend winter's damage. By now I had moved on to *Black*

Beauty, and spent hours studying my father's atlas or history books. Dad and I had both joined Leigh library, a simple act that opened up a whole new world for me. Having little knowledge of modern books for children, he introduced me to classics he had enjoyed during his long voyages at sea twenty years before.

With the warm weather, I would make us copious cups of tea to drink on the sunny front porch and, for reasons I can't even guess, spent hours sweeping dirt from the path. In the weeks leading up to Dunkirk, my father was employed full-time in Southend, with the sandbagging and tank traps and other war-related work.

At home I did a few chores, went shopping with Mum to Southend, and if the bus wasn't due for half an hour or so, we would stop for tea in Rossi's. Knowing enough to make faces at Dr Nicholls and the truant officer who stopped by regularly, I had no intention of going to school ever again.

Although there was nothing too startling happening on our home front, the war did intrude on our everyday lives. There was ugliness of some sort wherever we went. In addition to the tank traps and barbed wire, and dung-coloured sandbags around Southend's buildings, giant above-ground water tanks were installed on street corners. Providing ready water for firefighters, they became the unsightly homes of algae and mosquitoes and final resting place for other small creatures unfortunate enough to fall in.

Grass squares and verges gave way to allotments that were bright for only a small part of the year. In fact, colours seemed to disappear from our lives altogether. Clothes were utility brown, blacks and greys. Dishes, those we could get, were white, replacing our floral-patterned chinaware now kept in a cupboard for the special occasions that never came.

Until this time I didn't consider us to be poor. True, there had been a certain stigma to living on a council estate. But we were never hungry, and while our play-clothes were faded hand-me-downs, at school we were among the best dressed of its students. I guess it was a case of 'what you don't have you don't miss' because I never felt hard done by for not having a holiday or not owning a family car or telephone. In those years we didn't know anyone who did.

But then came the war to divide us into the 'haves' and 'have nots'. We were now in the latter class as we couldn't afford black-market foods or safe country homes or extra coupons for winter coats. Even the blackout was complicated for us. Those who could simply bought heavy velvet drapes to draw across their windows at dusk, or had black cotton linings made for their present curtains. Instead we made do with black tarpaper Dad nicked from a building site. Attached to frames made of laths that had also been 'salvaged' from nearby construction jobs, they bent and warped within weeks. As a result, we were constantly shouted at for showing slivers of light.

Each frame was numbered to match a certain window, and if put into the right place worked well enough. But tell that to Mum when she came home from a fruitless afternoon of scouring Southend's shops. Or Violet after twelve hours in the factory. And, not only were these monstrosities awkward to fit, but by day they were stored behind the settee or against a door, ready to be tripped over or roughly kicked aside. This meant the tarpaper had to be constantly taped and patched.

Some mornings Mum had neither the time nor the patience to pry them out of the windows, so would leave them in place. Then there were evenings when she didn't bother putting them up, preferring to sit in the dark listening to the wireless. On these occasions, one of us might come home, put on a light, and all hell would break loose as wardens came running, blowing their whistles, shouting for us to 'Put that bloody light out!'

One day, if you can believe it, a man came

calling in a trench coat and trilby hat like Humphrey Bogart in *Casablanca*. Seriously! A neighbour had reported us as probable spies. True, this was later in the war when the bombing was insistent, and a single crack of light from a window was all the German pilots might have needed to recognise us as a housing estate. Worse still, they could well assume they'd stumbled upon row after row of army barracks.

Considering how long we had lived on the street, this just went to show how jittery everyone had become. When she became a warden, Rose didn't bandy about her home address to any but her immediate teammates. Our house, she learned, was considered a threat to security.

Raids aside, it was quite dangerous to be walking at night. Street lighting was no longer turned on at dusk, while bicycles and motorised vehicles wore headlight covers. Even our torches, so essential for locating kerbs, were fitted with cardboard punctured with pinholes to provide the minimum light. Bus windows were covered in netting to prevent flying glass in the event of a hit; their interior lights were so dim we could hardly see them till they were almost upon us.

As white stripes were painted around trees and telephone boxes, pedestrians were encouraged to wear white clothing or armbands. In well-travelled areas, traffic accidents increased fifty per cent during our blackout years.

From early on, shortages, for which we knew there was no real solution, were part of the bad dream in which we lived. German U-boats had been sinking our merchant ships carrying food and other supplies to Britain. Losses were terrible, not only in ships and lives, but also in goods and materials necessary for us to keep going.

Food rationing was introduced during the first year; coupons for a clothing allowance came later. Instead of buying new clothes, we were asked to make do with old. 'Is Your Journey Really Necessary?' screamed posters at train stations and bus stops to anyone who may have frivolous travel plans. Most of the shops on Leigh Broadway, where Mum did her shopping, displayed signs telling us there were 'no sweets' or 'no cigarettes' or 'no butter'. Every so often an assistant would accidentally knock down one of the signs before closing up. Next morning a queue would have formed in the mistaken belief that the sweets, ciggies or butter were now in stock.

Butter and bacon were the first foods to be rationed, giving us four ounces of each per week. Sugar came next, limiting customers to twelve ounces each. Meat was rationed by value rather than allocated amounts, enabling us to choose quantity over quality. Tea hit us the worst, coming in at only two ounces a week. Oranges, bananas, peaches, fresh and tinned fruits were no longer being imported, and by war's end there were children starting school who had never tasted a banana. (When my niece Valerie, at age six, was given her first banana she tried to eat it with the peel on.) It made little difference to us that sweets weren't rationed for the first two years, because they simply weren't available.

Had my comfortable world continued in this manner, with nothing more than the blackout and shortages disrupting my home life, I would say the war wasn't all that bad. But then came Dunkirk and everything went pear-shaped.

CHAPTER THREE

Evacuation Gets Underway

Most people hearing the word Dunkirk will conjure up images of our troops waist deep in water, scrambling to board British vessels aiding their escape from enemy-occupied France. Unlike them, my mind commands a picture of the estuary awash with little boats heading towards the channel for the rescue operation.

The evacuation of British forces from France started on Sunday 26 May 1940, and continued for nine days, in which time almost a quarter of a million British and over 100,000 French troops were picked up from the beaches and water around Dunkirk. Destroyers and other large ships did most of the retrieval, but there was also an over-whelming response to a call for help from private boat owners. Leisure craft from Leigh Yacht Club put to sea, as did South-end's lifeboat based at the end of the pier; even our cocklers went across the channel in full force. There's no disputing that Dunkirk brought the war closer to our front door in dramatic style.

One morning during the Dunkirk evacuation Dad and I rode his bicycle (he pedalled, I sat on the crossbar) to Leigh Broadway. There, at the top of Church Hill, we watched the drama unfold. 'Those poor, poor buggers ... those poor boys,' Dad murmured over and over. The butcher, wearing his blue-and-white striped apron and straw hat, came out of his shop across from the church to stand with us. Putting his hand on my shoulder, he said he knew they would all come home safely. They didn't, of course. Today a plaque inside the churchyard tells of cocklers who set off so bravely on this mission, and did not return.

Dunkirk heralded the end of my long holiday from school. On the following Friday, Iris brought home her letter telling us that all children under the age of fourteen should report to their classes on Sunday morning. Fearing imminent invasion, the time had come for evacuation of children from the south-east coast.

By this summer of 1940, there were still seven of us living at 19 Kent. Rose was a warden with the ARP. At seventeen, Violet was ensconced in the unhealthy atmosphere of a local factory producing rubber dinghies and barrage balloons. Although she lived at home, we saw little of her, due to her long days and irregular hours.

Connie longed to find more interesting work. Serving cheese all day was tedious at best, but when a customer accused her of putting her thumb on the scales, she impolitely suggested he took his business elsewhere. Before the manager had the chance to sack her, Connie took off her over-sized white coat and walked out. In a matter of weeks, boredom led her to an army enrolment office on the High Street. Convincing the enlistment officer she was eighteen, when she was really two years younger, she was accepted for the Auxiliary Territorial Service, basically the women's army. Mum was so furious she threatened to go down to their recruitment office in the High Street and set things right. Dad was as pleased as Punch, though he felt she should have chosen the navy's WRENS. I don't think Connie had given it much thought. Her triumph was to get away from the cheese counter and its grumpy customers.

As the only family members of school age, Iris and I were prospective evacuees. On reading the letter from school, my mother wept for the first time since the war began. Evacuation was not compulsory, but advisable in view of our vulnerable location, and she said it was right that we should live in safety.

We were instructed to carry one small suitcase each, plus our gas masks, and food for our journey to an unknown destination. Recommended clothing included a change of underwear, nightdress or pyjamas, house shoes, socks, a toothbrush, comb, towel, soap and face cloth, handkerchiefs and a warm coat or macintosh.

Saturday saw Mum hunting up and down Southend High Street for new toiletries and underwear. That night she and Rose diligently sewed our names on everything, carefully ironed a couple of extra dresses, then looked around for something to put it all in. Dad came up with the answer, by providing us and our neighbours with sandbags.

Few children from our estate had suitcases because they were never called for. Who needed a holiday, when we lived by the sea, and had Southend Kursaal for thrill rides and candy floss? Hospital stays were usually as far as our neighbours went, and then their necessities could fit into brown paper carrier bags.

That I was about to leave home indefinitely really didn't sink in at first. After all, I hadn't been to school in a year, and had no class to report to. Surely I would arrive with Iris and, not finding my name on any of the lists, the teachers would send me home. So I wasn't too concerned when we set off for the school.

As sad little groups passed our house, Mum was out front pretending to dead-head her flowers. Iris's friend Lilah came tripping along, on her own and ready for adventure, saying her Ma told her to go with us. Rose came on to the porch hugging my teddy, which she promised to keep safe. My mother looked to be on the verge of collapse as Dad walked us determinedly down the path, joined by two neighbours with five children between them. When we reached the gate I turned, crying out, 'Mum ... what if I come back and you've only got one leg?' Where that stupid thought had sprung from I can't imagine. She straightened up. 'Nobody's having my leg or any other bit of me. I will be at the station to meet you, looking just like this when you two come home. That bloke Hitler will be long gone, and we'll all be back to normal.' And so she was. Though I have to say she looked decades older, and nothing was what we knew as normal.

When we turned the corner of Kent Avenue, I looked back for one last wave, but she had buried her head in her pinny. It was a year before I saw her again.

We were a forlorn little caravan. Two or three groups had joined us by the time we reached Manchester Drive, and more as we trudged along Darlinghurst Grove. On the London Road where our school was located, the trickle had become a flood of grim-faced parents and apprehensive children, constantly being told to pull up their socks, keep off that wall, try to stay clean.

Some children no older than me had preschool siblings in tow; adorable little girls in pretty dresses and pastel coats and ankle-strap patent shoes reserved for special occasions. Most carried a toy squeezed under their arms. I regretted leaving Ted with Rose, and asked if I could run back for him. My father shook his head. The children with toys, he said, were younger than me and I needed to look my age. That's why I had my *Black Beauty* book.

For all the time we had spent together this past year, Dad and I really weren't close.

When I was five, six, even seven years old, I loved to sit on his lap on the old shoe box in the back porch, listening to stories about his travels and children he'd met in far-off lands. When I came home from hospital though, I irritated him. Bad enough that I, his last chance at a son, was another girl. Worst than that, I had become a girl he could no longer understand. Where we used to talk about his adventures at sea, I now blinked and pulled grotesque faces, and was underfoot when I should have been at school.

Not that he had a lot to say to his other daughters. Doubtless he felt out-numbered, surrounded by so many females arguing about who took whose hair clips or fighting over the last of the green gooey Amami shampoo. When I think of him during that past year, it was of the times we cooked dinner together while my mother worked and he didn't. And on Sunday mornings, before he started in the garden – or perhaps because it was too wet to work outdoors. That's when he would sit in the back porch, mending our shoes.

I can see him now with the wooden leg upside down between his knees, its iron foot fitted into a shoe. He would put a bunch of tiny nails into his mouth, retrieving them one at a time to attach a sheet of Rubberox to the worn sole. Sometimes, when our footwear was really good for nothing more than the dustbin, he would transform the uppers with a shiny paint, even though the cracks came through within a couple of wearings.

As the war continued, there was nothing with which to repair our shoes, other than old bicycle tyres cut into shape. For the most part we just stuffed paper or cardboard inside, replacing it every few days. Over the past few weeks Dad had repaired my left shoe far more often than the right, because I had finally realised my dream to travel more swiftly than my two feet would carry me.

There was little possibility of having a new bicycle, until I was old enough to buy my own. The best my mother could promise was to talk with the Rag-a'-Bone man about a second-hand one. What the 'bones' were about I never did ascertain, but the rags were given to him along with old tyres, chairs, kitchen utensils and quite often bicycles as he drove his horse-drawn cart around the streets of Leigh.

On our council estate, youngsters often sat on their porches with a bowl of water and a couple of old blouses or coats, wanting to exchange their clothing for a goldfish from the rag man. More important transactions called for cash, with or without a goldfish.

No suitable bicycles turned up in the

weeks during which I waited every Thursday afternoon for the rag man to come by. Then, one day he had a rusty scooter, with part of the rubber tyre dangling from one of its two small metal wheels. My mother watched me scoot awkwardly along the footpath, bargained down the price, and bought it for a few pennies. Once Dad worked his magic on it, I was the happiest kid on Kent Avenue.

To me it was freedom – to run errands on the London Road, and eventually go twice as far to Leigh Broadway shops, with a half-crown and a note tucked in my knickers' pocket. With the sun or rain, even sea winds attacking my face, to sail along the virtually empty pavement was my idea of heaven. My world was near perfect for those few weeks in late spring. But now, even I, with my unreasonable expectations, didn't think that a scooter would be permitted on this evacuation journey.

The schoolyard proved daunting, as students had been led out to stand tidily in groups. Lilah located her class, and called for Iris to join her. I found the noise and number of people distressing. It had been a long time since I had been with more than a few people at one time. Now there were hundreds.

As the neighbours' children dutifully said their goodbyes and joined their classes, Iris tried to shake free of me. My hopes of returning home were dashed, when Dad handed me over, telling my sister not to let me out of her sight. 'She's to go in the same house as you. Be sure to tell your teacher, and the new people.' Iris nodded, impatient to join Lilah, and we boarded the buses heading for Southend's central railway station. I turned to wave to my father, but he was already lost in the crowds.

Somewhere in the region of 20,000 school-aged children were evacuated from the Southend area that day, as well as pregnant women and mothers with pre-schoolers. It was a procedure carried out with all the precision of a military exercise. Each of us had our own gas mask and clothes bag, and wore a name tag either around our necks or pinned to our jacket. Every child had a stamped postcard addressed to their parents. Upon arrival at our destination we would write our new address, hopefully adding a few words to say we were happy before mailing it home.

Nobody had been told where we were going. My mother was sure it would be Wales, where they grew lots of sheep. Not that our destination really mattered, because we would be back soon. Now that Winston Churchill – whom she already called 'Our Winnie' – was prime minister, she was certain the war would be over before we knew it. For my part, such reassurance meant little.

Until I boarded the bus with Iris's class, I had been convinced I wasn't going anywhere.

After warning me not to make weird faces, Iris, true to her word, hung on to my hand as we waited on the station. Her teacher, Miss Brant, came by counting her students. On seeing me, she paused momentarily, shook her head and moved on. I learned later that Iris wasn't the only girl to have a sibling clinging to her. Some had sisters and brothers as young as four years old.

Eventually, after lots of shouts and whistles and banging of doors, we were on our way, flying past recognisable scenes, such as the cockle sheds and quaint pubs of Old Leigh – the ruins of Hadleigh Castle where Iris had once climbed to the upper turret to scratch her name for posterity – through villages and towns with familiar names. At railway crossings, and from back gardens beside the tracks, people waved to us. As we waved back, I remember thinking how normal their lives were, while mine had turned upside-down. Children raced by on bicycles, dads paused in their gardening to wave, mums left their Sunday dinners cooking. I could almost smell their roast lamb and mint sauce to be followed by spotted dick with custard. All of a sudden it seemed grossly unfair.

We passed signs of a Britain preparing for an invasion, as soldiers stacked sandbags around signal boxes, and dug deep ditches across meadows to prevent German aircraft from landing. Names of railway stations were either obliterated completely, or had their middle letters painted out, to confuse invaders as to their whereabouts. On the outskirts of London, large placards advised mothers to send their children away to the country. Then, as we continued deep into the countryside, more posters proclaimed that caring for evacuees was a national service.

'Why are all those mothers crying?' I naively asked his of the women standing by the railway tracks.

'Because they're sorry for us little sods being taken from our loving homes,' Lilah retorted. 'Go on, Pammy. Blink one of them big blinks of yours and pull a funny face. Then they'll feel really sorry for you.' Iris shot her one of her killer looks, then glared at me so I didn't dare to cry as I would have done had I been at home.

Normally, trains from Southend would puff into London's Liverpool Street or Fenchurch Street stations, and from there passengers for northern England crossed the city by Tube, to board another train at Euston or St Pancras stations. Since ours was not a normal train, it took us beyond London and into some of the most beautiful countryside I had ever seen. We passed lovely old houses, set in lush emerald-green fields shaded by big old trees, and contented-looking sheep and glossy-coated horses grazing peacefully, impervious to our wheezing train. I began to think I might like country living.

Eventually, when we pulled into a tiny station where porters ran alongside telling us to get out, leaving our things behind, I thought we were having a fire drill. Instead it was what Lilah – whose brothers were fans of motorcycle racing – called a 'pit stop', or a place to refuel, in a neighbouring field. Volunteers had set up portable tables crammed with plates of sandwiches and cakes.

Gathering us around her, Miss Brant said we should use the public lavatories here, since we may not have another opportunity before our final destination. Tell-tale wet patches on the seats of some of the younger children showed they hadn't been able to wait. Two or three more had been sick down their nice clean clothes.

Whether the train driver had gone missing, or the local newspaper's photographer was late in showing up to snap some big-wig posed with a few students, I couldn't say. I do know we were stuck in that field longer than planned, which meant trouble for those in charge of a bunch of energised children.

Several began climbing up the hillside and rolling back down, so before long we had very grubby youngsters with grazed knees and dirt-smeared arms, legs and faces. When spit on handkerchiefs didn't help, Miss Brant sent those from her group into the lavatory, which at least had running water. They emerged reasonably clean, but soaking wet, and were told to flap their arms to shake off excess water.

Iris and Lilah scoffed at such antics until a lad called Norman made the mistake of taunting them. They chased him up the hill, and I had no recourse but to follow. At the very top, higher than anyone else, they stood arms outstretched shouting 'I'm the king of the castle.'

I had barely reached them when Norman kicked out his boot to touch my hand, yelling 'Get down, you dirty rascal.' Which I did, sliding uncontrollably past shrubs, over thistles and prickly weeds.

I don't think it was very far. No bones were broken, but I looked a real mess, as scratches oozed blood on to my dirt-caked legs. Stinging nettles brought instant welts on my face and arms, and oh, how I wanted to cry. I couldn't, of course. Iris was shouting at Norman, asking him how – after promising to look after me – she could face my dad if I'd gone and got killed before we even got there. When Lilah started on him too, he began sobbing loud enough for both of us.

Miss Brant blew her whistle, causing everyone to stand still, except for two nurses who came galloping over with a canvas stretcher. By the time they arrived I was upright, holding twigs and dandelions I had clutched at on the way down.

Until now, the zealous nurses had had nothing more than upset stomachs to deal with. This was their golden opportunity to jump into action, what with real blood to swab and scratches to disinfect. Iris was allowed in the medical tent with me, while the rest of the children soberly climbed back on to the train. By the time the medics were through, I had several rolls of bandages wound around my legs from thigh to below the knee. My face and arms were daubed with pink medication to treat the stings. I looked as if I had barely survived a bombing raid, before stumbling into a hive of angry bees.

It was only when the last piece of bandage had been snipped and tied did the unthinkable happen. It dawned on Miss Brant that she didn't know me. I obviously puzzled her. It was one thing for a pre-schooler to tag along with an elder sister, but surely I was old enough to be with my own class. I looked at Iris, now sheet white.

'You see, miss,' she told her teacher firmly, 'she hasn't got a class because she had the dip, so our dad said we must stick together.

And we are,' she ended resolutely.

My hero. Miss Brant told us not to worry. She would sort it out later.

A strong young man carried me over to the train, where Lilah was frantically waving us to our seats.

'Looks like your drawers are hanging down. Who's going to want you looking like that?' she demanded.

Miserably wondering what would happen to any left-overs not chosen by the new parents, I closed my eyes to shut out the world – and fell asleep for the rest of the journey.

Somewhere around late afternoon I was jerked awake by clanging and banging, screeching and hissing as our train came to a halt. Iris opened the window, stuck out her head and reported that a man carrying a clipboard had come aboard. It took a while for the first twenty or so children to stuff their belongings back into their bags and to disembark. From the train they moved in a neat line to a waiting bus.

More hissing and fussing, and our train started up. It was only then that I noticed Iris's face, garishly made up with mascara, rouge and lipstick. Lilah had done even more damage; her eyelids were a brilliant green.

'Who will want us with you looking like that?' I wanted to know.

'Look who's talking,' Lilah growled back,

showing me my swollen sting-blotched face in her compact mirror.

They were laughing like drunken sailors when Miss Brant counted off the next twenty or so children for disembarkation. Looking at Iris and Lilah and then me, with more dismay than amusement she told us to sit tight for the next stop, adding that the two girls should try saliva instead of the Tizer they had used to wipe off the rouge as their faces were now a distinctly odd colour. Years later I reminded Iris that we had been delayed on the train because of her poor make-up skills.

'Fancy that,' she grinned, 'our whole lives changed because I nicked Vi's lipstick and rouge.'

True enough, children disembarking earlier went to a different village, and perhaps stayed there for the war's duration. Leaving the train at the next stop we were less fortunate.

Iris proved a real brick. Her tongue was so sharp at times, her retorts so flippant, her language so unacceptable, I cringed often in her presence. But when all was said and done she looked after me, a timorous child fearful of everything new, who made fewer strange faces as time wore on, but still read in my spare time and aimed to excel at school. Goody Two Shoes, first to come running when called. We were as different as chalk and cheese, but my sister made sure we stuck together, as if with carpentry glue, for as long as was humanly possible.

Decades later, when our lives took very different paths, and we met only briefly once or twice a year, Iris still tried to look after me. She's gone now, but I remember clearly our last get-together at the historic Peter Boat in Leigh Old Town. She explained the menu, recommended certain dishes, fetched our drinks from the bar, and insisted on paying the bill. I loved it. We were both in our seventies, and I had travelled the world, but for this one last time, I was the little sister she had long ago promised to look after.

CHAPTER FOUR

We've Arrived

We were an unattractive group shepherded into a single-room schoolhouse with desks stacked against one wall and a row of chairs lining another. Ranging in age from five to thirteen, none of us was in the best of shape following our harrowing journey.

I was not the only child attached to an older sibling. Next to Iris, six-year-old Peter hung his head, whimpering pathetically into his grey jersey while his sister stared glumly ahead. He had clearly soiled himself and smelled awful. Too weary to cry, I found myself consoling him. 'It'll be all right. You'll see.'

Miss Brant, who was to live with us in Charbury, picked him up, holding him to her so his stained trousers weren't visible to the villagers. Taking his sister too, the trio moved away from the puddle at my feet. Horrified that anyone might think it had come from me, I hastily kicked my sandbag in front of it.

We were invited to sit on the chairs, while volunteers served us milk in enamel mugs, and chocolate biscuits such as we hadn't seen since the beginning of the war. Except for Lilah, I didn't recognise anyone from Kent Avenue.

Eyeing us with what I felt was suspicion, villagers mumbled among themselves. Some had brought their children, so they too might have a say in who would be living with them for the rest of the war. After a short welcoming speech from the vicar, and whispered thanks from us for our snacks, a young couple decided on a tall blond boy at the end of the row. Each of them spoke briefly to him, he nodded, and – watched by the rest of us – the three of them moved to a woman with a clipboard. Richard's name was ticked off, and they left without so much as a backward glance. These days it can be more difficult to adopt a puppy.

In ones and twos the children were chosen. Pretty little girls with Shirley Temple curls went first, and strong boys who could help out on the land. Iris and I had poker-straight hair, cut by Dad, whose ambitions exceeded his skills in that department. At the best of times we looked pleasant enough, and healthy, but not what you might call desirable.

Over the years I have read a lot about the inhumane manner in which evacuees were selected by prospective foster parents. Nobody here asked to look into our mouths, or checked our hair for nits, but several from our group were asked to stand up, turn around, and then, now rejects, told to sit back down. If appearance was a deciding factor I would have said that most of us looked nice. Girls had ribbons on their plaits, or slides on shorter hair-dos, and cotton frocks that had obviously started out clean. Boys were dressed in grey serge shorts and white shirts, some with ties. We all had decent footwear, whether they were boots, patent-leather shoes or plimsolls.

But, I suspect we were preceded by stories about children from London's slums whose families kept coal in the bath, and kids who had never slept in a bed or sat at a table to eat a meal. Rumour had it they seldom changed their clothes, invariably wiped their mouths and noses on sleeves and stank to high heaven long before boarding trains to their new homes. What's more, they stole everything that wasn't nailed down, swore like stevedores, and were jumping with head lice. Whether these reports were true, false or exaggerated I can't say. I do know we weren't like that.

Would it have been better if the billeting officer had given more thought to assigning children to foster parents according to family backgrounds? In our case, no. Had they done so, Iris and I would have gone to a large family in a small house, and probably wouldn't have been given a fair shake.

I remember the deep humiliation of sitting there as others were selected. If you've ever been the only one left when sides are picked for a team sport, you'll know what I mean. Except that this was ten times worse. On that day I likened myself to a bruised apple at the Co-Op, being passed over by fussy shoppers.

'Think perhaps we'll get sent home to Mum?' I whispered hopefully.

'More likely we'll be sold for half price tomorrow,' was Iris's response.

Surprisingly, Lilah was chosen quite early on, by a toothless old woman who took one look and said, 'Ye'll do.'

Lilah turned furiously to Iris. 'I'll be back

home tomorrow. Wait till I phone my mum and give 'er an earful.'

That brought a hint of a smile from us both. Lilah didn't have a telephone in her house; there were even doubts as to whether she had a mother.

Four of us were left. Alan wore an ortho-paedic boot because one of his legs was shorter than the other. Iris's face was a garish orange, from the rouge mixed with Tizer, while her frock and formerly white ankle socks were filthy. I definitely didn't look like a good prospect as a long-term guest. What with my bloody bandages and swollen face I could have had some dreadfully contagious disease. And that was before I started blinking.

I forget what was wrong with Bernie, who sat smiling lopsidedly two empty seats from me. The tiny twelve-year-old was not movie star quality when it came to looks. His huge flapping ears and bottle-top glasses made him look comical when he wasn't, and a shaved head may have indicated an earlier propensity for fleas. I suppose every parent wants to have a beautiful child, even when it is only for the war's duration.

Although it wasn't compulsory to have an evacuee, the billeting officer saw that you did. In these small communities where everyone knew how many rooms you had in your house, and how many beds were empty, householders were pretty much shamed into taking in at least one child.

Initially anyone accommodating evacuees was paid ten shillings and sixpence for the first one, and eight shillings and sixpence for each additional child. Not much when you consider a male factory worker could earn around six pounds (or twelve times as much) per week, plus overtime, while women in factories were paid approximately three pounds. Parents reimbursed the government with six shillings a week per child, or less if they couldn't afford it.

I was becoming really hopeful of being sent back home, when Joe and Cissy Simpson came into the hall. Ignoring the few remaining adults, she eyed the four of us. Joe stood back, leaving this to his wife, as he did with all the shopping. We heard her telling a neighbour next morning that we looked like good girls, who wouldn't give her any trouble. In any case, the other two were lads, and she couldn't abide the thought of noisy boys in her house.

I thrust out my legs wrapped in the grubby bandages. Iris turned the most artistically challenged side of her face to Cissy. Both of us were thinking she looked too stern, and a little bit strange with her short grey hair and weather-beaten face. Close to six feet tall, she wore a long dirndl skirt and men's boots over thick black stockings. Our mum wasn't into the latest fashions, but she wouldn't be caught dead dressed like that.

But as we learned, Cissy wasn't one to be fazed by appearances.

'Eh, lass,' she said in her husky voice, 'ye look as if ye've been down t'pit. Will ye like to come home wi' us then?'

She had a nice smile. I nodded, and turned to pick up my sandbag. Defiantly, Iris pulled me down.

'My dad says we have to stick together,' she said somewhat ungraciously.

'Well, then, I'll take the two of yer,' Cissy said without a second thought, or consulting with Joe, who was fiddling with his cap. With a no-nonsense 'Thank you, miss,' to Miss Brant, she led us away, agreeing to send us over to the school next morning at nine o'clock.

Across the street and two or three houses down, we were taken into a large white house with fields on two sides and a cottage on the other. A glass of lemonade and a currant bun the size of a football were awaiting my arrival. Cissy brought a second bun and drink for Iris, who was uncharacteristically quiet. She told us the lavatory was at the end of the very long garden, then helped us to wash our hands and faces in the scullery before seating us at the table.

Although it was still light outside, and the sun was shining, we didn't protest when

Cissy suggested we went to bed. Kissing me lightly on the cheek, she told me we could hear about the rules of the house tomorrow. Had I not fallen asleep within minutes, I might have worried about what they entailed.

Hundreds of thousands of good souls opened their homes and hearts to evacuees. In some cases they had to put up with youngsters whose personal habits were appalling and whose language was even worse. Country dwellers had to cope with children who were frightened of farm animals, often refusing to drink milk. (When they saw where it originated, they assumed it to be the cow's 'wee-wee'.) Language too proved problematic, because of the different dialects. And there was abuse. Wrenched from loving families, some children were taken in as cheap farm labour or servants. They were under-fed, refused access to the home's more comfortable rooms, bullied by foster siblings, physically and sexually assaulted by strangers they were supposed to trust. But, in view of the shortage of billets, teachers often turned a blind eye to what they considered minor difficulties.

Children too may have been at fault, keeping their woes to themselves. School personnel and similarly authoritative figures were seldom warm and fuzzy beings a child could confide in. Some letters written home were censored, or destroyed by foster parents. Often, money sent by parents never reached their children.

But let us not forget the flipside to this coin. I have friends who, in their late seventies and early eighties, are still in touch with families they lived with during the war. They have attended the weddings of foster sisters and brothers, and invited them to their own; they continue to exchange Christmas cards and emails and visit for holidays.

Some evacuees fought hard to stay in the countryside at war's end. I knew a little boy called Bobby whose mother suggested he came home in 1943. She was mortified when he wrote that he couldn't bring himself to leave his dog and Uncle couldn't manage the farm chores without him, and in any case he shook like a leaf in the wind at the thought of the bombs. He was not an isolated case when he chose not to return to his family two years later.

As the war continued so did evacuation, subsequently leaning towards the elderly and disabled, pregnant women and some quarter of a million Londoners who had lost their homes during the first six weeks of the Blitz. Free travel and billeting allowances were offered to those who made private arrangements, and by February 1941 London's population was reduced by a quarter.

It wasn't to last. After the expectant

mothers gave birth, boredom and loneliness caused them to return to the cities. The government used various means to persuade evacuees to stay put. One was the introduction of Cheap Day Return tickets on railways, which enabled parents and children to visit each other. Not that these were of use to us. During wartime we were a four or five hours' complex journey away.

By the end of 1943 there were just 350,000 people officially billeted. This number increased when the V1 attacks started in June '44, but within three months the evacuation process was halted. The return of evacuees to London was officially approved in June 1945, one month after the war in Europe ended. A year later the billeting scheme was abandoned, leaving 38,000 former evacuees homeless.

CHAPTER FIVE

Settling in at Charbury

For the life of me I couldn't think where I was when I woke up next morning. Although it was some comfort to find Iris beside me in the bed, everything seemed wrong. The thick patchwork quilt, barnyard smells outside the window, an aroma of baking bread. Sounds were unfamiliar too. I could hear animals. Crowing cocks, a whinnying horse – mooing cows so close they appeared to be right in our room.

Making sure they weren't, I cautiously left our bed and tip-toed to the window. Three russet-brown cows with sorrowful brown eyes and saliva dangling from their mouths stood with their heads over the garden fence. Hanging from a rope line stretched along the garden's length, the clothes we had taken off the night before were billowing in the breeze. Even my blood-stained bandages trailed like pretty white streamers playing against a chalk-blue sky.

I woke Iris and told her I needed a toilet. 'So go,' she said, pulling the covers up around her ears.

'She's taken our clothes.' I reminded her of the lavatory's whereabouts, adding that a couple of cows were watching.

'Oh, for Christ's sake...' Iris threw herself out of bed and began rummaging in her sandbag for a new set of clothes.

By now I was shaking, not only because I needed a bathroom in a hurry, but because of my sister's swearing. A painting of Jesus holding a lantern hung above the bed, and another on the dresser showing him as a baby told me these were religious people. Unlike me, Iris spoke her mind in no uncertain terms. Her swearing would surely get us off on the wrong foot with our new parents.

Unconcerned, she waited for me to get dressed before deciding we should go and 'rustle up some grub from the missus'.

I pushed her ahead, treading carefully on the narrow stairs. Cissy was there in the main room, lifting small loaves from the hearth, her face wreathed in perspiration.

'There ye are then,' she beamed. 'I was just coming for you. I've baked these cobs, see.'

I blurted out that I needed a lav.

'Off ye run then. We'll wait on ye. Everything ye needs is down there.'

With Iris close on my heels I thankfully made it in time to the little toilet shed, spotlessly clean and smelling of disinfectant, complete with an enamel jug of water beside the wooden seat. Not sure whether this was to wash in, or to flush, I left it for Iris to decide.

On the way back, we agreed Mrs Simpson was nice. Different from our mother, but still nice. Softly humming one of her favourite hymns now, she dished up oat cakes and sausages, followed by a cob slathered in home-made butter and jam.

I looked appreciatively at Iris, who was on her second cup of tea.

'You're a really good cook, missus,' she

said happily.

Cissy looked surprised. 'Does yer Mam not bake then?'

'No. She doesn't have the time,' Iris said airily, smirking at thoughts of Mum baking bread at eight in the morning.

Obviously pleased with our appetites, Cissy sat down to have a cup of tea with us. Instinctively I warmed to her. She was a big-boned, ungainly woman, dressed plainly in a blouse and skirt, with thick stockings in spite of the summer's heat. Her hair, a mottled brown and grey, was tied back from her face with black wool. Burned to a nice light tan, her face was sprinkled with freckles. She said we should call her Aunty Ciss and her husband was Uncle Joe.

Aunty Ciss told us that Uncle Joe worked in the nearby colliery, and because his section of the pit was too low for him to stand in, he was either on his stomach, or in a crouched position, for hours on end. I felt sorry for him already. At the end of the day, she said, he would come home as black as the coal he dug, and she would fill a tin bath with hot water for him beside the fire in this main room. While he bathed, we would go upstairs or out front until he was clean and dressed. We nodded our agreement. He seemed far worse off than our dad, who worked with dirty materials, but at least had a proper bathroom with a nice long tub to soak in at the end of the day.

Joe was a quiet man, his wife confided, not much for words, but a good man and a holy man. She went on to tell us they had never been blessed with children of their own. Last night though, the pair of them went on their knees to thank God for sending them two ready-made daughters. She seemed to enjoy our company, and was about to elaborate when a knock on the door interrupted our cosy time.

It was Lilah, all smiles, saying teacher wanted to meet us outside. For this one time, Cissy told us, we were let off the washing up. After such a slap-up breakfast we had no quarrel with washing the dishes, even though it meant fetching water from a garden pump, heating it on the fire, and working in an unheated scullery. That first morning, I don't remember feeling particularly sad at being away from home. A little anxious about starting a new school after such a long absence, but otherwise rather excited about it all.

Outside the Simpsons' house an iron gate straddled the gravel road leading into the village. At one time this was considered a toll gate, and whoever lived in the white house unlatched it for approaching motorists. So few vehicles came this way now, Cissy left the gate open, and now Lilah and two boys were swinging on it. She beckoned for us to join her as we waited for Miss Brant to finish talking to an auburn-haired girl who was sobbing convulsively and gasping about wanting to go home.

I began to feel very fortunate. Red-headed Muriel was billeted with a family that included two small sons who so far had delighted in pinching and punching her when their parents weren't looking. Then there was Audrey, who had brought an infant grinning wetly from a pram. As an only child, with no experience of babies, she felt the need to jiggle the pram non-stop. We watched, mesmerised, as the little boy slowly turned pale green before vomiting down his linen coat. Audrey was told to take the wailing Reggie home. She didn't come back that day. Later we learned the baby's mother had gone off somewhere and didn't return until evening.

Lilah, to our surprise, was delighted with her billet. The elderly woman it turned out was the gran, collecting an evacuee for her daughter who on Sunday had gone to Derby to visit friends. The daughter 'Call me Tess' – ran a hairdressing 'salon' from her home and, according to Lilah, people came from all over Derbyshire to have her style their hair.

What's more she was going to pay Lilah for helping out, after school and on Saturdays. Gran had her own cottage in the village, so there were just the two of them. And it got better. Tess was going to teach her how to apply make-up, do cuts and curls and everything. Before the morning was out we were fed up with hearing about the wonderful Tess.

We didn't know what to say of the Simpsons. She seemed really nice, but would take some getting used to. Our mum had grown-up daughters to keep her on her toes with the latest trends. Cissy seemed to be in her own world, far removed from traffic and busy shops and young adults squabbling about hair clips and shampoo. A big plus was the food situation, which proved better than we had ever known. At this early stage I felt it could be quite pleasant here – even though it seemed disloyal to our family to say so.

With the summer holidays fast approaching, we had no formal schooling at first. Instead, we met with our fellow 'vaccys' each morning in the field adjoining the Simpsons', or under a voluminous tree in the schoolyard. There, Miss Brant would keep us busy with art, reading, simple arithmetic and writing. When our regular education resumed in September, I went with four other younger children to Charbury's one-roomed school, which already had fifteen or so students of varying ages.

Iris always said she couldn't remember where she went to school, though I believe she and most of the evacuees were bussed to a senior school in a nearby town. Certainly they went somewhere, with Miss Brant, five days a week.

Charbury was then and is now a compact community. Its current population is around 400, and I'd guess during the war it had half that number of residents living in the clutch of houses fanning out from one main street. There was a small grocer's-cum-post office, a church, the school and several farms on the outskirts. The Simpsons' house, as I remember it, was the village's second best, the first belonging to the vicar, who lived across from the church. Mr Farrow, our village schoolteacher, lived down the hill beside the main highway. There was a pub, too, called the White Horse, which had been the villagers' local for more than a century.

When we assembled with Miss Brant that Monday morning, our first assignment was to write our postcards. I can't even imagine the depth of their anxiety, as parents waited to receive those cards. Or the distress, if their child wrote of being unhappy.

I gave my new address as The Lodge, Charbury, Near Derby, and in doing so could visualise Dad getting his map of Britain out, and his magnifying glass, to see just where his two youngest daughters were to spend the rest of the war. To this I added that we arrived safely and were billeted together with a nice lady we called Aunty

Ciss. I understand my postcard brought Mum no joy at all.

Some foster parents wrote to their new charge's parents, starting a correspondence that continued through the war and beyond. The Simpsons never did. In all his life, I don't think Joe ever wrote more than his name. Cissy, quite shy with outsiders, simply said she hoped our Mam would understand as how she wasn't very good with a pen.

Within a week we settled into our new routines. I can only assume that children are extremely adaptable. Without argument, we did the chores assigned to us. Nothing too onerous, they included errands, which I enjoyed. Mostly messages to the vicar and women from Aunty Cissy's church, and the picking up of fresh produce from a neighbouring farm.

My favourite place was the farm, where I would take a metal billy-can every morning before school, and sometimes again in late afternoon, for our milk. Local kids were able to swing the lidless cans like catherine wheels without spilling their contents. I tried it only once, and emptied the lot. Mrs Gee the farmer's wife hustled me into her kitchen. There she hastily washed off my dress, telling me to run about in the sun to get it dry, while she refilled the can.

If Aunty Ciss noticed the damp patch down one side of my dress, she never did say so. But, since absolutely nothing happened in the village without everyone hearing of it, my ineptitude surely would have reached her at some point.

Gossip was a major pastime in Charbury. With no preliminaries, I would hear women on their way to the shop or church, asking 'Did ye hear what so-and-so's lad went and did...' and then recount what likely started out as something small and grew with each telling. Inevitably it concerned an evacuee, confirming unfounded suspicions that we were not to be trusted.

One of the biggest tongue-wags was the elderly spinster, Miss Beer, who lived in a cottage beside The Lodge. Unlike my mother, who professed to have eyes in the back of her head, Miss Beer had radar to alert her to whatever Iris or I were doing a mile away. At that point in my life I had never disliked anyone more.

'Who was playing with the kittens in the hay and spoiling her newly washed frock,' she'd call after me as I scurried by on my way home from the farm.

'Was that rouge I'm to tell Cissy I seen on your cheeks this morning, you hussy,' she'd cackle to Iris.

'Afternoon, Miss Beer,' Iris would reply with a cheery wave. 'Nice to see you too.'

My love for nature grew from those early years as an evacuee as I quickly came to appreciate the countryside and wildlife inhabiting it. From The Lodge, I could simply slip through the hedge into a world shared only with birds and rabbits and farm animals. It was heady stuff. I'd lie on the grass listening to the buzz of small creatures I knew so little about. I marvelled at the delicacy of primroses and violets, growing wild with no gardener's help. I learned how to milk a cow. I knew the wonder of lifting eggs from beneath the soft warm bodies of hens. And virtually tingled with excitement when Uncle Joe and I checked nests in our hedge, to see if their pale turquoise eggs had hatched.

Iris liked very little about her stay in Charbury. Still 'lippy', as my mother referred to her quick retorts, she later told me she had spent a lot of time working out ways to get home. Within days, she and Lilah wrote off the local boys as prospective friends. For one thing they 'talked funny', the central England accent being far different from our own. For another they were farm lads, and dressed accordingly. Also, Iris was of an age where she yearned to go to the cinema on Saturdays, and perhaps a local dance chaperoned by her older sisters. Unfortunately for her, Charbury offered no such entertainment.

Older boys worked in the fields, while the three or four more youthful villagers played cowboys and Indians endlessly in a big yard behind a row of farm workers' houses. We had little to do with them, in part because Miss Brant invited all her evacuees on Saturday hikes and picnics throughout the summer.

For us, it was a time of abundance. With Cissy, we gathered red and blackcurrants, and plump blackberries from hedges separating the fields beyond our house. Next we helped (or watched) her make these berries into jam and preserves, sealed into jars which Iris and I labelled before lining them up on the stone shelves of the larder.

There was something very satisfying about being self-sufficient. Most of our vegetables were grown in the garden and, as well as our milk, we bought meat and poultry from the farm. Cissy was an impressive cook, making everything from scratch, of course. I can still remember the taste of her rabbit and chicken pies enhanced by thick creamy gravy heavily laced with Bovril.

Derbyshire's seasons are more clearly defined than those in the south. At home, winter usually brought nothing harsher than sea mists and fogs and occasionally a thick frost to decorate holly bushes with sparkling webs. Winter in the north came with bitter winds, and thick fluffy blankets of snow on the fields. It lasted for months, and we loved it.

After school while it was still light, we built

elaborate snowmen and flew down the hill on a piece of old ply-board, and when it was time to go home we trudged back to The Lodge for hot cocoa and sponge cake by a crackling fire. Hands and feet tingled from the warmth, our cheeks were as pink as Mum's roses, and we gave little thought to food shortages and bombs and air-raid sirens piercing the night air.

Cissy spent her evenings knitting thick socks for soldiers. She even made some for us to put inside our wellies. We didn't have any snow boots. I doubt Mum knew such things existed. With Aunty's mismatched socks (made from left-over wool) inside our wellies, we really didn't need them.

When she wasn't knitting, Cissy made rugs from scraps of cloth we would cut into strips, using scissors so blunt our fingers were permanently blistered. The multi-hued plaited mats could be seen in most of Charbury's houses, following the church's fund-raising sales and raffles.

CHAPTER SIX

At Home with the Simpsons

That's the good stuff. The bad, for us at least, was that this was a very religious household. Every evening Cissy would read her Bible aloud for a good half hour before we went to bed. From the slight tapping of Iris's feet, I knew she spent this time running tunes she'd heard at Lilah's through her head. I tried to understand Cissy's recitations, truly I did, but my thoughts inevitably escaped to compositions for school and planned letters home.

Sundays, a favourite day at 19 Kent, were no fun at all in Charbury. We wore our best clothes from morning to night, and weren't allowed to play or read our comics. Cissy didn't knit or sew on the Sabbath. Against her better judgement she did once, she said, and – lo and behold – the baby's leggings she was in such a hurry to finish ended up with two left legs. Like us, Uncle Joe looked thoroughly miserable, sitting quietly in his uncomfortable three-piece suit and starched-collar shirt, his black boots so shiny we could see ourselves in them. Formal clothes looked oddly out of place on him. Perhaps it was his face, so sad, permanently ingrained with coal dust.

Nobody thought to ask if our parents would want us to attend church every chance we had. Like it or not we were paraded through the village, in our Sunday best - 'a real credit to you, Cissy' the villagers used to comment – twice a day on the Sabbath and religious holidays. Cissy was in no doubt that she was saving us from evil.

It was a lovely nineteenth-century church perched at the other end of the village from our house, on the hilltop above the highway. But while I could have enjoyed carol singing at Christmas, and maybe an Easter or Harvest Festival service, it sometimes seemed as if we lived there.

I marvelled at Iris's restraint on Sundays as we sat on the black leather sofa, cold and stiff as if it had died like the cat I found in the field some days after it had been hit by farm machinery. Since work of any kind was not allowed, we couldn't make so much as a cup of tea. No rashers or pork with crackling, no oven-warm sponge cakes dripping in jam for Sunday tea in this house. Instead there were eggs for breakfast, hard-boiled the night before, cold cuts for dinner and sandwiches for tea. Home entertainment came from our Bibles.

Aching so much from all the sitting, we

welcomed performing what few chores were permissible. Mostly though we stared into our laps. In my head I wrote stories and did sums. Iris reckoned she honed the finer details of our escape. Even Lilah knew not to come knocking at our door on Sundays.

This was the only day of the week when I felt an unshakable melancholy settle over me like a voluminous black cloak. It was the one time I wanted so much to be home at 19 Kent – in that crowded front room with our sisters dancing to their gramophone records, the make-up sessions where they took turn as models. The happy confusion. Sunday dinner sizzling in the oven. And Dad almost, but not quite, winning the football pools that would make us filthy rich.

'This is it Ede. I've done it, old girl. I mean this time we've really got it,' he would say, barely able to contain his excitement while skimming over football results in the *News of the World*.

'That's nice,' Mum would reply, not pausing in her chores. She never checked his numbers. Her hopes of winning anything had long passed.

Reading them more closely, he let out the inevitable sigh of disbelief.

'Blimey, I thought we'd gone and done it, Ede,' he would say. 'One number wrong. Shows we're getting close, though.'

'Oh dear. Well you'll just have to try again

next week...' Thump, thump, thump, she would continue to pound the mashed potatoes, straight-faced, probably miles away in her thoughts.

Iris told Aunty about Dad and his pools, and how nobody ever believed him when he thought he had won. Cissy was aghast. It was sinful to throw good money away like that. If he didn't need it, he could have given it to God's work.

On pre-war Sundays, nobody strayed far from 19 Kent until they'd had their dinner. This was the one day of the week when we all sat down together, with extra leaves extended in the front-room table covered with a snowy-white damask cloth. It gave us a ton of washing up to get through before we started on tea. Christmas Day was more of the same, only better.

Christmas in Charbury was as cheerless as a typical Sunday. Cissy softened enough to say we could unwrap our parcels from home, then clucked disapprovingly that the two of us would receive so much when children were starving all over the world. From that point on, everything skidded rapidly downhill.

We spent just one Christmas with the Simpsons, and I remember it well. The only time I ever saw Uncle Joe grin from ear to ear was when he brought our present in from its hiding place in the shed. A wonderful two-person sledge, fire-engine red, with a steering bar and hooter he had scrounged from heaven knows where. His eyes glistened at our delight. He even managed to stutter that he thought he might like to ride it down the hill with us later in the day.

That's when a scowling Cissy stepped in to say church was in fifteen minutes, and he could take 'that thing' outside until tomorrow. I guess we should have been more effusive in our thanks for the little white leather Bibles she gave us with such great ceremony.

I suppose it could have been worse. We could have been shut in the cupboard under the stairs, or screamed at for waking the household at dawn, as were two of our friends. For us, Christmas 1941 was merely sad and lonely, when it could have been a lot of fun.

Abiding by Cissy's rules, we trekked to church three times that day, and then listened to a fourth service on the wireless. The turkey, cooked on Christmas Eve, was served cold with vegetables that were practically raw. After the evening church service, Cissy urged us to read our new Bibles. Joe stared glumly into his black leather-bound copy; his wife smiled benignly down at hers. For the first time in months I wanted to blink and twitch, and cry.

No crackers to be pulled, no paper hats,

no cheap decorations from Petticoat Lane or home-made paper chains. No tiny tree, its bucket wrapped in red crepe paper and branches thick with baubles that had been passed down through the generations. No ribald songs or charades or Dad's imitation of Adolf that had us in stitches.

In Charbury as we undressed for bed on Christmas night, I stared through the window prettily laced with ice, and felt dreadfully cold. Snow continued to fall, resting heavily on trees, weighing down the holly hedge with its bright red berries. The scene was hauntingly beautiful, the silence daunting, but Iris was too angry to come for a look.

'Give me the bleedin' 'eathens any day,' she snarled, they're more Christian than this lot will ever be.' When she added that we would never spend another Christmas in this bloody awful place, I was seriously worried. Supposing her escape plans were nearing completion? Would she expect me to go with her?

At the junior school across from The Lodge, I was one of the more fortunate students in that its only teacher, Mr Farrow (known as Gaffer) liked me. My lack of schooling for the past year proved no handicap in so mixed a class, where some ten-year-olds were still struggling to read. Eager to learn, I soon caught up to a boy called

Edward, who was the school's star pupil.

Gaffer was a man with a wild temper, who cowed the children with a bamboo cane he carried hooked over his arm. Two brothers, who strangely enough were two of the school's brightest students, received most of his abuse. For no reason I could see, this madman would suddenly tell one or the other to stand up, then proceed to whack him mercilessly around the head, legs, body – anywhere he could reach on the dancing boy. Edward, the elder of the two, had permanently red eyes from crying. Why their parents didn't complain, I will never know. Gaffer had more sense than to attack any of the evacuees, though his threats often had us shaking in our shoes.

It happens that I owe Gaffer Farrow a debt of gratitude. Perhaps, in a classroom where most pupils were destined to work in the colliery or become farmhands, it was my keenness to learn that caught his attention. For whatever reason, he began tutoring me for a scholarship. Twice a week he drove me down the hill and along the highway to his tiny home, where his wife had milk and biscuits waiting for us.

Here, I saw a different Gaffer, one who showed none of the cruelty displayed in his classroom. In his cosy front room my studies included new maths problems and areas of history not covered at school. When we were done, some two hours later, I would walk home – occasionally meeting Uncle Joe wearily pushing his bicycle up the bill towards our village. Usually he said no more than ''Ello, young Pam' and we continued in comfortable silence. One day though, in his slow way of speaking, he said he was no older than me when he started work in the pit. He described that first day on the job, and his fear at being underground. And in a surprisingly firm voice he added that I was a very lucky girl, and must be sure not to waste all this education.

My tutoring, application to sit for the scholarship, and all it entailed, were arranged between Miss Brant and Gaffer Farrow. I assume my parents agreed, although nothing was said to me. In early spring we counted down the weeks to the Saturday I would take the required exams in Heanor, a sizeable town north of Charbury. Since Edward, the elder of the two brothers assaulted daily by Gaffer, was also going, Cissy insisted that we walked together. Just as well, I suppose, because he knew the way.

Edward was not my friend. He was surly, and sneered at the evacuees as if we were from some lower planet, and bullied younger children. I have to admit though that on this day he was quite likeable. Along the way we tested each other with questions and, having set off early, stopped for a sandwich and milk from our flasks beneath a tree. Here we checked our satchels to be sure we had the requisite fountain pen and blotting paper, an eraser, sharpened pencils, and clean hanky.

Both of us wore our Sunday best, which meant Edward was in his grey serge suit with knee-length shorts and high grey socks held up by garters. He had a ruler stuck down one sock for safe-keeping. I wore my favourite light brown dress with orange flowers embroidered on the yoke. Mum had sent it for me to wear over Easter, along with new patent ankle-strap shoes – totally unsuitable for a long walk on dirt and gravel roads. Iris gave me a rabbit's foot for good luck.

As I recall, the exams took up the best part of the day. When Edward and I met for our walk home, we both agreed we were pleased with the questions. I told him how, during the lunch break, I had met two girls who were at school with me when I first started in Infants. One said matter-of-factly that she had heard I died of 'the dip'. Edward thought this amusing.

Looking back, yet again I am astonished at how much was left to chance. Would I have let my eleven-year-old daughter go off to such an important event without an adult escort? I don't think so. Yet Cissy wasn't the least concerned. Afterwards, she didn't even want to know about the exam. Gaffer, on the other hand, went over every question and my answers, and was pretty certain I had passed with flying colours.

Forty years later I met Edward's mother in Charbury's crowded little shop. She took me to her house, brought out family albums, and proudly told me that her elder son taught at university while his younger brother was doing very well in London's world of finance.

When we parted company on the scholarship day, Edward surprised me by asking if I'd go to the pictures in Ilkeston with him one Saturday. I said I would talk to Aunty, even though I knew she didn't approve of cinemas, or boys.

It never occurred to me that some of our villagers might go to the cinema on their weekend excursions to Ilkeston, the market town just east of Charbury. After lunch on Saturdays, a double-decker bus came to the village to take passengers into town. Around four in the afternoon it brought us back.

In Ilkeston, for those few hours, Iris and I enjoyed being on our own, spending pocket money sent from home. Cissy went off to the market, to buy what bits and pieces were available in the way of knitting wool, sewing supplies, and anything else she might need but couldn't make for herself. Then we'd meet her in a café for a cup of tea, before our ride back home.

This was the only chance we had to shop for ourselves. Usually Iris bought a magazine called *Girls' Crystal,* and I looked for a *Dandy* or *Beano* comic. We loved the market being so crowded with shoppers, and hawkers yelling things we couldn't understand. It reminded us of Southend. At Christmas there were even street performers, totally unsophisticated by today's standards, but still they enthralled us with their juggling and banjo music. On a really good Saturday I would find someone selling crayons and notebooks, and a few pieces of sticky peppermint rock to eat on the bus ride home.

Considering ourselves particularly clever, one Saturday we bought Aunty a boxed set of lavender water and matching scented soap wrapped in mauve paper. Until her birthday, we hid the package in one of the sandbags under our bed, occasionally taking it out for a luxurious whiff. When the big day came, she told us sharply that only fools wasted their money on such frivolity. So far as we knew, she never even took our presents from their box.

Cissy made her own soap, horrible hard blocks of it, which we hated to use on our skin. It produced virtually no lather, yet made dirty clothes clean and bright as new, when she scrubbed away with it at her corrugated washboard in the bath kept in the backyard.

We had a big decision to make on Saturdays, because that's the day Miss Brant escorted her evacuees on hikes through the countryside. I loved them. I loved being with her. She knew so much about ferns and flowers, and told us stories of her own childhood in the Lake District not far from here.

We carried picnic lunches that we ate under a tree, or in pouring rain beneath a bridge scattered with human and animal waste. Miss Brant was more approachable than other teachers I met later during my evacuation. On our walks she actually encouraged us to talk about our foster families, any problems we had or concerns about war news from home.

Although she was barely older than some of my sisters, she knew how to assuage young Peter's fears, and made us feel good about small achievements in school. She also assured us that this old war would not last for ever. And, yes, she would definitely let us know if she heard that streets our families lived on had been bombed. With Miss Brant as her teacher, I never understood Iris's lack of enthusiasm for school.

Neither of us saw much of Lilah as time went on. Iris's friend had become totally boring apparently, with endless stories about the salon and its customers. She kept up to date with the latest hairstyles designed to keep female workers' tresses out of factory machinery and above uniform collars. She even took to wearing a snood, something like a black fishing net, which looked quite silly considering her bobbed hair.

At thirteen, Iris had developed an interest and skills that went beyond new hair-dos and singing the latest songs to her mirrored self. The singing had to go anyway, because the Simpsons had only one small mirror in the house. It was cracked and worn, and often splattered with Uncle Joe's shaving soap. Also it was propped up in the scullery, which was too uninviting to hang around in unnecessarily.

For the next few months, cookery became the love of Iris's life. Here in the country, while some foods were in short supply, others were so plentiful she could enjoy the challenge of creating tasty new dishes. Alter school she might come home to find Cissy poring over cookery books, looking for a recipe we would all enjoy and that Iris could adjust to whatever supplies were in the pantry.

Apparently when Mum received my letter saying Iris's bread had risen better than Aunty Cissy's, she thought I was pulling her leg. When another mentioned that her pastry was as light as air, she was dismayed to realise how much the cheekiest of her

106

seven girls had changed.

Most of the time Cissy seemed to enjoy having two ready-made daughters. I had become handy with a needle, while my sister took genuine pleasure in her new cooking skills. We were the first children the Simpsons had come to know so well. Neither of them seemed to have relatives.

Our lack of interest in formal religion aside, we caused her little angst. Iris was sometimes too quick with her retorts in the early weeks, but with passing time she became more tolerant of Cissy's ways.

For my part, I was grateful to be left alone in our room while the pair of them pondered the latest recipe. So long as it was light outside, I loved nothing more than to curl up in the window, reading books borrowed from Gaffer Farrow's house. Or I'd write lengthy descriptive letters home. Some were so long I had trouble fitting them into their envelopes.

Not only did I write about everyday happenings, animal births and deaths at the farm but, showing no sensitivity at all, I described in detail the wild raspberry pies and lamb stews and those warm cobs dripping with butter. Mostly, though, I wrote of the countryside, which changed so dramatically here with each passing season. There were also exciting tales of our expeditions with Miss Brant, and trips into Ilkeston on Saturdays.

My mother reciprocated with thoughtful letters telling us about our sisters; where they were, what they were up to. Dad was away a lot of the time now, repairing bomb damage. Rose was kept busy with her ARP duties, patrolling on the lookout for blackout leaks, attending bomb and fire victims.

Although our part of England's south coast was not intentionally targeted by German aircraft, it was attacked anyway, when they were prevented from getting through to London. Instead of taking their 'eggs' home, they would unload them on Essex and neighbouring counties. Some were wasted at sea; others deliberately dropped on civilian sites.

Mum's letters said little about local raids, or food shortages that had her queueing at shops for hours on end. When she wrote asking about specific evacuees whose parents were worried by their scrappy little notes home, I would gleefully report on their activities – usually exaggerating about their fun-filled days, which kept them too busy to keep in touch.

Winter reluctantly gave way to a late spring without real crisis in the village. There were few links with the war raging in Europe, or the bombing of industrial areas. As close as we came to the war first-hand was when a German plane crashed into a field beyond the Simpsons' house, and we joined villagers gathered around the bewildered pilot whose parachute had tangled in a tree.

Children, who knew they shouldn't, took pieces of the aircraft as souvenirs. Grown men who should have known better prodded the young man with their pitchforks. Nobody seemed to know what to do with him, until someone's brother, who was a policeman in Ilkeston, arrived and took him away. For days it was the talk of the village. Until Brenda in the end cottage gave birth to a stillborn baby.

Brenda, little more than a child herself, married soon after leaving school and lived in Derby until her husband volunteered for the militia. She was staying with her mam in Charbury when her infant was born. Cissy decided we should see the body. We were horrified.

Iris said she was sure it wasn't something our mum would want us to do.

'She would,' Cissy assured us. 'Death is part of life.'

And so we did. In our Sunday best we dragged our feet through the village to where neighbours were coming and going from the tiny row house with 'Brenda loves Barry' scratched on the chipped brick beneath its front window.

As a mark of respect, all curtains on the street were drawn. And there in the front room was a little white box, no more than two feet long, lined with white satin. Inside was a doll-like figure in a white cotton bonnet and gown. I stared at its face and wondered how anything that looked so squashed, more like a turnip than a child, could be referred to as 'my Cheryl' even by its own mother. But it was Iris, not me, who woke up screaming that night saying shrivelled rubber faces were chasing her through the field.

A few days later a letter from home told us we were to be aunties. Our sister Kath was expecting a baby. The news was joyous, but worrisome too, because Kath continued to live in east London, which was being heavily bombed. Aunty Cissy thought it very wrong for us to be told of the pending birth, which was still months away. I believe 'disgusting' was a word she used, adding that we were too young to know about making babies.

Iris piped up that our sister was married, and that's what married people do. This comment caused considerable tutting and head shaking, along with a threat to wash our mouths out with soap.

That night I admitted to Iris how little I knew about making babies, even though I'd seen the pigs give birth at the farm.

Her 'Yeah well ... another time. I've got to sleep now,' spoke volumes on how little she knew on the subject herself.

Stories of London's Blitz filtered through to us in letters from home to our fellow evacuees. No Pathé News at the cinema for us these days, but we were permitted occasionally to hear the grave voices of the BBC announcers. The Blitz, a term given to the bombing of London and other industrial centres throughout England, had started in September 1940 and continued to May of the following year, with the main concentration on London. Before they were through, German bombs had killed 43,000 civilians and destroyed or damaged more than a million houses.

By mid-November, more than 13,000 tons of high explosive, as well as a million or so incendiary bombs, had demolished many parts of London. Probably the most devastating raid was on the evening of 29 December 1940, creating what became known as the Second Great Fire of London.

The last major raid on England's capital came in May 1941, when 541 German bombers destroyed or damaged the historic British Museum, the Houses of Parliament and St James's Palace. The raid inflicted more casualties than any other: approximately 1,500 killed and 1,800 seriously injured. None of these details was given to us in our quiet little corner of the world. Not that it was to be quiet much longer. Here in Charbury that May it was scandal, not bombs, that forced us from our homes.

CHAPTER SEVEN

What Have We Done Wrong?

Although cheap day and weekend rail tickets were available for parents wanting to visit their evacuees, and even allowed children to go home for special events, we were told we lived too far from Essex for our families to make use of these. I don't recall any friends or relatives visiting Charbury's vaccys. With petrol increasingly hard to come by, and then permitted only for journeys considered essential, nobody expected parents with cars to drive three or four hours to reach us. Perhaps had they been able to do so, things might have worked out differently.

Something I have never understood is how our evacuee destinations were chosen. Some Londoners were sent to Chelmsford in Essex, just eighteen miles from my home, a distance my sisters had ridden often on their bicycles. Yet our school was sent on what amounted to a whole day's journey during wartime. Also, children from northern cities such as Liverpool, Manchester and Birmingham were evacuated to Norfolk and Sussex, an easy commute from my home but a long way from theirs. Derbyshire, where I was, is an easy distance from industrial cities in central and northern England, yet children from those areas were sent south, or south-west to Wales.

Because we were told to write cheerful letters home, few of our parents knew exactly what went on in their evacuated children's everyday lives. Perhaps if Miss Brant had been more observant ... or Beryl's parents had visited ... or Uncle Phil had chosen to spend his shore leave somewhere other than his sister's house in Charbury... Oh, isn't hindsight lovely?

At first I was unaware of a new man in the village. Commonly known as Uncle Phil, he was a naval officer who sometimes stayed in a terrace house across from the school. I had little to do with him at first. What with my extra homework and tuition at Gaffer Farrow's house, along with daily chores, there wasn't a lot of time to socialise during the week. Even less on weekends, being confined to the house except for church on Sundays, and off with Miss Brant or Cissy on Saturdays.

Still, at some point I understood Uncle Phil to be the source of American chocolate bars such as I had never seen before, and large juicy oranges. This was in the late spring of 1941, by which time such luxuries were in desperately short supply. Every villager had access to farm produce, local fruit and vegetables, but imported fruits and sweets were out of the question. Unless you had an Uncle Phil in your life.

Once I knew the drill, and time permitting, I too joined the happy children prancing around him, hoping to get a Hershey bar or packet of Wrigleys chewing gum.

With warmer weather upon us, Uncle Phil would hold sports competitions in the field. Who could do the most cartwheels or handstands? Who could walk on their hands, or run fastest in the wheelbarrow race? Not me, but I gave them a good try anyway. These were innocent children's games, for which we girls tucked our dresses in our underwear to get them out of the way. And that pleased Uncle Phil no end. Flushed with excitement over our chocolate, nobody noticed how upset Audrey looked on one occasion, emerging from the woods with a second bar of chocolate while Uncle Phil followed nonchalantly a few feet behind. Next day it was another girl who earned an extra prize. Had I given it any thought at all, I would probably have concluded he had a second stash hidden in the trees.

Iris and Lilah had a friend called Beryl, who along with her younger brother Wilf was billeted with Uncle Phil's sister. It was young Wilf who spilled the beans about Beryl's unwanted attention from the naval

114

officer during the night when they were trying to sleep.

According to Wilf, at first they believed the house to be haunted. Sometimes he saw the outline of this man in the darkness of their bedroom. Once Beryl woke up to find all the buttons on her pyjama jacket undone. Then the other morning she discovered she wasn't wearing her pyjama trousers at all.

Lilah, who was more worldly than Iris and Beryl, put two and two together, and decided this was no ghost. It happened only when Uncle Phil was home from America, right? Then obviously he was the culprit. What's more, they should tell Miss Brant. Beryl refused, so when the situation worsened, Lilah and Iris approached her on their friend's behalf.

They were frightened for Beryl after she whispered that she had gone to sleep wearing a nightie, and woke up in the morning with nothing on. Was she being drugged like Veronica in their latest copy of *Girls' Crystal?* Worse still, would she have a baby from all this touching? Who could know, when she was unable to say exactly what happened?

Beryl was furious when Miss Brant asked her to explain what was going on. Obviously there was something. The poor girl was pale, tired, inattentive in class and, when tackled on the subject of Uncle Phil, frightened of reprisals from her foster family. Tearfully,

115

she told her story, and however unlikely it sounded, Miss Brant knew it was true.

Uncle Phil had gone back to sea when the teacher called on his sister, who claimed it was all a pack of lies. Her evacuee was an ungrateful brat, who could leave her house immediately unless she took back the hateful accusations. With her predator out of the way for the next month or longer, Beryl apologised, and stayed in her unhappy billet.

Blissfully ignorant of child molestation, I thought little more of it although it did seem odd that Iris, Beryl and Lilah had several dental appointments in Ilkeston accompanied by Miss Brant. After one such visit, when it occurred to me that none of the girls returned with frozen or swollen faces, I asked to see Iris's fillings. Uncharacteristically, she told me to mind my own business.

Then one awful Saturday morning in early June, I went for the milk as usual. Mrs Gee at the farm did not respond to my cheery 'Good morning'. Her son, who filled my can, looked everywhere but at me. As I walked home I realised nobody was about. Usually a few village boys would be racing noisily around the courtyard behind Miss Beer's cottage. And on such a nice Saturday morning, three or four girls should have been playing Double Dutch or Hopscotch in the communal yard. On this day everything was eerily quiet. Until I arrived at The Lodge, where an unholy row had reached hurricane force.

As I stood stunned, comic books came flying through our bedroom window. Our precious comics that we swapped and re-swapped with our friends. Cissy was screeching obscenities such as I had never heard anywhere before, least of all from her. Clearly she had gone stark raving mad.

Leaving my milk on the scullery table, I raced upstairs to our bedroom, so foreign to me a year ago but now a comfortable haven. Just yesterday I had stared at the gardens below, and the field in which colts and calves were growing sturdier every day. The gnarled old apple tree was experiencing life anew. Uncle Joe's vegetables prospered. Wild flowers had been allowed to flourish among them, bringing golds and reds and royal blues to mingle with the many shades of green.

A safe harbour no more, our room looked as if a tornado had swept through it. Cissy continued to empty the contents of our wardrobe on to the bed; Joe sat miserably on the worn wicker chair. I stood there in dumb horror. A white-faced Iris was attempting to stuff far more than would ever fit into our sandbags.

According to Aunty Ciss, Iris was an ungrateful slut. She turned and saw me, cringing in the doorway. 'You too,' she screamed.

'Go back to the bombs. It's what you deserve. Leave us God-fearing people alone. Nothing but trouble since the day you came...'

The tirade continued. It was all untrue, but I couldn't say a word in our defence, because I had no idea what was going on. I supposed it had something to do with the trio's mysterious visits to Ilkeston. But how could they have turned my cosy world upside-down?

It had to be bad. As well as the swearing, for which Aunty Ciss would certainly repent next day, there was Uncle in our bedroom wearing his mud-caked boots and gardening clothes. The picture of misery, he held his head in his hands.

Calmly, Iris explained that we were leaving the village. Some bloke, from the courts or schools or somewhere, had come banging on the door and handed Cissy a printed notice. It read that, in the light of recent events, and hostility directed at all evacuees in Charbury during the last twenty-four hours, for our own safety we were being taken out of the community for relocation. We would leave at two o'clock today, and there was to be no further communication between us and Charbury's residents until after the war.

With not so much as a glimmer of understanding, I dutifully began stuffing my sandbag.

118

'She dunna mean it, luv,' Joe said unsteadily, when his wife stomped off to the scullery to crash pots and pans around in the sink. 'Right now she sees it as a terrible shame you've all brought to the village. In time she'll think different.'

'But why? What have we done?' I wailed. I could smell a shepherd's pie simmering on the hearth, and suddenly concluded I liked it here too much to move on.

Briefly, Iris told me how the 'sodding pervert' known as Uncle Phil was arrested when he left his ship in Liverpool, and there had been a court case. Now he was in the clink. Beryl and Wilf had already been moved to an undisclosed destination, but since it had been in the papers and brought shame to the village, everyone had turned on the rest of us.

Iris was in hot water for urging Beryl to talk to Miss Brant about it. She and Lilah had spoken to the police, during their 'dental' visits to Ilkeston, and the three girls he had molested in the woods gave evidence. It was too much for me to take in. I couldn't believe all this had gone on without my knowledge. Nor could I begin to understand why we were being punished for Uncle Phil's actions.

'Seems we're more the enemy than Jerry,' Iris concluded.

With our sandbags overflowing, she instructed me to wear two vests and pairs of knickers, and a jumper over my dress in spite of the early summer heat. I wanted to know about my scooter, which had arrived here – at great expense to my mother – just two weeks earlier. Joe lifted his tear-streaked face long enough to say he would get it to me, once he had word of our new address.

'When pigs fly,' was my sister's muttered response. He was called for his lunch. We remained upstairs, waiting for two o'clock. Iris's face was unfathomable. I was both sad and scared. I wouldn't see the baby birds in the hedge take their first flight, or the chicks grow into hens. I wondered if Gaffer Farrow had heard of our plight, and whether the scholarship people would know where to reach me. Most of all I was fearful of being the last to be chosen by our new pretend parents.

At a quarter to two, when we heard a bus chugging noisily outside the school, we hoisted our sandbags and gas masks on to our shoulders. I also dragged my satchel, bulging with schoolwork and the latest books from home, and we bumped down the stairs for the last time. Without hesitation, Joe came forward to relieve us of our bags and walk us to the waiting bus.

Cissy sat at the table, as if made of granite. Not a word. Not a grimace. She didn't even have her Bible in front of her.

'Thanks for everything,' Iris said with a

dignity I didn't know she had. Still no response.

'Yes, thanks,' I gulped, following my sister
out of the door.

Helping us to board the bus, Joe said
haltingly how much joy we had brought to
his life. It was the longest speech I had heard
him say in all the months we lived under his
roof. Movement across the road caused me
to turn back to The Lodge, and there was
Cissy banging my beloved scooter against the
wall. A wheel went flying across the garden. I
just hoped it didn't hit one of the nests in the
hedge.

A cluster of hostile villagers stood silently
by.

'Good riddance, then,' someone called
out. The bus was barely on its way when the
first stone was heaved, causing the back
window to crack.

CHAPTER EIGHT

We are Welcomed at Ivy House

Once again we found ourselves sitting in a
school hall on a row of folding chairs, this
time in the village of Kirk Langley, just twelve
or so miles from Charbury. None of us smil-

ing hopefully. Nobody crying this time around. No sense of an adventure about to happen. We had become war veterans, hardened by events, suspicious of strangers who we now knew may not be as nice as they looked. Our gas mask cases were torn, our bundles tatty. There was no time to have haircuts and baths and be given clean hankies for our journey, as there had been a year earlier.

Later Iris told me she was ready to snarl at anyone who looked remotely like a pervert, as farmers and their families came forward to claim the more desirable among us. Most of the good billets had been taken a year ago. Now, on this warm sunny day that had held such promise earlier, villagers had been called from their chores and asked to open their doors and hearts a little wider. One couple brought their two evacuees with them, so they could choose a third who would be sharing their room.

My sister and I sat at the end of the row, near a door. Suddenly it burst open and a short, round man who looked rather like a well-fed tramp burst through it. I can see him now, wearing baggy old tweed trousers held up by braces, a sweat-soaked chequered shirt, and muddy brown boots. Wiping perspiration from his face with a grubby handkerchief, he looked from the short row of adults to a longer line of children and, realising he had come in through the wrong door, he announced to nobody in particular, 'Never could find my way around a school.'

When Iris smiled, in a few quick steps he was at our side.

'Would you like to come and live with us, then?' he asked, still mopping his apple-red face.

Grabbing me, my sister told him we were a pair.

'Loovely. My Min will be right pleased to have two instead of one.'

A young man in charge galloped over, spluttering that Mr Dean, sir, was down for a teacher. Possibly two. Funny what you remember seventy years later. I clearly see the saliva at the side of his mouth, the lank blond hair a shade too long for wartime fashions and an unhealthy pallor to his skin.

Mr Dean, sir, shook his head. 'Can't stand 'em. Teachers,' he replied breezily, beckoning us to follow him through the side door clearly marked 'no exit'.

'Car's this way, young ladies.' All three of us ignored the billeting officer, now practically foaming at the mouth.

'Crikey, he's got a motor.' Iris was grinning from ear to ear. I felt less optimistic. For a few wild moments I'd had the idea once again that we might have been sent back to Essex.

Manoeuvring his little Austin out of the lane, Fred told us his wife couldn't be with him at the school because he had come straight from his brother's farm.

'In any case,' he added, 'she's in her wheelchair, so it can be difficult.'

Aha. This is why they were passed over when the first batch of evacuees arrived last year. Iris rolled her eyes at me. So that's the catch, she wanted to say. We are going to be pushing some fat old woman around in a wheelchair.

'She'll be really pleased to see I've brought two instead of one,' Mr Dean – 'Call me Uncle Fred' – assured us, turning into an ivy-covered house, which to us was a veritable mansion. Seemingly over the moon at what he considered such a good catch, he lightly patted Iris's knee, in a gesture not missed by either of us.

Out of nowhere, an orderly line of small fluffy ducklings came waddling towards him. 'Their mam will be after them,' Uncle Fred cautioned, 'so we'll just wait a minute.' Sure enough, an agitated duck raced into view, and literally shooed her family around to the back of the house. Fred's smile would have lit the sky on a moonless night, as he switched off the engine, raised his head and announced: 'Here's my loovely Min.'

Min was not lovely in a physical sense. Her thin face was lined with pain. A thick bush of unruly grey hair made her head appear too large for her body. Her legs were so crooked, as far as they were visible below the unstylishly long frock, I wondered how they could possibly be attached to her body. In the doorway she stood, a diminutive woman leaning on two canes.

Awkwardly, holding the sticks in the air, she hugged us both, saying we were her 'poor wee looves'. Going on to explain that Vera had made us cakes and lemonade, and how blessed she was that her clever Freddy had managed to get two such lovely girls, she beamed from one of us to the other with obvious pleasure.

'I thought looking so dirty, he wouldn't be trusted with any,' she continued.

Her Midlands accent was so strong we couldn't get every word, but the voice was unmistakably warm, while her blue eyes set in sunken cheeks were shiny bright with joy. As we gratefully accepted her hugs, we caught the first whiff of eau de cologne, which we associated with Aunty Min throughout our lives. She playfully admonished her husband.

'Freddy, you should've come 'ome for a wash loov. I'm right surprised a dog would follow you home, let alone two beautiful young ladies.'

Harbouring unsettling thoughts that this was turning out to be too good to be true, we walked into a dim, cool room where a low table was set with plates of iced cakes and tall frosted glasses of lemonade. Min, assisted by her husband, moved to sit in a wheelchair across from the settee, on which Iris and I sat together as if still nervous of being separated.

Min continued to smile happily, while telling us that her Freddy had been helping at his brother's farm at the time she received the urgent call. When she telephoned him, well, she thought he'd have come home to get washed up. But then again, if he'd done that, all the children might have been snapped up before he got there. Not much chance of that, I thought, recalling the sullen looks on the faces of the would-be foster parents in the school.

'And then what does he do?' she exclaimed. 'Clever old boy that he is, he manages to bring us two.'

It was definitely too good to be true. Perhaps misinterpreting our suspicions for weariness, Min called for Vera to meet us.

Vera, the housekeeper who came in daily, led us upstairs to two bedrooms. We could have one each, or share and keep the other to play in. We decided to share a room.

I don't remember a lot about the house as it was then, other than the outside walls being covered almost entirely with ivy. I do recall it being cool and quiet and often empty on schooldays when we came home for lunch. Two places would be set in the dining room then: linen napkins in silver rings, cold cuts and fruit with fresh home-made bread, Vera's baked goods, and a cold lemon drink all on two trays with inverted bowls on top to keep off flies.

Where Aunty Min and Vera went on those days, nobody ever told us. Perhaps Min went for treatment, or did volunteer work; we couldn't tell from her clothes when they returned in late afternoon, because she always wore long floral print dresses or skirts.

The sense that our lives had taken us into a fairy-tale world continued, when Fred took us on a garden tour of the orchard and emerald-green lawns, the duck pond and chicken coops. And space, so much space everywhere. Gooseberry bushes would soon be heavy with juicy green berries. The vegetable garden kept him so busy, he said he often called his brother, Stanley, to help out. Across the lane, Fred rented a field in which he kept pigs. One huge sow was close to giving birth on the day we arrived, necessitating a visit to the sty every hour or so to check on her status.

On our first morning at Ivy House we came down to a cooked breakfast served by Uncle Fred, while Min sat at the end of the table in her wheelchair. Vera fussed with home-made rolls and butter, and a choice of jams to follow fried slices of thick ham and sausages and eggs. I couldn't help feeling guilty, thinking of Dad, if he was home on Sunday mornings, frying his fatty rashers helped out by a pan full of fried tomatoes. Invariably, he would be squinting into smoke generated by one of his skinny hand-rolled cigarettes. Mum would be scraping her marge on day-old bread, with Clarabelle looking on. It didn't seem right, to have so much while they had so little.

Accompanying Uncle Fred on a trip to see the pigs, I managed to ruin my black patent ankle-strap shoes that had been sent from home to wear last spring. Had I been given time to think clearly, I would have left these in Charbury and, instead packed my plim-solls and wellies. Now, without questioning the whereabouts of my more suitable footwear, Fred nipped along to the farm and brought back a pair of his niece's boots for me to borrow. Days later he came home from Derby, grinning with pride that he had managed to buy new boots *and* plimsolls. Shortages of rubber being so desperate, he had reason to be pleased with himself.

Exploring the garden on our own during that first day in Kirk Langley, we came across Lilah standing morosely by the front gate. She was furious to be billeted with a woman and two young children. She urged us to ask if she could move into Ivy House. Iris shook her head sadly. The missus was a cripple and couldn't handle any more kids.

It really wasn't definite that we would be staying. In any case, she lied, we had to wheel the old lady about in her chair and she knew Lilah would hate that.

On the following weekend, Lilah came back, this time with two adorable little blond moppets clinging to her skirt. We led all three of them into the orchard, where the girls delighted in chasing the ducklings. Vera brought us lemonade and her speciality cupcakes, and Lilah admitted it wasn't so bad in her billet once she got used to the half pints following her around.

When Iris considered it safe to introduce her friend to the spare room, without having her want to move in, part of it became a beauty salon of sorts where they spread out filched make-up from Lilah's Charbury home and Violet's shelf at 19 Kent, and had a high old time with it. Vera contributed lipsticks gritty with age; Aunty Min found metal clips that produced sausage curls if left long enough in our hair.

Uncle Fred's niece Sylvie had no need for curlers. According to our chief stylist, her thick wavy hair would have lent itself to the latest fashions of film stars. Sadly for Lilah, Sylvie wasn't interested in sitting before a mirror for more than two minutes at a time.

Both Aunty Min and Vera tentatively asked where we had lived before coming to Kirk Langley, and why we had left so suddenly. To jog our memories, Vera showed us a couple of paragraphs in a Derby newspaper. It said simply that all evacuees had been moved from a village in Derbyshire for their own safety, and there was to be no further contact between them and anyone from that community for the war's duration.

Having promised Miss Brant we would not talk about our unplanned departure, we said we didn't know. It was adult gossip. I didn't want to think about a deranged Aunty Ciss smashing my scooter against the wall. In any case I hadn't fully understood what all the fuss was about.

As I grew older, I remembered the kindnesses Cissy and Joe bestowed on two little strangers. Who was I to judge their lifestyle, their profound religious beliefs, their simple ways? Even before war's end, when my life as an evacuee spiralled downwards, I came to realise what good and generous souls they were.

Once I returned home I wrote to them every Christmas, and since my cards and letters were not sent back, I assumed they were read. Then one February, in the early sixties, I believe, my envelope came back unopened, stamped 'deceased'.

Whether one or both of the Simpsons had died I didn't know until I returned to the village many years later. That's when a neighbour told me Joe was so lost following Cissy's death, he moved away to be with a distant relative. As an afterthought, she added, 'He was a child. She did everything for him, you know,' and I could see the truth in what she said.

Meantime in Kirk Langley, Fred and Min Dean had longed for children of their own. In view of Min's crippling arthritis, which she attributed to heavy-duty work in a military hospital during the First World War, they never thought to adopt. Despite her disability, they filled their lives with love, laughter and joy.

I had never known a family with a social life. My parents were always too busy and perhaps they considered their home too crowded for entertaining. Except for Mrs Hardy, whose house backed on to ours, my mother had no true friends. She settled for lots of acquaintances who would stop and chat in the Broadway, or pause by the garden to discuss her roses.

With an erratic mail service as our only means of communication, it was even hit and miss when our out-of-town sisters wanted to visit. Once the war started Kath and Wally came less. Edie found it too much to bring her infants by public transport, and was disinclined to put them in the sidecar of Sam's newly acquired motorbike. In consequence the twins were in their third year when we first welcomed them to 19 Kent.

On that occasion Edie had written a week ahead to tell us when she would be visiting, but her letter wasn't delivered until after the trio's arrival – putting Mum in a real old flap.

It was even worse now, with Connie turning up unannounced on forty-eight hours' leave, often with a friend or two. And Dad's timetable, dictated by the when and where of bomb damage. If he was home, his idea of entertainment was not to receive friends in his home, but to meet them in a pub following a football game in Southend.

Once the war heated up he often joined Mum and Rose at the Odeon after the game, not for the sentimental movies they so enjoyed, but to see the Pathé newsreels with up-to-date footage of the battles raging in Europe and at sea.

One of the three letters we received from Dad during the war years was in June 1941.While we were settling in at Kirk Langley, Germany had invaded Russia on a huge 1,800-mile-long front. Dad wanted to be sure I looked at my atlas and saw that, in their march through Poland and the Baltic states on their way to Moscow and Leningrad, the Germans had foolishly diverted forces from western Europe. In so doing, he wrote, they gave Britain a chance to regroup. Like Napoleon before him, Hitler was a silly little man who bit off more than he could chew, and we would be home sooner than we thought. I wasn't at all sure this was what I wanted.

The Deans had good friends, and a house that was splendid for entertaining. What's more, they encouraged us to invite other vaccys to Ivy House. On Saturday evenings Sylvie and Lilah inevitably joined us in our spare room, where we'd practise dance steps to the wireless, and sing along with Vera Lynn or The Andrews Sisters. Most Saturdays, too, the Deans had friends and relatives drop by.

On those afternoons Vera didn't go home until she had covered the worn oak dining table with plates of cold pork and ham and crisp chicken legs, new potatoes dripping in butter, cheese platters, bowls of fresh salad from the garden. And baked goods. I had never seen so many outside a cake shop: fruit pies liberally sprinkled with sugar, custard tarts, rhubarb pies and sponge cakes.

Eating off trays upstairs with our friends, we would hear the laughter, bantering over a game of cards, records on the gramophone. Often we would be called down to watch Fred and his friend's wife attempting to jitterbug. On those Saturday evenings, I felt that all was well.

It wasn't, of course. Mum's weekly letters told me of bombs and casualties and how the Andrews boy along the road had come home from the front without legs. And the queues. Here we were with all this food, while she went on about two skinny pork chops she'd managed to get from the Co-Op, or an extra piece of cod slipped to her from under the counter by her favourite fishmonger, Good Alf.

I no longer hovered around the end of the drive waiting for the postman as I did in Charbury. Not only was I too busy, but I was losing interest in happenings at home. I hated this being so, because these were kind, thoughtful letters, telling me who in the family was where, and what they were doing to bring the war to a successful conclusion. Accounts of queueing, and attempts to make meals from few ingredients, Mum's ongoing war with the local wardens about chinks in the blackout, were described with humour. But the truth was I read her news with a twinge of guilt, because a part of me didn't want to be there sharing the shortages and bombs and all the other worrisome stuff going on at 19 Kent.

Not that Mum could have found my letters particularly riveting. Years later she told me she felt she was losing me, but wasn't unhappy because she knew I was getting a taste for the good life. The letter that had her wondering if had gone quite barmy, was one in which I told her about my pet pig, who smiled when he saw me and rolled on his back to be tickled. Barmy or not, it was true.

When the sow had a litter of five piglets, the smallest, who was always pushed out of the way at mealtime, looked so forlorn that Uncle Fred let me feed him with a bottle. From then on, the tiny cartoon-like creature followed me everywhere within his compound, and around the garden if I brought him across the road to be with us. We called him Mardi, a local word meaning 'soft' or 'silly' because he would prance about like a puppy whenever he saw me. And, instead of the traditional snort, he chortled when he wanted me to tickle his belly.

CHAPTER NINE

I May Like to Stay for Ever

Uncle Fred's workload wasn't confined to the animals and gardens of Ivy House. Although his hours seemed erratic, he did have a full-time job in Derby, where he was in charge of the Co-Op's stables. Horses here included magnificent shires, massive beasts employed to pull drays and canal barges loaded with coal. Each horse had its own stall, with a name such as Rita and Betty (for film stars Rita Hayworth and Betty Grable) painted above it, and every horse appeared to love Fred as much as he loved them.

When he couldn't sneak a few lumps of sugar from Vera's supply, he would bring home-made biscuits, for which these huge gentle creatures would nuzzle into his hand – or his pocket if he was slow in bringing out their treat.

About once a week that summer, he would take me to work on days when he knew he could leave for home after lunch. I loved it there; the smell of wax and leather and fresh hay. Watching him check the horses' feet and run his hands down their legs, I felt tremendous pride at being with 'the guy' making his rounds, receiving reports from the stable lads, who were literally boys because the older men were off at war.

In his office a glass-fronted cabinet displayed numerous ribbons and silver cups won by his horses in parades and competitions. Pictures of Uncle Fred standing triumphantly beside the winners crowded the walls. He told me of a parade in October, which could well be cancelled because of the war; but if it wasn't, then I could ride up front on one of the drays alongside him. He demonstrated how we would plait the horses' tails, attach brasses to their harnesses and rosettes in their manes for the big day. We might even sleep in these stables the night before, to work on the horses bright and early next morning. This was heady stuff for an eleven-year-old, a story good enough for me to write for *Girls' Crystal*.

Sometimes on the way to work Uncle Fred picked up a young man called Eric, who needed a lift into Derby. At seventeen, he was in the Home Guard, receiving training to defend us if the Germans ever landed. This was a voluntary force, ridiculed in the beginning when dedicated men and boys – usually too old or too young to be called up – assembled to train with nothing more threatening than pitchforks and rakes. Now they were organised, with over a million recruited across England, and like Eric almost all had uniforms and official weapons.

One thing I remember about Eric was that he could recite his mother's Co-Op number. I could too, both then and now, although it's a good sixty years since I last used it. Why I remember such trivia when I falter over our postcode is one of life's little mysteries.

I told Uncle Fred how Leigh's Co-Op had sawdust on the floor, and dried beans and raisins in sacks with mouse holes in them. It wasn't my favourite shop. For one thing, adult customers were served ahead of me even though it was my turn. This could have been because they were spending money, while I was collecting a halfpenny for a returned jam jar, or perhaps the shop assistants simply gave preference to adults. For another, aesthetics were not the store's strongest point.

But the Co-Op's appeal had nothing to do with service or appearance. People like my mother shopped there because they believed that most items cost a halfpenny or so lower than elsewhere. The society bought wholesale, passing on savings to retailers, and every member/shopper had a number (ours was 48563) identifying who spent how much, and annual dividends were awarded accordingly.

By the 1930s, Co-Op customers received bread and milk deliveries from horse-drawn carts. (Mum loved them because they provided manure for her roses.) Also coal, which the coalman carried through our house in half-hundredweight sacks to tip into the backyard shed. Before the war I never looked twice at those huge horses waiting patiently in the street for their master's return. After the war, I never saw one without thinking of Uncle Fred.

Following several trips to Derby with Eric in the back seat of Uncle Fred's Austin, I had a secret I felt I should pass on, since Home Guard members were trained to tackle any Germans who came our way. Time and again I wrestled with my conscience, but could never bring myself to tell him about the Sunday morning Iris and I were convinced we met a German spy in the village shop.

Kirk Langley wasn't a compact village with a central hub, so much as a smattering of farms on a few country lanes just off the main road. There was the obligatory pub on the main road itself, and a small grocer's across from it. On the way to this shop, we walked past the fourteenth-century church and Sylvie's parents' farm. Then, had we continued, we would have come to the school and meeting hall. But there was no core to the community. No neighbours peering through lace curtains, no watching the comings and goings as in Charbury. Which is why nobody but us, and Marie, knew about our 'spy'.

Marie was an evacuee from London who had rented a cottage in Kirk Langley for herself and three children. Her sister ran the store, except on Sunday mornings when Marie opened up early, stacking the weekend newspapers outside to catch a few motorists. We were regulars, getting there soon after opening for our *Beano* comic and *Girls' Crystal*. For an added treat, if she had any sweets, Marie would save us a bar of chocolate or package of wine gums.

On this particular Sunday we arrived to find her, puzzling over the gesticulations of a tall blond boy, dressed in baggy farm-worker clothes, and carrying a brown paper bag. He spoke virtually no English but eloquently indicated he wanted something to eat. Marie showed him her ration book, then held her hand out for his. I half wondered why he didn't simply jump the counter and grab what he wanted but, as Iris pointed out later, almost everything there required a tin opener and he wouldn't have had one. In the end, Marie gave him her sandwich brought for lunch, and a packet of wine gums. He had no money. She shrugged as if to say 'what else can I do' before waving him out of the door.

'Well, I don't know about you, but I reckon he's a spy,' Iris said immediately he was gone.

'He's some mother's lad, that's what he is,' replied a grim-faced Marie.

We hadn't heard of a plane crashing in the vicinity, so how had he got here? From the sea?

'Shouldn't we report him?' Iris wanted to know.

Marie took a pile of newspapers outside, furtively glanced in each direction and said he'd scarpered. Disappeared into thin air. On second thoughts, perhaps he was a Brit on a training exercise, seeing how far he could get without an identity card or ration book. 'You know, practising to be a spy in Germany or France or somewhere.'

We didn't believe it for a moment.

'So don't you two go blabbing to anyone about me aiding and abetting the enemy,'

Marie warned, handing us each a package of wine gums, 'or I'll get shot and my kiddies will have no mum.'

She was breathing rapidly and had turned bright red at the realisation of what she had done.

'He's a young boy far from home, frightened out of his life, and he'll be picked up without our help before the day's out.'

We nodded in unison. If Marie was shot, we doubted her sister would supply us with comics. In any case, look where speaking up had got Iris and Lilah back in Charbury. We didn't want to be sent packing a second time.

For me this was an idyllic summer of long warm days spent mostly outdoors. Iris often preferred to mess around in the playroom with Lilah or Sylvie, and to help Vera in the kitchen. Everyone, though, wanted to go on outings in the car. With Iris and me, we could take Lilah and Sylvie at a squash. If Aunty Min was well enough to join us we left Iris's friend behind.

These trips were so memorable, I sometimes brought them to mind to cheer me up when things were bleak in the months ahead. If his wife came, Fred was in fine form, telling us silly jokes

'Oh give over, Freddy,' Min would chide him, not appreciating that he meant to be funny.

Petrol was in very short supply by now, allowing for only essential journeys. Somehow Fred managed to eke out a little for our picnics, and by keeping to the back roads was never stopped for questioning by police patrols. Petrol to be used in agricultural vehicles was dyed red for easy recognition if used illegally. Apparently, it wasn't difficult to filter out the dye, though I can't say I ever saw Uncle Fred doing this.

In any event, our outings were fairly close to Kirk Langley. Even the beauty spots such as Dovedale, where we shrieked hysterically when a boy took us across the river on his donkey – all five of us and the hamper for a threepenny bit. Vera's picnics, packed in a suitcase-sized wicker basket, would have done Henry VIII proud. Gleaming silver cutlery was tucked into chamois sleeves, china plates and cups and real glasses safeguarded in individual pockets. As for food, we feasted on sliced ham and breaded chicken legs with salad fresh from the garden. Fruit from the orchard and home-grown berries had been baked into individual tarts, accompanied by little pots of thick cream to be spooned over them. For the adults there was wine that Uncle Fred poured into delicate long-stemmed glasses. These were leisurely lunches. Nothing like the thick cheese sandwiches we packed for our trips to Hadleigh Castle. There, we ate and ran to avoid the flies that zeroed in on us, and hurried to get our blackberries picked with one eye on Mum's watch for the next bus home.

It was Vera's picnics that caused us to drop out of Miss Brant's Thursday-afternoon hikes for her evacuees. Other children had brown paper bags containing rough-looking sandwiches, while we had delicacies packed in a smaller version of the large wicker basket. Not only were we uncomfortable to be eating this carefully prepared feast with our less fortunate pals, but a particularly obnoxious boy called Simon tended to target us with his snide remarks. The last time I saw him was after his visit home, when he told us almost all of Kent Avenue had been demolished by a bomb. And was it number 17 or 19 that received a direct hit, killing all the scabby people who lived there? He wasn't quite sure of the house, but he did know most of the street was flattened and casualties were high.

We were so upset we ran all the way back to Ivy House to tell our sorry tale to Aunty Min. She called Freddy right away. Lord luv him, he came panting into the kitchen three hours later, to report there had been no bombing of the laundry, the high school, or Kent Avenue alongside it. His lovely round face, always perspiring, was alight with joy. More seriously he added that we must not be angry at Simon, whose own house had

143

been destroyed and his dear mam killed. We didn't go to any more of Miss Brant's outings.

Saturday was my favourite day of the week in Kirk Langley, because for me they started while most of the household was still asleep. If I wasn't already awake, Uncle Fred would tap softly on our bedroom door to get me up soon after dawn. Following a scalding cup of tea and thick slice of bread and jam, we would set off: Uncle carrying a rifle, and me with a basket, for we were about to go hunting. It was a magical time of day, with practically nobody else about. Black and white magpies lined up on gates and overhead wires, a fox or two lurked under a hedge, dew glistened on our wellies as we squelched through the grass.

Fred was after the huge brown rabbits hopping about the open fields, and sometimes a nice plump partridge. My job was to collect wild mushrooms the size of his cap, trying hard not to break the crowns as I tugged them from the ground.

I felt sorry for the rabbits sitting up so still, right in the line of fire, their whiskers twitching, eyes nervously searching for the enemy they sensed nearby.

At first I would cough quietly to frighten them off when Fred raised his rifle. It was the only time I recall seeing him angry, as he threatened to leave me behind next time.

Usually he shot three or four good-sized rabbits, which were hung from a tree branch to be collected on our return journey. A puzzlement to me was how he always knew which were his if there were other hunters about, and nobody ever stole them.

By the time we returned with the rabbits it was around eight o'clock. I would collect half a dozen eggs from beneath the hens while Uncle Fred got started at the stove, and soon the smell of fried mushrooms, eggs, tomatoes and bacon would bring Iris and Min downstairs. On Saturdays Vera joined us at the table, for a jolly meal during which Fred could sometimes report that he had seen one of her brothers during our early-morning expedition.

'If young Pam hadn't pointed out he was wearing a cap, I might have shot 'im for a rabbit,' he would lie or, 'Young Pam 'ere persuaded me to let him have the biggest rabbit you ever saw, so I didn't shoot it meself.'

Always he ended his little stories by giving me far more credit than was my due. What a dear kind man he was.

Although the Deans were not regular church goers, I became familiar with the village's Church of St Michael, because Uncle Fred and I decorated its interior with flowers from Ivy House gardens. If there was to be a christening, Aunty Min would have us pick lupins and delphiniums, pink for a girl, blue for a boy. For Harvest Festival, Fred and his brother donated enormous baskets piled high with fruit and vegetables. He told us we would all go to church for that autumnal festival. Iris and I would wear our best frocks, and walk with the village youngsters down the aisle to place more of the harvest by the altar. How proud he and Min would be, he said, to have their two girls in the procession. We would choose our offerings with care, and polish them shiny bright.

It didn't happen. In that autumn of 1941, when the harvest was in and Kirk Langley's celebrations were underway, I was no longer there.

CHAPTER TEN

Visitors from Home

We were shelling peas in the back garden one warm summer's day when Aunty Min shocked us both by announcing she had written to our dear mam, inviting her and our dear dad for a visit. Iris said something like 'yippee'; the steady ping, ping, pinging of my peas into the colander provided my initial response. Uncertain that I wanted them intruding on my new life, I reminded

Aunty Min that parental visits were not allowed.

'We'll not tell anyone, so as not to make the other vaccys jealous,' she grinned, pleased as could be with her plan. 'If any nosey parker asks, I'll say they are my sister and her husband.'

'I don't think so.' I rambled on about them being unable to get train tickets, and how Dad was likely away doing bomb damage work. What's more Mum had never been further than London, so she couldn't possibly come this far on her own.

Dismissing my objections, a few days later Fred came home from Derby triumphantly waving rail tickets to be posted to 19 Kent right away. My equally determined mother wrote back to tell us Dad was busy in Ipswich but, if it was all right with all concerned, she would bring Violet, who needed a rest from the factory.

Neither of them had ever been on holiday before. Vi had visited London with her friend Gladys. And as a young girl Mum was invited, but declined, to join her Londoner friends on their annual hop-picking trips to Kent. Some of our Leigh neighbours also turned to the hop fields for their summer holidays. At the season's end they came home looking as if they'd been sunbathing in the south of France, but Mum would never go with them. Said she didn't fancy the

147

camp atmosphere. Every summer Dad made us stilts, useful for picking hops from the taller vines, should we ever get there. Iris and I became adept at walking tall, but we never did get to use them in Kent's hop fields.

Now, in mid-July, Mum and Vi were coming for a week in Kirk Langley. With so many railway delays and cancellations, we couldn't be sure exactly when they would arrive in Derby. Even so, on the big day, Uncle Fred and Iris left Ivy House in mid-afternoon and, with Lady Luck looking over them, their train from London pulled into the station by early evening.

It was still light when they reached Ivy House, where I was anxiously waiting on the front lawn with Tipsy, the Deans' three-legged dog. All doubts about the visit vanished when I saw Mum – red-faced and uncomfortable in her best rayon dress and tightly laced shoes, a little straw hat askew on her head – struggling to get out of the car. Violet was only a little less formally dressed, her face ashen.

Later my mother confessed that she hadn't recognised me. Thought it was a boy, she said, wearing those flappy old shorts and sandals, when she had expected me to be dressed in my best frock with the patent ankle straps and white socks she'd sent for Easter.

Aunty Min greeted her guests as long-lost

friends. Uncle Fred brought out some of his Johnny Walker, kept, he said, for such grand occasions. Mum said she would prefer a cup of tea if it wasn't too much trouble, while Violet gulped down her whisky as though it was something she did every day.

Clearly overwhelmed by their surroundings, and tired from the journey, they talked little throughout dinner, smiling benignly at our promises of a tour next day, and a picnic at Dovedale. Mum did summon enough energy to comment how she would love to serve Dad a dinner such as this, instead of the bread-filled sausages she had to give him after a hard day's work.

Every now and again she glanced at her little gold watch, probably wondering where he was, or if Rose had got off all right for her ARP duties. Even whether Clarabelle was missing her.

Next morning she was her old self. Never having slept in another person's house, she said she couldn't believe she had gone out like a light, not waking again until past nine. Violet was already up, lazing in a striped deckchair in the back garden, drinking tea and smoking a cigarette. Mum had warned her not to smoke in Aunty Min's presence. It wasn't ladylike. These people weren't factory workers. She mustn't let us down. Yet here was Aunty Min, talking nineteen to the dozen, smoking alongside Vi.

'This is a vice the girlies don't know I have,' she admitted, tucking her Players packet back into her apron pocket.

It was a wonderful week. On most evenings the Deans invited friends and relatives over. For our outings there wasn't room enough for all of us in their car, so for larger parties Fred commandeered his brother Stan to drive behind him with Iris and Sylvie and me. They were the jolliest occasions. We children would go off into the woods, or across the fields with Violet, returning to find the remaining adults had got through a bottle or two of homemade wine, talking excitedly about everything from food rationing to Mum's man of the hour – Winston Churchill.

At one point both Min and Fred were close to tears, over my mother's vivid descriptions of bomb damage she'd seen in London: houses sliced in two, exposing wallpaper and toilets, and bits and pieces of furniture dangling from upper floors. Entire families sleeping in the Tube stations.

For most of the week we relaxed in the garden. Uncle Fred and I went about our usual farm chores; Iris and Violet took off on long walks through the fields and along country lanes. Mum and Aunty Min hardly ever stopped talking. I would not have believed they had so much in common, but here they were animatedly discussing subjects as diverse as keeping hens and how

Violet had bouts of pneumonia as a child just like Min's little sister, who died when she was eleven.

Flowers became a favourite topic. Mum told Aunty of the gypsy fortunetellers who came to the door on the pretext of selling pegs. One had advised her to put rusty nails under the tulips to change their colour. And wouldn't you know, the very next spring they came up black as coal and the local newspaper sent a chap to photograph them.

On about her third day at Ivy House, Mum shyly handed over some rose cuttings from 19 Kent which Vera planted in the front garden. Min was choked with emotion when she was told 'You seem to have everything already, so I didn't know what else to bring.'

'Not everything, my dear,' she replied, looking down at her crippled legs. 'But I do have these two lovely girls you have lent us for now. What dear Fred will do when young Pam leaves us, I hate to imagine. She sticks to him like a shadow.'

At dinner, talk turned to war. Mum was so impressed by Churchill, you'd have thought she was his press agent. My mother, I soon realised, had the gift of listening and appearing interested, even when she couldn't offer much by way of response.

A subject upon which she was knowledgeable enough to talk at length was the Co-Operative Society where Uncle Fred worked.

She had shopped at Leigh Broadway's Co-Op store for years, she said, and before that at another in Greenwich. In fact she and Jack had been given membership – which she believed cost all of half a crown – as a wedding present. It proved far more useful than the silver tray they received from her former employer, though even that came in handy since she hocked it for the train fare to Leigh when she left London with the two kiddies during the First World War.

On their way home following that first visit, Mum and Violet were loaded down with a large ham, butter and a dozen eggs, which for safety Violet carefully placed in her gas mask case. It was my turn to go to Derby station with Uncle Fred. We all stood awkwardly there, hoping the train would arrive soon, joking about what would happen if Vi had to get her gas mask out in a hurry. When the London-bound train did arrive, it was crowded with soldiers, many of whom were sitting on kitbags in the corridor. Fred pushed his way through to find a space for Mum and Vi, and managed to hop off just seconds before the train carried him away.

As they waved excitedly, he commented on how different they looked. He was right. Neither of them wore hats or stockings. Both were tanned by the sun, and appeared to be years younger. It was a wonderful thing my foster parents had done for these two war-weary souls. How could I possibly have had second thoughts about their proposed visit?

Towards the end of our happy, carefree summer, the postman brought distressing news contained in a square envelope addressed to me. It appeared to enclose a birthday card – a mystery, since my birthday is in October.

Inside was a congratulatory card, etched with good-luck symbols: black cats, gold horse-shoes, silver wishbones and the like. Both parents and two sisters had signed it. In her neat, familiar script, Mum had added 'I knew you had it in you'. I could think of no reason for the card. Aunty Min and Vera were puzzled. Iris took one look and said, of course, I had passed the scholarship.

I felt sick. Hopefully it was a mistake. Or, in the unlikely event that Mum had told nobody else, possibly I could ignore it. If not, I would have to move further north to a town near Buxton where Westcliff High School for Girls was evacuated.

I was distraught and angry. How could everyone expect me to leave the Deans where I was loved as their own? I wrote as much to my mother, expecting her to see my dilemma. She replied that I would thank her in the long run. Next, Miss Brant came calling, in part to convince me of the wonderful opportunity afforded me. One that would open all kinds of doors in the future – a future I wanted no part of.

Uncle Fred made frantic telephone calls, trying to get me into a Derby high school for the war's duration. Even though he promised to take me there every day, the school authorities saw no wisdom in such a plan. The scholarship was for Westcliff High School for Girls, currently located at Chapel-en-le-Frith. I must report there within two weeks or forfeit the opportunity.

There were days when I dismissed all thoughts about the life-changing event fast approaching. Until my uniform arrived, sending Iris and Sylvie into hysterics. Each in turn pulled the Panama hat down over her eyes, and paraded in the baggy black bloomers I would be wearing for gym class. My blazer bearing the school crest was scratchy, the tunic for winter wear unbearably heavy. A second parcel brought a sky-blue dress with a white clip-on tie, and knee-length white socks. Mum wrote that she couldn't find everything on the list, including canvas field hockey boots and proper tennis shoes, but would keep on trying.

So it was happening. There was my mother running all over Southend to get me whatever I needed for this la-de-da school, when she should be queueing for food.

Aunty Min and Uncle Fred, though less enthusiastic, consulted Miss Brant about my transport.

Iris and Sylvie were unfazed. Life goes on as usual, they said. Iris added that she might ask about going home, now that her job of keeping an eye on me was finished. It was unreal and unfair. I would be playing with Mardi or doing my farm chores, when tears filled my eyes. It had all been so lovely. Now I felt I was on a runaway train, and could do nothing to stop it.

On the Saturday morning I was due to leave, Aunty Min promised to phone if at all possible, and gave me a few pennies for a public telephone box in case I wanted to call her. I had never made a telephone call, and knew I wasn't likely to start now, but I did promise to write her long letters about my new school.

She and Uncle Fred gave me a small leather suitcase so I wouldn't have my smart uniform crushed into a sandbag, and somehow Fred had managed to find a geometry set for me in Derby. On a sad, bewildering day I said my goodbyes. Uncle Stan and Sylvie had come from the farm, Vera was there noisily blowing her nose, Iris stood forlornly holding on to Mardi – a brave thing to do, considering how much she disliked the 'dirty, smelly pigs'. Lilah, wearing her hair in a fashionable snood, held one of her small foster sisters up to wave.

I had grown strong in the past fifteen months. Wearing the uniform of a prestigious girls' school, at eleven years old I was about to set off on my own for a world I could not control with a monthly medical certificate awarded for a nervous tic. Fred put my case into his car boot. Everyone else hugged me goodbye. As my loved ones stood waving, two broke from the group to run after the car: Mardi and Tipsy sent dust flying for a good hundred yards, until they too stood dejectedly by the roadside.

They all looked so normal. And here I was off on a train to some strange new place. In my pocket I had a card with no more than my destination, Chapel-en-le-Frith, written on it. Aunty Min had wanted to pin a label to my blazer, showing my name and Kirk Langley address, but I felt I was too old for that. Anyone wanting to know who I was could ask me. I told myself I was fortunate in that there would be no school or community hall filled with picky foster parents, ready to choose anyone but me. Then I remembered there would be no Iris to stick up for me, no Lilah clowning around, and my heart plummeted.

Uncle Fred's eyes were moist, his wet hair plastered to his head when he removed his cap to hug me goodbye. I asked him to think of me when he drove Rita and Betty, in the

October Parade. And not to let anyone kill Mardi by mistake.

He busied himself with my suitcase; I clung to my satchel and gas mask. A soldier squeezed along so I could sit by the window, and Fred asked him to help me if he was still on board when we reached my destination. Both the train and station were too crowded for me to wave, but I fancied I saw him anyway, a dejected figure in his tweed three-piece suit and brown boots – wearing his Sunday best in spite of the heat, to say goodbye to his evacuee.

CHAPTER ELEVEN

I am a High-school Girl at Chapel

Despite its quaint name, Chapel-en-le-Frith is a bustling market community of several thousands, located between the grand Victorian spa town of Buxton and Stockport in England's Peak District. The closest major city is Manchester, some twenty-five miles distant. Not that I knew any of this on the sad morning Uncle Fred put me on a train in Derby, squeezing me into a window seat so I might better see where to get off.

On my map today I see this as a journey of

157

little more than thirty miles, but with wartime schedules and convoluted routes there was no knowing how long it would take to get there. On top of which, I quickly discovered that even up here names of stations had been removed or changed so as to confuse the enemy.

It seems inconceivable to me today that an eleven-year-old would be put on a train, and told to disembark at a town she knew only from its name on a postcard. Had I become lost, I presume some kind soul would have telephoned the school on my behalf.

My dilemma was not unusual. There were evacuees only eight or nine years old at the time, yet in charge of younger siblings whom they temporarily lost during their relocation. One I know of was afraid to tell her mother she had 'mislaid' her little sister, until she found her three weeks later, happily living with a group of kindly nuns.

Here I was then, not with a label around my neck this time, but one on my satchel and another on my gas mask, giving my address as c/o Westcliff High School for Girls, Chapel-en-le-Frith. Trusting as only a child can be, I decided someone from the school would be there on the station to meet me. Better yet, there would be several other students getting off this train at the right stop. So I dozed off. It was mid- or late afternoon when the soldier across from me shook me awake to say we had reached the destination I had written on my gas mask case. He knew it well, he said, because he lived just down the line.

Leaping on to the platform with my suitcase, he held up the train while I gathered my other baggage and jumped down. With a lot of huffing and puffing from the engine, and waves from soldiers hanging out of its windows, the train disappeared into the countryside leaving me alone in what appeared to be the middle of nowhere. I wondered whether to use Aunty Min's pennies to try to call her. Perhaps I was close enough for Uncle Fred to come and get me. Except that there was no telephone box.

I pulled up my sleeping sock, adjusted my hat that had been knocked sideways, and was putting my postcard into my blazer pocket when I heard a voice booming from behind the station house.

'Are you Pamela? Pamela Hobbs?'

Swinging around, I watched a stocky figure dressed in a black gym tunic and long-sleeved white blouse coming towards me. A woman of indeterminable age, who was to be my friend long after I left school.

Almost as wide as she was tall, she wore her steel-grey hair in a bun kept neat with a coloured band around her forehead. Her tunic was above her knees, revealing plump black-stockinged legs as muscled as those of a dancer. On her feet she wore soft black pumps, which allowed her to bounce along making no sound at all. A whistle dangled from an orange sash around her neck. She had an impish grin and the merriest blue eyes I had ever seen.

'You are Pamela?' she repeated boisterously, stopping a few feet from where I stood.

'Yes, miss.'

'Well, old thing, we do not wear our hats like that.' In one swift movement she reached up and straightened the offending Panama I wore at what I considered a becoming angle. 'And we do not stand with our hands in our pockets.' I thought to explain about the postcard but decided against it, when she continued: 'Also, I am not "miss". I am Miss White.'

Indicating that I should pick up my suitcase, she turned back towards the station's exit. Following behind, I wondered if she knew her navy fleece knickers hung below her gym tunic for a good three inches.

There were no cars outside the station. Just a pony and trap, which Miss White explained was her way of contributing to the war effort, since it enabled her to put her car in the garage and leave it there. The pony was named Tobias. As he clip-clopped along narrow lanes cut through superb countryside, he needed no direction from Miss White, who chatted on about the school's prestigious reputation and how everyone pulled together to make sure that rules were not relaxed simply because there was a war. The town's name she explained as being derived from the church erected here by thirteenth-century foresters from the Royal Forest. The community that grew up around it was known as the Church in the Forest, corrupted to Chapel-en-le-Frith.

Turning on to the High Street, I had hoped she would pay more attention to the traffic, but her relaxed pose remained unchanged. After a few yards I began composing in my head a letter to Iris and Sylvie.

'There was Miss White,' I would write, 'with one leg resting easily on the side of the cart, revealing a great expanse of navy bloomers, driving through Saturday-afternoon traffic in town as if she had the road to herself...' I was a travel writer, off on an adventure.

A twinge of excitement had intruded on my anxiety; sadness at leaving Kirk Langley receded to the back of my mind. My new surroundings, the strangeness of being with Miss White and Tobias, had banished thoughts of poor sad Uncle Fred walking away from the train in Derby. Was I unbelievably shallow? Fickle? Unfeeling? I really don't know. Escaping reality, perhaps, because all of a sudden I was one of the heroines in Iris's *Girls' Crystal* magazines.

Tobias, without instruction, turned into a short U-shaped drive leading to an impressive stone house. Blimey! A big house, a nice lady and a pony, all in one afternoon. How lucky could I be? Just to be sure, I asked Miss 'White if she was my new foster mother. Also, with thoughts of Vera's lovely meals, I wanted to know if anyone but the two of us would be living here. This suggestion brought a low gravelly laugh, such as I would hear often in the years ahead.

Cheerfully Miss White explained that this house was a holding station of sorts, where I would stay until a billet could be found. Most homes were taken when the school came to Chapel fifteen months earlier. Now first-formers like me, who were arriving daily, were put here temporarily. She added that I would enjoy living with other girls. It was like a boarding school.

Crushed, I nodded silently. How could my situation have gone from high to low within five minutes? Miss White hopped down, more sprightly than one would expect considering her size, and tied Tobias to an iron post beside the front door. Sensing my dejection perhaps, she told me she lived in a nearby cottage with the headmistress, Miss Wilkinson. Miss White was my gym teacher, and a friend.

With my heart somewhere down in my

solid black shoes, I followed her into what I deemed then to be a baronial hall. For its wartime role, several upstairs rooms had been turned into dormitories, each containing half a dozen or more folding cots. Our floor had one bathroom as I recall, where we lined up each morning, to be allowed only a few minutes inside. A prefect, who took me from Miss White that first afternoon, told me the dorms were full right now, so she had arranged for me to have a cot in the corridor. As an afterthought, she said it might be a bit noisy being on the path to the lav, but it would have to do for a few days.

The sound of a bell, followed by a sudden stream of girls pouring from the dormitories, led me to the main-floor dining room. The prefect who had shown me to my cot, and seemed to know me only as 'old thing', was about to take me inside when I spotted a vaguely familiar girl my own age.

She was Monica Granger, whom I had known briefly in Kirk Langley. Once the school broke up for summer, she said, she had gone to Devon for a family holiday. Her father had brought her to Chapel two weeks ago while delivering her brother to a private school nearby.

I told her about my train journey, and how Miss White had met me, and she said I was very brave. Monica, I quickly realised, was not a scholarship girl. Back home she lived down by the seafront in Chalkwell, where Daddy kept a twenty-six-foot yacht, and he paid a handsome fee to have her at this school.

The noise in the dining hall was more deafening than Uncle Fred's hen house at feeding time. After a meal, far less memorable than any of Vera's on even a rushed day, Monica showed me the grounds, and a library where I was to spend many happy hours curled on a window seat with borrowed books. I soon fell into a daily routine. In the bathroom queue I was envied for my fluffy pink flannel and lavender soap given to me by Aunty Min. Before the week was out, I was sharing a dorm with Monica and four other girls our own age.

Every morning at around 8.30 we assembled at the front door to walk in a crocodile formation to another house currently set up as a school for us junior girls. Standing on a hillock of neatly mowed lawns, its pale grey stone walls were interspersed with thick oak doors and mullioned windows. A brocade bell-pull, used in other times to summon a maid, was temptingly close to my desk. In late afternoon we formed another line to walk home. Once there, our time was our own to relax with schoolwork, write letters, and join our friends in the garden.

Back then, high-school students attended classes for six years, usually from age eleven to seventeen. In Essex, Westcliff High School for Boys was built alongside our girls' school, and although I knew nobody there I heard they were evacuated to Belper – close to Derby and some thirty miles from Chapel.

Much has been written about segregating the sexes during high-school years. Was it a good thing for me? I can't say, since mine was an all-girl society at home too. On the one hand we probably worked harder, without distractions from male students. On the other, as a young adult I blushed furiously when I met boys of my own age because I had never had the opportunity to interact with them.

I concerned myself with none of this as I settled in to my new life. I was busy trying to talk with the posher accent of my middle-class peers, to eat like them and think like them. It wasn't always easy. An advantage I had over some, though, was that I achieved high marks in almost every subject except social studies. A lot of my weekend time was spent on writing long descriptive letters to my family, and to the Deans.

My mother's letters, neatly written on blue flimsy notepaper, arrived every week. I liked to visualise her sitting at the kitchen table in the early morning, the back door open to let in a soft breeze, Clarabelle at her side on the table between the sauce bottles and tea cups. When we compared notes years later, Iris and I learned she had received exactly the same news, minus reference to my schoolwork. Dear Mum. On some days she missed her early bus to the Broadway because of the time she took writing her letters.

Aunty Min's notes were shorter. Although she had plenty to say that would have interested me, she obviously found writing difficult. In early December, she wrote that she had telephoned the school to ask if I could return to them for Christmas, but didn't hear back. Another letter told how Iris and Sylvie had started at a secretarial school in Derby. Neither of them liked it, and Aunty Min fretted that Iris wanted to be going home soon to our dear mam.

Every couple of days, Miss Carter, the teacher in charge of billets, came into our dorm to say she had a new home for some lucky girl. Monica had already moved on, but still joined us for our walk to school. I had no wish to leave my temporary home. I loved the boarding-school atmosphere, which I would never experience again. I loved the grandeur of the house and its garden. I loved being responsible for myself, and having other girls to join for homework sessions. I loved having space of my own, when I wanted it.

Feigning stomach pains and headaches

when Miss Carter dropped by, I managed to hold on for several weeks. Then, one day after school, she sought me out to say she had the perfect solution. At Monica's suggestion, her foster parents had kindly rearranged their accommodation so I could stay with them.

I had met the young couple earlier. They were friendly enough, but not quite what Monica was used to. Their tiny terrace house was cluttered with baby paraphernalia; their two-year-old son, Arthur, constantly suffered a runny nose. I thought of the grand houses on Chalkwell Avenue, and without knowing which one was Monica's home, could readily see why she had little in common with the young family who lived here.

They were the Drakes. Arthur Drake was in his early thirties, a short slender young man with a hacking cough. Whether he was ill, or if his work at the local Ferodo factory kept him out of the forces, I didn't ask. Despite his stature, he was known as 'Big Arthur'. His wife Mary stayed at home with her child. The house was rather like 19 Kent, though far less tidy. Baby Arthur was usually referred to as 'Little Arthur', but Monica and I called him 'Little Arser' because invariably he went about bare-bottomed, in the hope he'd use the chipped enamel potty under the table.

He took some getting used to, but I have to say I liked his mother instantly. She reminded me of my sisters, not one in particular, but all of them rolled together. She laughed at silly jokes, spent hours with her friend fussing around with hair curlers, ironed her clothes only when she needed them, and left us to pretty well look after ourselves.

'Oh Arthur. You little boogger,' she'd say cheerfully when he dribbled on our open exercise books. 'He looves them colours,' she surmised when he gleefully tore Africa from my atlas. And if I had a penny for every time he scribbled on my homework I would have been quite well off by the time we parted company.

With Big Arthur working Ferodo's night shift, Monica was moved from the small third bedroom into a larger one at the front, with a nice bay window and big double bed. I shared it with her, while Mary slept in the box room. When Arthur had a couple of nights off work we all switched around. Then I slept on the downstairs settee, and Monica had her original room, leaving the spacious front bedroom for Big Arthur and Mary. It suited us fine. None of us thought anything amiss that when Big Arthur slept during the day, he took the main bedroom because it was quieter than at the rear.

We had been there for about two months. Christmas was approaching. Chapel's weekly market was beginning to attract custom by displaying home-made toys and decorations.

Mum sent me a jumper for Little Arthur, which my eldest sister had knitted using red wool unravelled from her cardigan. I hid it in my suitcase, along with a cheeky-looking green bear I had bought in the market. Monica's mother had sent her a slab of Palm Toffee, which she generously saved to share on the big day. We even made plans for New Year's Eve: we would mind Little Arser while Mary went to a dance at the Ferodo works. In return, two of our friends could be invited over for the night. Compared to last Christmas in Charbury, this one actually looked like being fun.

Once we got used to having a small child around, we really liked Little Arser. Instead of having him scribble on our maths books, we sat him at the table with his own paper and pencil. On weekends we took him to the high street, where he enjoyed the bright shop windows. Although they held no particular joy for us, their displays of empty licorice allsorts boxes and fake bars of chocolate were bright enough to attract a two-year-old. In the market square, he liked to watch older children pretending to lock each other in the old-fashioned stocks, and if the day was sunny we took him to kick his ball about in the park.

Back at our foster home, nobody objected when we turned the wireless up loud, and we found we could do our homework well enough, even when Mary decided to dance with Arthur to her scratchy gramophone records.

A worrisome note around this time was that Mary's family lived in Manchester, being pummelled by what became known as Hitler's 1941 Christmas Blitz. A large part of the city's historic centre – including the cathedral – was destroyed. Casualties were heavy. Mary heard nothing from her sisters and their mother, as well as some of Big Arthur's relatives, all of whom lived close to the city core. With a fake cheerfulness, she replied to anyone who enquired, that 'no news is good news', or 'life goes on, right?'

Given a choice I would have opted to live at the school's hostel, but still we were fine with the Drakes. Mary had an endless supply of tinned beans and sausages that, together with thick fried bread, one of us could whip into a dinner in no time flat. Nobody was mistreated. In fact, more than once, Mary said she was grateful for our company since Big Arthur was working nights. An added bonus for Monica was that, with a little tutoring from me, her schoolwork improved.

Of course, all of this was before a big black shiny car stopped outside the house, and her mother stepped out.

CHAPTER TWELVE

Life Takes a Turn for the Worse

It was morning, around eight o'clock. Having done his good deed in the enamel pot under the table, Little Arser wore nothing more than a short cotton vest as he stood on a chair placed in the window for him to watch older children hurrying by to school. Monica was in the bathroom. Big Arthur was probably reading the paper, or coughing over his tea at the littered breakfast table. Hearing the unfamiliar sound of a car outside our house, Mary and I stared through the front window in disbelief.

The person stepping from it was tall and slender, dressed in a smart black suit, and a small felt hat with net covering her face.

''Tis someone's died,' Mary whispered.

'Doggie,' Little Arser shouted, pointing at the fox fur elegantly slung over her shoulder. On joining us, Monica let out a horrified 'Mummeee'. Mummy gave one withering look up at the outside of the house, stepped gingerly around Arthur's rusting tricycle and his tin bucket and spade coated in mud, then hammered on the door.

Little Arser, excited probably at the thought of patting the glass-eyed 'doggie', ran ahead of his mother – and promptly widdled on our visitor's expensive suede shoes. She squealed, grabbed her daughter, and the two retreated to the car while her driver, in army uniform, walked a discreet distance for a smoke.

A very embarrassed Monica came back into the house, saying her mother, Mrs Granger, wanted to see her room. Within minutes the woman was back downstairs and in the car, leaving her daughter in tears. Mummy had come and gone within fifteen minutes, and said not one word to the rest of us.

Monica mumbled her apologies to Mary and the two Arthurs. Her mother, unhappy about the sleeping arrangements, had gone off to see our headmistress.

Some time before lunch Miss Wilkinson called us into her study, where Eleanor Granger sat looking as cold as ice, holding a list of complaints in one hand and a bundle of her daughter's letters in another. She did not find her humorous descriptions of Arthur without his nappy at all funny. Nor was the picture she painted of Mary's two cats, Patch and Popeye, sitting on the table waiting for us to feed them some of our dinner. And when she learned that Monica was sleeping at night in the same sheets used by an adult male in the daytime, well, this was so unbelievably unsanitary she had to come right away to see how her girl could be treated in such a despicable manner.

With no understanding of our situation, she further demanded to know why Monica herself had not checked out the billet before moving in. Even our headmistress looked startled at such an outrageous suggestion. Did the woman have any idea what was involved in finding homes for girls of this age? Mrs Granger's final comment appeared to be addressed to me, when she stated imperiously that such lodgings might be adequate for some, but not for *her* daughter. We were dismissed.

It was all our fault of course. A scathing Miss Wilkinson called us back at the end of the afternoon to tell Monica that our school demanded more loyalty from its girls. And how could she show such utter disregard of the rules, by divulging so much in her letters home? Monica hung her head in shame. You'd have thought she was sending war secrets to the Jerries, the way Miss Wilkinson went on and on. Had I had the courage to interject, I might have replied that from what I saw, Monty's Eighth Army could not have stopped Mrs Granger from doing something once she had made up her mind to it. In dismissing us, the Head told us we must be ready to go to a new billet at five o'clock.

The only smile of the day, other than Little Arthur's, came from Monica when Mary told her they should put her mam up against Mr Hitler, and this bleedin' war would be over before we know'd it.

Right on the dot Miss Carter, the billeting officer, arrived in a shabby old car she borrowed for such occasions. There was little time to say our goodbyes. Mary, good-natured as ever, told us we could come over any time, and that Arthur would love us to take him out as usual on Saturdays. We in turn promised to mind him on New Year's Eve, if she still wanted to go to the Ferodo dance.

The amiable, gentle teacher who earlier had followed up Monica's request that I join her in this home, was no longer our friend. Apologising profusely to Mary, she strode ahead of us to the car, offering no help with our bags. Tight-lipped for most of the drive to the other side of town, she opened them only long enough to say she expected no complaints about our next billet.

I had hoped we were returning to the hostel, but no such luck for these trouble makers. Instead, we were driven through the dreariest of council estates, crammed with row upon row of dark grey stucco houses in blocks of four or six, every door, every windowsill painted an institutional green.

If houses are allowed to look forlorn, then

the dwelling we stopped at was downright miserable. Not a soul around, no lace curtain pulled aside to denote curiosity or perhaps interest at the unusual sight of a car stopping outside. Even the doorbell had a sad ring to it. The woman who opened the door was tall, six feet or more, gaunt-faced with long thin grey hair tied in a knot at the back of her head. Her eyes were as lifeless as those in the heads of Good Alf's fish laid out on his marble counter.

We were introduced to Mrs Barker, and the niceties ended there. Our new foster mother commanded us to remove our shoes and take them through to the scullery. Miss Carter began to slip off her own footwear, only to be told there was no need for her to stay.

'I will tell them what is expected of them,' she said curtly, closing the door before following us into the Victorian-style scullery-cum-kitchen.

In my long and eventful life, I have to say the months spent in the Barker home are the worst I can remember. Towards the end of our stay, when Monica and I seriously schemed to run away, I boldly asked my foster mother why she had volunteered to have us in her home. Without hesitation she told me, 'It was you or two Irish workmen, and I see now I made the wrong choice.'

Mr Barker was as dour as his wife. I knew

his name to be Alfred, only because his mail was so addressed. When his wife spoke to him in our presence he was 'Mr Barker'. Thinner than a rake, he spoke in short, economical sentences. Both appeared older, but were probably in their fifties, and like Big Arthur he too worked at the Ferodo factory. He ate as sparingly as he did everything else, but unlike us he didn't seem to be unduly hungry.

I wonder if things would have been different had we reacted with more warmth to Mrs Barker's little attempts at being motherly. On our first night in the sparsely furnished bedroom, I responded to her good-night kiss on the cheek with a demure, 'Thank you for having us, Mrs Barker.' But when she went around the bed to repeat her little act of kindness, Monica rudely turned her face away. 'Oooh,' she shuddered with the poor woman still outside the door.

'Didn't you see those revolting whiskers on her chin? My God, how could anyone let her kiss them?'

On another occasion, when Mrs B's hair was dangling like a lank rope down her back, I commented that I had no idea it was so long. Something akin to a friendly conversation started, when she said she had trouble brushing it as hard as she would like, due to arthritis in her arms. I told her Aunty Min had the same problem, and I used to enjoy doing it for her. Hesitantly, she handed me the brush. There was no comparison between this greasy stringy tangle and Aunty Mm's newly washed bouncy mane, which I could tame into classic waves. Still, I knew enough to recognise an olive branch of sorts, and went to accept the brush. But Monica's exaggerated 'Uggh' and grimace of disdain barely hidden by her textbook were not missed.

'Thank you,' I responded coolly, 'but I have to memorise a long poem.' At that I dashed upstairs, with Monica on my heels laughing her head off. So, upon reflection, we were not the nicest of house guests for hosts who would rather have had their home to themselves. Had I not been egged on by Monica, I could have made myself more likeable to the Barkers. As it was, I went along with my friend's rudeness, thinking it an attitude acceptable in affluent homes where children were raised to be leaders.

Most evenings we ate with the Barkers in their parlour, a meal remembered for its stinginess in both substance and accompanying conversation. The only sounds, but for the clicking of cutlery on china, were the loud ticking of a clock on the mantel and twittering from Joey, the green and gold budgerigar in a cage by the window.

I like budgies. We had two beautiful blue and green birds at home before the war.

Without success, Dad spent hours coaxing them to talk. A friend told him they would never do so as long as they had each other, but he kept on trying. Mum didn't care for the mess of seeds she swept from the floor beneath their cage several times a day, and once in a while we caught a chagrined Clarabelle with a tiny green feather on her whiskers, but all in all we enjoyed our birds hanging in the bay window. Although one was said to be a male, nobody thought it odd that we had named them for two female music hall entertainers, Gert and Daisy.

After England received its first bomb in Lowestoft in 1939, Gert and Daisy were evacuated. The government's overworked propaganda machine had spewed out pamphlets telling us it was cruel to keep pet birds and animals in areas where they could be gassed or injured, or at the very least frightened enough to run (or fly) away. There was no thought of sending Clarabelle to the country. (Had we done so, she would probably have walked back home.) But Dad did take Gert and Daisy to the railway station, with a note on their cage asking that they not be separated. Little did he realise he would be doing the same with his children a few months later.

Perhaps the Barkers, on the receiving end, had taken in Joey as their first evacuee. Did they go to choose him from the parrots, cats

178

and dogs lined up in a school hall? I never asked, but I have to say he was loved more than a child. When Mrs Barker talked to him in a sing-song voice sometimes reserved for babies, he responded with a lot of twittering and a few distinct words. 'How do' was his favourite, followed by 'ta very much'. His mistress even let him sit on her armchair by the fire as she did her knitting. We were seldom allowed to share this warm domestic scene, except during our brief walk through the parlour from the scullery to our upstairs bedroom.

I really didn't mind so much. It would have been difficult to pass our evenings with the Barkers, knowing they wanted to spend them alone – she with her knitting and he with the local paper. At nine o'clock, he turned on the wireless for an update on the war, while she made their two cups of Ovaltine. At 9.30 all lights were extinguished: they retired to their bedroom assuming we were in ours.

The unheated, stone-floored, brick-walled scullery became our home away from home. After school we did our homework at its scrubbed deal table, struggling to see in the light provided by one dim yellow bulb hanging high from the ceiling. After that we set the parlour table, and joined the Barkers for our painfully silent evening meal.

The tablecloth was always the same, white cotton with a silky sheen, trimmed with a faded blue and orange squared pattern. For something to do while swallowing our scrappy meals, I used to count the squares as far as I could see them. Twelve down and between eighty and a hundred across.

What random memories to have of our stay here. Squares on a tablecloth, Joey's vocabulary, Mrs Barker's greasy hair. No picnics, no home-made cakes and milk waiting for us after school, no Mardi, no happy faces, no music.

Sometimes on Saturday afternoons, we visited the local cinema, which had matinees for children, and for admission of three pence passed a couple of hours out of the cold. The highlight of our afternoon was the showing of a film, usually a very old western that we didn't understand, plus several cartoons. The soundtracks were scratched, the projector broke frequently, the youthful audience was rowdy and seats were rickety at best.

Very few girls from our school attended the afternoon shows. I would like to think they were enjoying outings into Buxton with kindly foster parents. In truth many were scared of the local boys who made a point of filling the seats around them. Gloves and hats would be tossed about, a lot of name-calling went on.

Although these lads did nothing more serious than to deliberately trip over our feet, pull our hair, thump us in passing, we found them threatening.

All rowdyism ended one Saturday afternoon when we arrived at the cinema, aptly dubbed the Flea Pit, to find Miss White seated plumb in the centre of the middle row, surrounded by juniors from our school. A few ripe words from the louts, or an 'ouch' from one of the girls, would bring her to her feet, whistle poised as she stared witheringly at the offender. So far as I know, she never did blow the whistle. Her presence as our would-be protector was enough to keep the peace, and on future visits we sat as close to Miss White as we could.

At the time I thought it sad that our teacher had nothing better to do with her Saturdays. It never occurred to me that she was generously giving up this private time in order to protect her girls.

Our daily routine in the Barker home, following what passed as a meal, was to return to the scullery to do the washing up and polish shoes with hard brushes and blacking. After that, with homework completed, and if the weather wasn't too atrocious, we would join a few friends from the estate in a field not far from our house.

Like the heroines in our books, we had joined a secret club, whose four or five members came from miserable billets in and around this unhappiest of neighbourhoods. On the side of the hill, one of the girls had discovered a cave of sorts, sheltered by an overgrown bush. Not a real cave carved from limestone cliffs for which the region is renowned, but more of a huge dark basin in the soil, where a bulldozer had long ago left its work unfinished, or perhaps tree had been uprooted. Whatever its origin, we found solace in sitting there on damp blankets, huddling for warmth till it was time to go home to bed.

I brought a torch; someone else provided a small lantern. Hidden from the world here, we talked about our teachers and foster parents, and fantasised often about being safe in our own homes again. And we laughed. Oh, did we laugh. I realise now how important that was, making light of our misery, repeating silly Adolf jokes, poking fun at our teachers.

Some of the girls were romantics, wanting nothing more than a handsome young knight (an air force pilot would have done nicely) to sweep them off their feet. Me, I dreamed of being a spy. A very heroic spy, dropped behind enemy lines to take a secret message from Winston Churchill to God-knows-who. My reasoning was that nobody would recognise a child on such an important errand. I was getting A plus for French, so I'd have no problem with the language, and when I came home I would be a hero acknowledged by Winston himself.

Somewhere in this fantasy I picked up a few pairs of silk stockings for Violet, and fresh lipsticks for Iris. So maybe my secret mission would be to America instead of France. Wherever, my daydreams saw me as a heroine loved and admired by all, even Miss Wilkinson and Miss Carter and Mrs Granger.

Two of the girls in our group were physically abused by quick-tempered foster parents or their children. Marjory always had a new bruise or two on her arms or legs. When Miss White enquired about these during gym one day, she admitted to being 'jolly clumsy'. True enough. Her nervousness caused her to drop plates or scorch her foster brother's shirt because he crept up behind her and made her jump while she was ironing. A carpet beater was kept in the kitchen for the sole purpose of chastising her. Marjory's was a Cinderella story without the happy ending.

We agreed there was little point in complaining to our teachers. Because of the war, their responsibilities had tripled as they took on the role of parents and counsellors as well as educators. They also had the personal worries of leaving their homes and families, perhaps a loved one fighting overseas. One weekend afternoon I was shocked to see our English teacher whizz by on the back of a motorcycle driven by a young man. Until that day I hadn't considered her as anything but a teacher; certainly not someone who could have a personal life. As a concession to the wartime shortage of unattached teachers, we had one with a husband tucked somewhere out of sight. Normally though, only single women were employed, and had to leave their profession when wedding bells rang for them.

Relocating girls to new foster homes was one of the biggest headaches facing our school's staff. In some homes, a child's puberty was an issue. Several students had been sent back to the holding centre once they started menstruating, because their foster parents were unwilling to cope with this crossing into adulthood. According to Monica, who overheard things when we volunteered to do lunch dishes in the staffroom, 'One ignorant clod likened a girl having a period to a dog in heat. She said all the boys would come sniffing around, and with two teenage sons at home she couldn't have that.'

'It's not as if they can keep their monthlies quiet,' one of our members confided dramatically. Her older foster sister, she told us, had to put her soiled towel napkins in a tin bath to soak until they could be boiled. Our friend was appalled that they didn't seem to be aware of Kotex pads. I was about to turn twelve when I heard this conversation, and had no real idea what they were talking about. I, too, was an ignorant clod.

Throughout my time at Chapel I was plagued with chronic colds and sore throats, and an ailment then generally described as catarrh. It caused considerable discomfort from a blocked nose and called for the spitting up of copious amounts of phlegm. The only relief came from black capsules purchased from the chemist.

For anything more serious our teachers took us to a local doctor or dentist, but when over-the-counter remedies would suffice they were usually bought by foster parents who would be reimbursed by parents. No such luck in our house.

At the onset of cold weather Mum sent money to Mrs Barker for a tin of ointment recommended for my chilblains, as well as cough syrup and catarrh capsules. She denied receiving it, so I went without the medication.

After one particularly bad bout of tonsillitis I began getting ten-shilling notes in my letters from home. My foster mother insisted on keeping the money safe – so safe I never saw it again, and nor did the chemist. Had I needed the dreaded Kotex, I can't imagine what she would have done.

It soon became clear that our foster parents couldn't stand the sight of us. They did not want us sharing their life; we did not want to be a part of theirs. We liked the scullery, cold and damp as it was, because there we could sit and whisper and giggle to our hearts' content – even use profane language without consequence.

When teachers admonished us for our sloppy writing we agreed we must try harder, without bothering to explain the difficulty of holding a slender pen while wearing gloves. Other than being cold, under-fed and occasionally miserable, I can't claim to being mistreated in this gloomy house.

For me, the really sad aspect of this billet was that for the first time in my life I knew what it was like to be unwanted. It founded fears of being unloved and created a lack of self-confidence that stayed with me for decades.

So far as schoolwork went, I was very sure of myself, mostly because I was diligent and wanted to learn. Social studies, though, could be less than comfortable. Some girls in my class had already had holidays abroad, and talked knowingly about the joys of Paris and hiking trips in the Bavarian mountains.

I would love to have let rip with my essays, especially stories in which I could exercise my imagination. It simply wasn't possible, because the best work was read to the class. No way could I do that, so my compositions remained mediocre.

A favourite class was one in which we were brought up to date with the war. With a shortage of teachers at Chapel, those who could do so taught several subjects, which is why our gym mistress sometimes conducted our Modern History classes.

On a morning in early December, enunciating every word slowly to savour it to the fullest, she told us rapturously that over the weekend Japan had attacked Pearl Harbor in the Hawaiian islands. In consequence, Miss White said – as wide-eyed as if she'd seen Father Christmas himself – America was with us, and now we would surely win. We all knew about the attack anyway, from BBC newscasts. Even the sober Barkers talked of it over dinner. But it took Miss White and her creased map of the world to show us the true significance of such an attack on the American island.

Hawaii. I positively drooled over its exotic scenery and colourful people in the school's dog-eared National Geographic magazines. Now we were told that on the day before, 7 December 1941, Japanese bombers had pounded the US Pacific fleet napping in Pearl Harbor. At last count more than 2,000 people had been killed, and over a thousand wounded.

'And now,' Miss White concluded, theatrically, 'with the help of our American friends, we will bring this war to a satisfactory conclusion.' I thought she was going to give us a little victory dance, but instead she threw her chalk into the air and caught it triumphantly. My thoughts were not on the aggressive Japs or our new American pals, but how soon we could go home.

On the following Wednesday Japanese aircraft sank the British battleship Prince of Wales, and the battle cruiser Repulse sailing from Singapore. By the end of our school week, the Japanese had captured Hong Kong, attacked the Philippines, Indonesia and Burma. And Germany declared war on America. The buzz around our little hide-away was excitement that 'The Yanks are Coming'.

CHAPTER THIRTEEN

Time to Leave

Good news of the war aside, it was a wretched winter for some of us at Chapel. Clothes that had fit me a year before were now too small, others totally inadequate for the frigid temperatures experienced in the English Midlands that year.

My feet became a source of pain, in part because my wellies were too small to acco-mmodate socks. On particularly cold after-noons, to break our forty-minute walk between school and home, Monica and I would stop off at the library to warm up. This wasn't a particularly good idea because, when my feet thawed, the pain was excruciating.

Mum knew I needed lined boots, but simply couldn't find any. Not understanding how much I had grown, she sent thick fishermen's socks to go inside my Wellingtons, and by January my toes were a mass of sores and chilblains that kept me awake through most nights.

I don't remember Christmas Day at the Barkers' house, which may be just as well. I do recall receiving an enormous scarf, which Mum had persuaded Edie to knit in the school colours of red and gold on navy blue. It was the size of a table runner, and wrapped around my neck twice. At night I bound my feet in it.

By spring I realised I had become very thin, a first for me in view of my love of food. After the bountiful harvest of Kirk Langley, I found my perpetual hunger now hard to accept. There was little chance to buy, or steal, our own food. Mrs Barker kept our ration books in her battered leather handbag. The scullery's larder was locked, literally, with a padlock for which only she and Mr Barker had keys. The neighbourhood had no orchards, the hedges no berries worth picking. In April, when the Barkers' garden started producing root vegetables, we could have sneaked some had we been really desperate, but we weren't. We simply felt the need for a cake or biscuit to fill a void after our single-course dinner; even a little goodie of some sorts in our lunch box.

Another sandwich would have been fine too, since Monica and I shared a lunch so tiny it packed into a red Oxo tin. Usually the contents included one sandwich cut into four, made from stale bread and a revolting spread. We also had a carrot apiece, and perhaps a couple of green apples. A real treat was a hard-boiled egg every week or so. Our inadequate lunch was an embarrassment as much as anything.

Most days we managed to sit away from girls with their multiple sandwiches and bacon buns. If someone joined us, Monica might say she had forgotten her lunch, so was sharing mine. Or we'd hold our piece of sandwich to our lips for a while before taking a bite, to give the impression we weren't hungry.

We became cunning, too. The teachers ate in a staffroom, which had a small kitchen attached. Our volunteering to wash their lunch dishes gave us generous apple cores, bread crusts and discarded pickles – even left-over chicken legs once in a while. By adding hot tap water to the Oxo or Marmite residue at the bottom of their cups, we had ourselves hot drinks. When early summer brought berries and tomatoes ripening in the school's kitchen garden, we could easily snatch a few while shaking tea towels and tray cloths outside.

'If Mummy knew I was subsisting on apple cores and stale crusts, she would be up here in a shot,' Monica grinned one day. Had Mummy arrived with a fresh loaf of bread and a jar of home-made jam, I would have welcomed her with open arms.

The shortage of food at our foster home was made more tolerable by snacks inadvertently donated by teachers, and the occasional sweets sent by our mothers. Not that many came into our hands. Parcels that arrived while we were at school were always opened, and left on the scullery table. New vests, socks and gloves went untouched, but more often than not the sweets were gone. When challenged, Mrs Barker would tell us blithely we couldn't trust the postmen these days. Most were women with no training at all.

It was a Cadbury's bar of chocolate that drew us to the attention of two neighbourhood demons. Few local children lived on the Barkers' housing estate, possibly because it was not close to schools. These two, a little older than us, came from several streets away simply to taunt and bully us.

Our first encounter with the boy called

Arnie and his sister Becky was during our walk to school one morning. Monica was dividing her chocolate to give me half, when out of nowhere this pair magically appeared. We were still wondering who they were, and where they were from, when the girl kicked Monica in the shin, took the chocolate and ran off.

During future assaults Arnie carried a penknife which he adeptly flicked open and held menacingly close to our faces. When he told us he had taken his mother's eye out with this very same knife, Becky urged him to do the same to us.

Our conclusion that both children were mentally deficient did nothing to allay our fears. They didn't go to school, but instead hung around waiting to do some mischief. Their joy was to throw our hats over a hedge or high into a tree.

Since students were not allowed into school without hats firmly planted on their heads in all seasons, we often arrived after the late bell had sounded. Our explanations fell on deaf ears. The general consensus was that if locals pinching our hats was all we had to worry about, we were luckier than most. My biggest nightmare was that I might encounter our tormentors when I was on my own.

This happened on a Saturday as I hurried, fearfully, through a wooded area to deliver a message for Mrs Barker. Monica had private piano lessons on Saturdays, so we set off together that morning before separating at the corner with a promise to meet later. Sensing danger as soon as she left, I comforted myself with memories of happier Saturdays when Uncle Fred took me hunting. Now I felt sure I was the hunted.

Soon they appeared, the girl with her filthy face and missing front tooth, Arnie with a maniacal laugh, his penknife and, on this day, a rope. I think I was close to fainting as they tied me to a tree.

'Arnie wants to fuck you,' Becky said, as he stood by snickering. I had only a vague idea what she meant. All I knew was that people up here used the word as a profanity, like we would say 'bloody hell'. Arnie pulled his sister aside to whisper in her ear. Turning to me, she warned that they were going for their big brother to show Arnie how it was done, and I'd better be there when they got back. With that she hauled him down the hill, berating him for his innocence.

In no time flat I was free of the loosely knotted rope. Streaked in mud, with a ripped blazer, and rope in hand as evidence, I stumbled through the back door to where Mrs Barker was chatting with Joey, who sat comfortably on the arm of her chair. Grim-faced she listened to only half my story before putting hands over her ears, and bellowing for me to go upstairs. She always knew we were trouble; should have guessed we were out there with the boys when we disappeared nightly after dinner. I felt dizzy. It was Charbury all over again.

Timidly I asked if we should tell the police, or someone at school. She was aghast. What would the neighbours think of her if a policeman came to her house? She pointed her bony finger to the stairs, and with a none-too-gentle push headed me towards our room.

I told a shocked Monica, of course, when she came home demanding why I hadn't met her as planned.

'What a bloody cow. Now we're definitely running away,' she said as she consoled me. 'Jesus. She thinks more of her sodding Joey than any human being.'

Sadly it was true.

For the rest of the weekend I was in disgrace, confined to the house. It suited me just fine, since my attackers could be out there plotting revenge for my escape. We saw them soon after we left for school on Monday morning. Instead of being ahead of us as usual, they walked a few feet behind, which I found so unnerving I could hardly breathe. Slowly, without missing a step, Monica passed me her satchel and gas mask, swung around and grabbed Arnie by the front of his shirt while kicking his sister to the ground.

Their astonishment was a sight to see.

Bringing a ruler from its hiding place down the inside of her knee sock, she swung it at their bare legs, then told them quietly that if they ever messed with us again she would kill them. Nobody would care because in London her father was the head of Britain's entire police force. What's more, as of this day he would be ordering the local plods to look out for these two. They were snivelling so loudly I actually felt sorry for them when she added that our teachers were on to them as well, so they'd better watch their backs.

All lies, but it worked. We seldom saw them again. If we did, they crossed the road to avoid us. Monica was amazing. She reckoned that's what Humphrey Bogart would have done in a similar situation.

By June 1942 Hitler was on the run. Our Royal Air Force boys took to the air in their Lancasters and Mosquito bombers, inflicting real damage on Germany's industrial areas. The Russians had halted the Germans at the outskirts of Stalingrad. Monty had Rommel turning tail in North Africa. And Monica's mother was back in town.

This time it was a photograph that brought her to Chapel. Very few were taken by civilians during the war. Films were almost impossible to buy for the few box cameras that were still around. Even so, someone had arranged for a class photo with all of us standing straight and tall, and of course smiling. A copy was sent to a parent, who happened to meet her friend, Mrs Granger. Could that emaciated-looking girl at the end of the front row really be Monica? And beside her, with the spindly arms and legs, surely it wasn't her roommate, who only last autumn had been on the plump side?

She came to take her daughter home. Had she been able to locate my mother in the telephone book, she would have asked if she could bring me too. But it so happened that when she left Chapel next day it was without either of us. During her chat with our headmistress, Miss Wilkinson revealed a secret, which Mrs Granger promised to keep to herself.

In telling her daughter why she should stay for another two months to finish the school year, she swore her to secrecy before passing on the news. After I 'crossed my heart and hoped to die' Monica confided it to me. And that evening four of our group members gathered in our dug-out hole were also told: the entire school was returning to Westcliff this summer.

Mrs Granger had been vague about the reasons, Monica said, because she and the Head had talked of many things. The threat of invasion had passed, so our part of the coast was relatively safe. Many of the girls were drifting home due to unsatisfactory billets. In fact almost everyone, including the teachers, was cheesed off.

According to my friend, plans were already underway. Soldiers who had occupied our school premises in Westcliff were given marching orders. The building would then be thoroughly cleaned, restored and equipped for the return of our school.

For me it meant the beginning of a new era. Evacuation had been a great leveller. Here in Chapel we were all in it together; sharing, grumbling, joking, looking after ourselves and each other. Now most of my peers were returning to spacious homes in which they had their own bedrooms, while I would live in a crowded council house. Theirs were middle-class families with middle-class values and conversations. Mine was working-class. Their fathers doubtless read *The Times,* while mine subscribed to the *Daily Mirror* and for a really good read enjoyed the *News of the World* on Sundays.

Before the war, their mothers likely had a 'daily'. Someone like Mum who would go out most mornings, with her pinny and slippers in a carrier bag and a subservient demeanour, to earn half a crown cleaning up another family's mess. England's class consciousness is like no other when it comes to reducing a person to size. For some the war would continue to minimise the gulf between the classes, but for me it was about to be widened.

When the day came, Chapel's station was packed with foster parents and their vaccys, several actually crying as they said their goodbyes. Monica and I had no such tearful partings. Mr Barker, who was in the garden when we struggled off with our assorted luggage, didn't even look up from his spade. His wife, slamming her knife down on the cutting board, beheading some poor vegetable or other, appeared angry. I couldn't think why. Surely it wasn't over the loss of income caused by our departure, since she received little more than a pound a week for the two of us. And it wasn't because she wanted us to stay. We cluttered her everyday life, crowded her little house with unwanted noise, took up space.

Still it didn't seem right to simply walk out.

'Thank you very much for having us,' I said politely. 'I'm sorry if we weren't what you wanted.'

'Yes, well, you'd better get along then. You have a long journey ahead.'

If she was struggling with the wisdom of saying more, perhaps even something nice, she thought better of it.

Monica was already outdoors, her hockey stick and tennis racquet under her arms, satchel and gas mask on each shoulder, her suitcase on the pavement ready to be kicked along to the station, and a bulging carrier bag in one hand. Assembling my gear in a similar fashion, I followed her down the street feeling far less enthusiasm than expected for this long-anticipated day.

'All we need now is to meet Arnie and Beck,' she called back to me as we turned the corner.

But we didn't. Instead we bumped into a fresh-faced young soldier home on leave, who relieved us of our two cases, as we joined the stream of traffic heading for the station.

PART II

I Return Home to War

CHAPTER FOURTEEN

Home at Last

Poor mum was devastated. On the very day
I was coming home, she had the chance to
buy new shoes, and there was no telling how
long it would take to get them. Word had
spread that 'Joyce' shoes, a brand of soft
leather footwear, were to be put on sale in
the local branch of Dolcis. Better yet, instead
of the utility blacks and browns to which she
had become accustomed, they were to have
some in mouth-watering colours. No telling
about sizes, but with a bit of luck she would
end up with two pairs of fives – red for Rose
and brown for herself – before coming to
meet my train.

We were due at Chalkwell station around
mid-afternoon. After queueing for a good
part of the morning, and through the lunch
hour, Mum was still in line outside the shoe
shop. The hands on her little gold wristwatch
turned relentlessly. At half past two she was
sixth in line. I wouldn't expect her to leave
now, surely? The young assistant came along
to say only size seven was left. No matter.
She would buy them, and stuff paper in the

toes. Her swollen feet, crammed into her best shoes, were killing her.

On our homeward-bound train, excitement mounted as we passed familiar scenery: the ruins of Hadleigh Castle, Leigh Old Town with its cockle sheds alongside ancient lopsided cottages, Leigh beach, and then Chalkwell all dressed up in its wartime finery of rolled barbed wire.

Finally we chugged into the small station. It was two years since I had left home as a nervous child with a twitch, hanging on to Iris. The platform here was choked, mostly with mothers craning to catch sight of daughters in a sea of girls all dressed alike. Almost immediately a strident Mrs Granger spotted Monica, and surprised us both by offering to drive me home. I shuddered at the thought, telling her thanks very much, but someone would be coming with a car.

The crowds thinned, and only a handful of us remained when dear old Mum came puffing along, red-faced, dripping in perspiration – triumphantly holding up her shopping. It had been a long time since I felt so happy. We fell on to each other, hugging as I hadn't been hugged in a year. Bring on the bombs, let Hitler invade – there was no way I was leaving home again during this war. We had to wait a little longer, she explained, because Dad had been to the football before going home to get transport for my luggage.

When he arrived, it was on his ageless bicycle that had served him well during all of my lifetime. Today, it pulled a wooden box on two large pram wheels. The last two years had not been kind to him. His hair had become sparse, his features thin, but his grin was broad as he loaded everything but my satchel and gas mask into the container and pedalled off. Not wanting us to struggle with luggage on a bus crowded with Saturday shoppers, he had made the carrier especially for this day. The journey home would take him at least an hour. And to my discredit, all I could think was 'Thank God most parents and our teachers have already left the scene.'

When I dreamed of reuniting with my family, I used to think everything would be the same. Now I discovered it had all changed. Faithful to the end, Mum had written me with weekly up-dates, but it took my homecoming for the reality of it to sink in.

Our little house seemed cheerless, without the wireless blaring and my sisters shouting up the stairs to 'come look at this'. Or to 'put that light out', because with more than three lights on in the house they flickered until one was turned off. Mum filled the brown teapot, capped it with a cosy resembling a thatched cottage, and proudly brought out three lemon-curd tarts as she explained who was where. Clarabelle, who had been waiting for us at the bus stop, sat beside her on the table staring stonily at me.

Dad said he was away all week, usually getting home for weekends. 'Still sand-bagging mostly,' he said modestly, glancing at an ugly scar across each of his hands. Not quite. It seemed that two weeks earlier he had been caught in a building during a raid, put his hands up to protect his head, and had slate roof tiles slice through them. 'Could have been me old noggin, but it wasn't,' he ended cheerfully when I insisted on hearing the story.

Violet's work hours were so erratic nobody knew when to expect her home. She and her friend Gladys worked at Skyborne Industries on the Arterial Road. When quotas had to be met she cycled home late into the night, often in the pitch dark, and was back on the job by eight next morning.

My father thought she had too much responsibility for a youngster, especially one who had been such a sickly child. But then again, boys her age were getting killed at the front. We reminded each other of local youths who had gone straight from school to fight in Europe. One of Vi's classmates had lost his right arm.

Last Mum heard from Connie, she was stationed in Shenfield, working on predictors to track the paths of incoming enemy aircraft

– the same as Our Winnie's daughter. 'Quite the lad,' was how Dad proudly described his daughter number five.

Kath had given up her work at Plessey's during her sixth month of pregnancy, and was now living in East Ham with her infant Valerie. Wistfully, Mum stared into her tea. It was hard, she told me, to think of them in London. They came to 19 Kent for a few days at a time, but not so often now there was less bombing. It wasn't convenient to stay longer, not with their ration books registered at East Ham shops. And Kath didn't like to leave her house for long, because of the looters. What pained Mum most, I think, was that she'd promised Wally she would keep his little family safe and was unable to do so.

The only good thing about Kath's being in London was that, until recently, she could visit Mum's sister and their mother in Camberwell to make sure they were okay. But no more. Her last journey had taken in so many detours, with Valerie in her pushchair she had found it too much. It had been months now since Mum had received news of her family.

Rose was the daughter who truly disappointed Dad. 'I can't understand it, Pam,' he confided. 'There's our Con who couldn't wait to be of age to fight for her country. And me, I'd go with bells on if they'd 'ave me. Yet,

207

'ere's Rose refusing to go...' A sharp look from Mum told him he'd said enough. Retrieving his tobacco tin and Rizlas from his shirt pocket, he concentrated on making a painfully skinny cigarette.

To some, the ARP was for cissies who didn't want to fight in the real war. After dark its members walked the streets making sure no lights were showing. They assisted air-raid victims and other civilians who might need help, directed us to the nearest shelter when the siren sounded. Often Rose came home exhausted, covered in grime if she'd been rummaging through the remains of a bombed building. On mornings following a bad night, she would stumble through the front door and go straight upstairs to bed, without saying a word to any of us.

On my first evening home I was beginning to feel unaccountably restless when Iris charged through the front door with her old sit-up-and-beg bike, and throwing it into the already crowded hall called for her 'baby sister'. Her appearance shocked me. She looked years older than the child I had clung to on that June morning two years earlier, and was barely recognisable as the carefree, tanned young teen I had left on the lane outside Ivy House only a year ago.

Like the rest of us, Iris had lost her innocence to this war. Until she could reasonably expect to lie about her age and join the forces, she was working in Woolworth's on the Broadway. Not much of a lark, she grimaced, but it meant she could help Mum out with bits and pieces in short supply.

After turning fourteen the previous February, Iris could have left school. Instead, she and Sylvie chose to attend a Business Academy in Derby, which, regrettably, turned out to be not quite as advertised. According to my sister, the academy was run by two old ducks who were short of both students and equipment, while trying to teach simple book-keeping, Pitman's shorthand and typing.

On weekday mornings Uncle Fred delivered the girls to their destination but getting home was dodgy, in view of the blackout and absence of street signs. During one frantic evening, when they found themselves totally lost, Fred ran out of petrol looking for them. Another time Sylvie sprained her ankle, tripping down an unseen kerb. By the third week, it was decided that attending Business School was more trouble than it was worth. Sylvie chose to stay home to help out with a new baby brother. Iris concluded it was time to return to her own family.

It was a harrowing journey for a young girl on her own. Crossing London for the Southend-bound train took her several hours because of transport delays and station closures. Dispirited and disorientated, she reached the historic City area only after the last of its office workers had left for the day, and found herself having to detour through its narrow twisting lanes with nobody in sight to give her directions.

Reading about the bomb damage while sitting under an apple tree in Ivy House's orchard was one thing, but seeing it still raw from 1940 bombings was another. Office buildings had roofs and upper walls sheered off to expose missing stairs and broken furniture wedged into crevices. Windows were still taped or boarded up. Small businesses that had survived for centuries were now silenced by the Blitz.

It was spooky enough, she said, even before ghostly moans sent her into a darkened doorway as a torch light and running footsteps went to its source: a young woman cradling an unconscious child, victims of a hit and run. 'Came out of nowhere, then left us to die,' she wailed to the policeman who had rushed to her aid. 'Probably didn't know he got you, luv,' the copper told her, "appens all the time.' Iris's sudden appearance, probably resembling a Dickensian waif, startled them both. When she told them she thought the moaning came from a ghost, he said there were quite a few around there. He saw them all the time.

Following his instructions to get on to

Lombard and then Fenchurch Street, Iris was able to catch a late-night train home. And there on Leigh Station, Mum and Dad were waiting at the top of the steps. They had been there since three in the afternoon. Anxiety had turned to worry, then despair, and finally relief during their six hours' wait. Dad took time out for a snack and a pint in the adjacent Old Town, but Mum refused to leave. 'What else could I do?' she now interjected. 'Any mother would do as much.' Patience and worry, that's what this war meant to my poor beleaguered mother. How could I have possibly thought I would return home to find everything unchanged in this summer of 1942?

Trying to keep it all together, Mum had a hard time putting meals on the table. She spent a good part of each day in queues, on Leigh Broadway every morning and in Southend several afternoons a week, never knowing what she would buy.

Fortunately when we moved from the Old Town years before, she had continued to shop on the Broadway even though London Road shops were about half the distance. Now her loyalty paid off.

'Come back in an hour and I'll have a nice bit of cod for you, Mrs H,' Good Alf the fishmonger would whisper.

'I've saved the end of the bacon for you. Or three sausages. Or an egg,' Iris's friend

Ruth would tell her. 'Act normal. Don't say anything when I slip it into your bag,' she always added, as if she were handing over the crown jewels.

Iris's job at Woolworth's was a real blessing. Often she cycled home for lunch, rushing in breathlessly to announce they were putting out cups and saucers or tinned pilchards or Yardley's soap at two o'clock. Word would get around, and by the time Mum had trudged back to the shops, queues trailing along the street had mingled with each other. Still, she knew that by the time she reached Iris or one of her mates, a little extra would be brought out from under the counter for her. If she didn't need it herself, it might be something she could pass on to the butcher or fishmonger in exchange for food beyond what her ration books allowed.

Spam began appearing in the shops around this time, sent to us from America as part of the war's Lend-Lease programme. One of the few meat products not included in the meat-rationing allowance, it became a great bartering tool for my mother, who was able to buy several tins at a time from Woolworth's. At first it was quite a novelty, battered and deep fried, served cold, or hot with gravy and mashed potatoes. It wasn't long though before we were heartily sick of this mixture of pork and ham, which tasted like neither.

Lord Woolton, Minister of Food, really went to town when promoting Spam, offering us ingenious recipes distributed by area food offices, printed in women's magazines, broadcast on the BBC. We were also given recipes for meatless pies and carrot jam. And nettle tea – which we were assured lost its sting once the leaves were put in boiling water.

Although rationing of certain foods had been introduced soon after the war began, even these goods could be in short supply. Butter, bacon and sugar had been rationed first, then meat, but by Christmas 1941, tea was down to two ounces a week, sugar cut to eight ounces.

Fruit, unless home-grown, was non-existent. Ships were needed for goods more important than bananas and oranges. Cheese was a miserly one ounce per person, and in 1942 sweets were rationed. Only two ounces a week, but that was more than some of us had seen during the preceding years. In the weeks leading up to sweet rationing, we drooled long and hard in anticipation of what we would buy with our precious coupons.

Shop windows were meagrely but creatively decorated. Sweet shops were the most inviting with their pyramids of Cadbury's purple chocolate boxes and Bassett's multi-coloured allsorts, artfully arranged around red and green plaid packages of Macintosh toffees. Dummies, every one of them, but still they had us thinking of better times ahead.

Before we knew it to be so harmful, smoking was actually encouraged. Cigarettes were never rationed, but for civilians they became scarce enough to be sold one at a time. Popular brands such as Players Medium Cut and Senior Service remained available only to the armed forces. As the war moved along, American cigarettes were a favourite with illicit dealers, who offered them on the black-market. Often army deserters, they were known as 'spivs' and recognisable from their long coats, big enough to conceal several cartons.

Since Britain had no vineyards, wine soon disappeared from the off-licences. However, the government knew the importance of keeping up morale, so Dad and his mates could still nip into their local pub for a pint of beer, which they scornfully described as being as weak as ants' piss. Gin, distilled from various grains, and even potatoes, became the only widely available 'short' drink offered in pubs.

Posters urging us to Dig for Victory were aimed at encouraging Mr and Mrs Public to grow their own food, but they had little meaning for us. Ever since we moved to 19 Kent, Dad had worked on a prolific vegetable garden. His greatest pride was his tomatoes, often the size of tennis balls, and small white potatoes that clung to the plants in clusters of a dozen or more. Now Mum and I tried to keep it going, with less success. Even so, between spring and autumn we supplied the family with root vegetables, runner beans, peas and tomatoes. Adding an Oxo cube to provide the broth, they contributed to a tasty enough stew, especially on occasions when flavoured with rabbit or pork.

Our milkman's horse, Ernie, played an important role in our gardening successes. Before the war he provided fresh manure for Mum's exquisite roses. Now it was lavishly spread, still steaming hot, on the vegetable patch. Occasionally, we received a bonus from the coal and bread delivery horses (no motorised delivery vehicles back then, at least not in our area) but none was so regular as Ernie.

We did have a problem with Mrs Jones, who lived across the road. She would stand in her porch with a bucket and shovel, as did Mum in ours, waiting for this wonder horse trained to do his business in front of our two houses. Then, like boxers out of their corners, the two women bore down on Ernie, actually shoving each other to get it – straight from the horse's arse. A bigger embarrassment for me was when Ernie wasn't in the mood. I would be handed the shovel and pail and instructed to follow him around the streets, for as long as it took.

CHAPTER FIFTEEN

Where Do I Fit in Now?

I didn't expect to feel this lonely. For months I had literally dreamed of being home, back with my family in a noisy kitchen and cosy front room. Now nothing was the same. Not the house, not my family, not the daily routine – and definitely not me.

At Chapel we laughed over our embarrassingly small clothes, grumbled good-naturedly about miserable foster parents and excessive homework, made fun of our holey socks and shoes lined with paper to keep out the rain and snow. This was possible because we knew our hardships were temporary. Some situations would be rectified after the war, but others would end once we could bask in the warmth and love of families grateful to have us home.

For me it simply didn't happen, not right away at least. I felt disassociated from my family – like a person on the outside looking in. A stranger. It was the war, of course.

Everyone was busy doing what they had to do. But then as summer wore on, thanks to Mum, so was I.

I was not alone in feeling this way. In fact, many men and women, returning from war duty to even bigger changes, felt the same as I did – in spades. Husbands discovered wives enjoying a new independence that came with earning their own pay packets. For many there were no homes, and often no jobs. If there was work, chances were it was far less exciting than being an integral part of a fighting unit.

Well, I wasn't looking for excitement or more independence or to be a member of anyone's team. I just wanted us to have time for each other. On my first morning home, coming downstairs to nothing noisier than the loud ticking of the kitchen clock, I felt abandoned. I couldn't remember ever before greeting a new day alone. No Monica. No Little Arser. No Iris. Everybody gone. Selfishly I saw it as a personal slight.

I couldn't even unpack my few clothes, since the wardrobe bulged and dresser drawers were already overflowing. Even wall and door hooks were already overloaded with coats and dresses. Next, I thought to have a bath, only to discover there was no hot water.

In the kitchen I half expected to find my breakfast laid out on the table, but no luck there either as I confronted dirty plates and cups left by my sisters. My thoughts turned to Kirk Langley. How different it would have been had I gone to Ivy House, with its roomy lavender-scented cupboards containing lots of empty hangers. Vera would have cooked me breakfast, Uncle Fred would have stayed home to show me his latest farm animals, and Aunty Min would be fawning over her 'little loov'. Even Mardi would have been all over me, squealing with joy. Not like Clarabelle, who tried with all her might to push me off Mum's favourite chair.

At ten o'clock sharp the cat jumped down to head for the front door, seconds before the key turned in its lock and Mum came in, red-faced and smiling because she had managed to buy a 'nice bit of cod'. With a hint of sarcasm that went undetected, I agreed it would be a real treat with a few potatoes. Mum added boiling water to the teapot's contents, and over a cup of weak tea she said it was lovely to have me home. But then, just when I thought we had settled down for a nice chin-wag, she looked over at the tin clock that had stood on the mantelpiece for ever, and now told her she had to get a start on the dinner.

Instead of offering to help, I stared moodily at my anaemic tea until Mum suggested I visit some of my little friends. How about this Monica I used to write about? She seemed to be a good mate.

Good mate. Yes. Good idea. I fished her address from my satchel pocket. It seemed so long since we had sat in the Barkers' scullery swapping such vital information. Now I realised I could actually walk to her house. We could sit in the park and reminisce, hop on a bus into Southend if she had any money or walk to the shops on Hamlet Court Road. Such freedom.

The last time I had followed this route I had been accompanied by Dad, Iris and Lilah with our sandbags and – for me at least – a sense of trepidation. So much had happened, so many people had come into my life during those two years. Past Chalkwell School where I had lined up in my sister's class in the now deserted playground, I rounded the park. Soldiers were practising some sort of drill where Rose used to take her employer's toddler to feed the pigeons. Continuing alongside the dentist's house and surgery with its windows boarded up, I came to Monica's street sloping down to the seafront.

Looking at the house names and numbers I heard a familiar laugh some four or five doors away. Caution stopped me as I made to run towards my friend. She was joined by a tall sandy-haired man in civvies – it was her brother Rob, whom I recognised from a photograph. Mummy came next. No mistaking her as she folded herself into a small green car. Monica climbed into the rear while, waving cheerily to a neighbour, Rob hopped into the driver's seat. In view of petrol rationing, and because they appeared to have no luggage, I felt they couldn't be going far. Should I wait for their return or come back later in the day?

Monica glanced through the back window as I raised my hand. Instead of a smile, a frown creased her face. Surely it was puzzlement, not recognising me in Iris's blouse? The frown accelerated to a scowl as she turned away, touching her brother's shoulder in a gesture that seemed to indicate he should hurry off. Blinded by sudden tears, I turned and hurried off too – in the other direction.

Now what? I could wait in the park for an hour or two, then tell my mother I'd had a lovely morning with Monica, or I could walk into Southend on my own. Or should I simply get on home? Suddenly 19 Kent, with Mum in the kitchen sweating over her nice bit of cod, seemed rather attractive. What the heck, it might even be time for another cup of tea. I found myself smiling again.

'What a shame,' my mother sympathised when I told her Monica wasn't home. She was on her own eating a small slice of Spam with mashed potatoes, tomato and gravy. The rest of the family had come and gone, and presumably eaten her cod. My Spam was being kept warm on the stove top. 'Well then,' she continued, 'we'd best go into Southend after we've cleared up this lot. See what we can find in the shops. Maybe go to the Odeon. I bet it's a long time since you've seen a good film, luv. Let's see what's on, shall we?'

I finished my meal and started the washing up while Mum drank what passed for tea. Looking beyond the sink to the cluttered backyards, the neat rows of vegetables and behind them the dismal air-raid shelter, I decided I need never be lonely so long as I had this woman in my life. All I had to do was let her in.

As the days wore on I participated more in household chores, buoyed by my mother's constant reminders that it was lovely to have so much help. It fell on me to muck out the chicken shed at weekends and prepare the smelly mash eaten by Arthur, our cockerel, every day.

On Mondays we did the family wash, which meant confronting the horrible great tin boiler kept under the draining board. Fed with water from the kitchen tap, it was larger than your average dustbin and, aided by a gas flame underneath, literally boiled our towels and bedding and smaller 'whites'. Every now and again Mum or I would lift the boiler's lid to stir its contents with a wooden stick, causing the kitchen to fill with steam. When several loads were finished and lugged out to the backyard, a cast-iron monstrosity known as a mangle was hand-turned to wring the water from our washing.

From there the soggy bedding was hung on the line, propped up by a pronged pole so it could fly high in the wind, and we had the unwelcome task of emptying the boiler into the gutter. By the time we were through, we were steaming as much as our laundry, and in dire need of a cup of tea. That was Monday taken care of. With the help of a stiff breeze or a fire in the hearth to dry this lot, on Tuesday we could do the ironing. It was hard to believe this was my mother's life, and had been for years.

Housework was remarkably time-consuming through the 1940s and early '50s. Engineers were creating all manner of clever stuff to destroy or maim, but when it came to labour-saving equipment for the home we were in a time warp. Small clothes were laundered by hand in a footbath on a rickety table in the backyard, the water coming from a rubber hose tied on to the tap in the kitchen and led through the window. My help was appreciated here, because without a second person to hold it on tight, the hose would leak over the floor. (Dad repeated the procedure of tying his hose to the kitchen tap when watering his garden. Not that it always worked, because if Mum was cooking she would disconnect it without warning when she needed water.)

During my first week home I found there was very little time for leisure. On most mornings the ground floor of 19 Kent was swept and dusted, the red tiles in the hall and front porch buffed vigorously with a mop. And since every cup of tea brought into use a cup, saucer and spoon, we were washing up three or four times a day. Add to this the endless trips to Leigh Broadway or Southend High Street for food, the cooking of meals for Dad and my sisters who rarely kept similar hours, and the tending of the vegetable gardens. Well, you get the idea. The list was endless, giving us no chance to be bored. Even at night, while listening to the wireless, I would pick up the darning or mending, kept in a basket by the hearth.

Although I quickly became my mother's first mate, I seemed to have little in common with my sisters. We all went about our daily tasks, returning like homing pigeons to the same house, but there was no longer that cohesion necessary for a happy family. It was as if we were a broken necklace, its thread severed, the beads scattered. When this war was over, some would be lost for ever.

CHAPTER SIXTEEN

I Go Back to School

As the summer of '42 drew to a close I cleaned out my satchel, sharpened my pencils and read through old textbooks I had last looked at during the final weeks of evacuation. Other than my glimpse of Monica through her brother's car window I had seen none of my friends from school. Not surprising really, since they didn't live close by. Now, with the naivety of youth, I was eagerly anticipating a reunion. Who would be in my class? Would I be considered prefect quality?

Three days before school started I ironed my uniform and hung it on a hook behind my parents' bedroom door. My black shoes shone so brightly Mum said I needed dark glasses like those American film stars wear. White socks were placed carefully on the back of her turquoise wicker chair. I was ready.

Come Monday morning my mother gathered up her baskets ready to leave for her bus stop at the end of our road. 'You coming, then?' She eyed me up and down, and said I looked smart. In response I looked at her mottled legs and run-down shoes, her dress rucked up at the back. 'No, it's early, I'll wait a bit.'

We kissed, as we always did when we parted company. 'Tat-ta then,' she smiled fondly. 'See you for dinner. It'll be ready so you can be back at school in time. I'll try to get some fish. It's good for your brain.'

I swallowed. How could I be such a cow, not wanting my friends to know this shabby-looking woman was my mother?

Watching from the front window I waited for her bus to come and go before I left the house. Kent led on to Middlesex Avenue, which separated our estate from the school. All I had to do was turn left for a few yards and I was steps from the main entrance. Waiting until our street was deserted, I made my dash to Middlesex and joined a group of older girls coming off a bus. On that first morning, by the time I reached the school bulletin board for classroom information, I was a dithering mess. Monica and Marjorie were there, already talking of their 'summer hols', and I knew right then that I didn't fit in here either.

Still, I didn't want to believe my friendship with Monica could not survive the differences in our home lives. By now convinced she hadn't recognised me through the car window on that miserable July day (I was, after all, wearing an unfamiliar blouse), I enquired about her summer. It was busy, she said. She meant to look me up, but had been in Devon where she was put to work scraping her cousin's boat until her hands were raw. I told her I had been busy too, and was about to quip that my hands were raw from washing and cleaning, but decided she might not appreciate my humour.

A couple of weeks later, when she was given a disastrous mark on our maths test, I offered to help her. That's how I came to be sitting at her family's polished dining-room table with our books spread out at one end. A vase of pink roses scented the room, classical music wafted in from the carpeted lounge. Mummy served us fizzy lemonade and digestive biscuits.

Come teatime I was told the table was needed, and we should pack it in. As I prepared to do so Monica's mother handed me a crinkly paper bag bulging with used clothes. 'I know it must be difficult with so many children,' she offered, 'but if these don't fit you or your sisters and brothers, another family in your neighbourhood will be glad of them.' Beet-red by the time she finished her Lady Bountiful speech, I grabbed the bag and ran. 'Your little friend should learn some manners,' Mummy called over her shoulder to Monica as I sped down their path.

Instead of being insulted, Iris laughed out loud, tossing a blouse made to fit a three-year-old for me to try on. It had what looked to be a gravy stain down the front. In stretching a red jumper over her now sizeable breasts, she pushed her hand through a hole in the elbow, causing more laughter. Like me though, Mum did not share Iris's hilarity. Momentarily examining the pile of clothing from which buttons had been carelessly removed, belts were missing and jumpers shrunk beyond wear, she simply pursed her lips as was her fashion, and told me I would do well to keep clear of the likes of Monica from now on. Together we stuffed the softer items into the rag-bag under the stairs to be used as dusters and polishers.

I suppose Mrs Granger meant well, and truly believed we needed her moth-eaten, stained cast-offs, but I didn't see it that way at the time. The truth is we were well-dressed children in pre-war years. Mum or Mrs Hardy made us cotton outfits for summer, and my sister Edie knitted us jumpers and skirts that even our teachers admired. On a shopping spree twice a year my mother returned from Southend, her wicker baskets spilling over with green Marks & Spencer bags. In spring they contained white ankle socks and underwear, patent ankle-strap shoes and leather sandals. For winter she bought knee socks for me, stockings for Iris, navy-blue bloomers and cosy vests and liberty bodices.

We had more new clothes, including smart winter hats and coats, when Mum's club was due. Weeks ahead of these purchases we would be dragged into a certain clothing shop to try on their latest coat collection. The last outfits we bought there in the winter of 1939 were rust-coloured cloth coats with matching hats. I loved the coats, but not the club enabling us to buy them.

Almost every family on the estate belonged to such a club. Ours was for a general clothing shop, and since it was run by my mother, Iris and I had to collect a certain sum – I believe a shilling – every Saturday from its members. I found this humiliating. When we knocked at some doors, conversation in the house would stop to give the impression nobody was home. Or we might hear, 'Don't get that, Doris. It's only the little Hobbs girls for the club.' If we were unsuccessful after two attempts, Mum would visit the errant member, who would pay her because she wanted to join next year's club. And when everyone had paid up, Iris and I would get our new hats and coats free.

With the onset of war our club ended, and afterwards we had no need for one. Limited by rationing, my sisters bought their own clothes after endlessly studying shop windows and magazines. Most of the time I wore my school uniform, in an era when there was no chance to customise it with earrings or brooches or multi-coloured scarves. The only jewellery allowed was a house badge and a wristwatch. I had both. The badge was mandatory and, when I needed to pace myself during tests and exams, my mother lent me her Rolex Oyster watch.

Also, out of sight under my blouse, I wore a small cross. At one time or another during the first years of the war Mum gave each of her daughters a cross and chain. Mine was silver, its inscription reading 'Pam, with love, Mum, 1940'. Iris and I each received one for Christmas, much to Aunty Cissy's delight. I kept mine until the mid-eighties when I returned home from a bicycle ride and discovered it gone. In the 1950s I spotted Rose's gold cross in a Westcliff pawn shop and I wear it still. I also wear Connie's, which I found in her belongings following her death in the 1990s.

The Rolex brought us grief and pleasure. I was around seven or eight when Mum spotted it on the pavement outside Chalkwell School and, believing it was a toy, gave it to me. At a glance it resembled something you might try to win by activating one of those slippery claw devices at a fairground, or even find in a Christmas cracker. Nobody thought to wind it, to see if it was real. A few stitches repaired the broken elastic strap and I wore the watch to school for a week or so before an eagle-eyed teacher took it from me, studied it carefully, then slipped it into her handbag.

Two days later a policeman visited 19 Kent, for 'a serious conversation'. I can only imagine Mum's ashen face when she saw him. An accident at Dad's building site? Had one of the kiddies been hit by a car? No. The nice teacher assumed our little watch to be stolen. How else would a child from a council estate come to be wearing such an expensive piece of jewellery? Mum laughed in the copper's face, then invited him to share a pot of tea. After hearing her story he said if the watch remained unclaimed after six months it was hers to keep. She told him he could keep the rotten thing. She preferred Dad's pocket watch with its nice big face, which she kept handy in her bag.

Winter came and went, allowing spring to paint our landscape in brilliant style, and before we knew it Easter was upon us. This meant chocolate eggs for everyone at 19 Kent, except Dad, who received a chocolate cigar. On this particular occasion though my mother left her egg-filled shopping basket on the bus. At the end of the day, when the transport company didn't have it, she rushed over to Woolworth's to buy a second batch of eggs.

Finding herself across from Leigh's police station on Easter Saturday, Mum decided it

wouldn't hurt to pop in. The same policeman who had questioned her about the
wristwatch now told her a good Samaritan
had brought in our Easter eggs. And wasn't
she the lady who'd found the Rolex? Well
he'd been meaning to drop by, because it
was hers now. A bumper Easter for the
Hobbses: two lots of chocolate eggs for us,
and an expensive watch for Mum.

CHAPTER SEVENTEEN

Overcoming Shortages

Although many of my favourite foods were
no longer available we had enough to eat at
home, and soon I was back to my normal
weight. All over England people were
discovering they could grow their own food.
Sports fields near us were divided into allotments – small plots where entire families
would toil away growing root vegetables and
berries. Many of those allotments are still in
use today.

During the war, even Londoners in the
wealthiest neighbourhoods turned the soil in
their communal mini-parks to grow carrots
and runner beans, peas and potatoes. Famous flower gardens such as those at Hampton

Court were planted with vegetables. Here, horticulturists maintained demonstration gardens where they shared their knowledge, as well as seeds and cuttings, with visitors.

Many a vegetable garden prospered on the roofs of Anderson shelters piled high with soil. And if you had looked up, way up, you could even see hens staring moodily from tiny terraces and roof gardens, wired in to keep these producers of tomorrow's breakfast from flying away.

We had kept two hens before the war. A neighbour moving from the estate had given them to Dad, who built them a little run beside the coal shed. They were useless old things, didn't lay eggs and when they weren't looking for grubs and worms in Dad's newly dug soil, they sat contentedly in the elderberry tree watching life go by around them. One day both disappeared, either frightened off or stolen by workmen who used to trundle their building supplies along the alley at the end of our garden.

A few weeks before my return home in 1942 Mum had purchased Arthur, a magnificent-looking young cockerel who grew rapidly to become all of three feet tall. A bad-tempered greedy bird, he would peck at anyone arriving with his food. My mother managed to keep him at bay with a broom, while she lowered his dish to the ground. On the days I took over this chore, I'd throw it in and hope for the best.

When Arthur escaped along the alley, and it took two labourers to get him home, Mum in her wisdom – or lack of it – thought it a good idea to buy him an amorous hen. Not only would she sweeten his disposition, but they might also give us some chicks. Since Mum couldn't go near him without brandishing a broom, I didn't see how a hen would let him fertilise the eggs. Still, we agreed it was worth a try. Neither of us knew how this worked, but hoped to learn as we went along.

A small advertisement in the Southend paper offered Grey Leghorns and Buff Orpingtons for sale. The address was in Rayleigh, a fair distance for us on erratic public transport, but we went anyway. The owner, a young woman whose husband was at sea, said she was packing it in and moving to South Wales, where her sister had a farm. My mother took one look, and wanted to buy several of the speckled pullets, but with no means of transporting them home she had to settle on a comfortable-looking buff-coloured bird with a delicate pink comb. Buffy, as we named our new purchase, was tucked firmly under my arm, while Mum carried two fresh eggs in her gas mask case. It's hard to believe now that we trekked all the way home with a live chicken, because no buses came along to give us a lift.

Arthur proved such an obnoxious and aggressive suitor that Buffy was afraid of him. On his next leave, Dad spent all weekend making a separate run for the hen. There she continued to lay lovely brown eggs several days a week, which was just as well because I had forfeited my egg ration in order to buy her food.

Arthur became impossible; the day he strutted after Mum pecking her bottom we agreed he had to go. Dad admittedly didn't know how to kill a chicken – or any other creature. My mother hated the bird so much by now she said she'd be happy to aim a chopper in his direction, had she not been terrified of missing. So, two days before Christmas, Mr Beardsley, who lived three houses down and kept both poultry and rabbits, came to our rescue. With one sharp twist of the neck, Arthur became no more threatening than an impotent heap of brilliant plumage shining against the greyness of our backyard.

Mum and I decided to pluck the feathers, rendering him unrecognisable as he hung in the pantry by the time the other girls came home. On Mr B's instructions we loosened the feathers with boiling water and, hunched over the footbath containing his body, began pulling them out one by one. The stench was unbelievable. Clarabelle went missing for two days after seeing us strip

Arthur's body, possibly thinking it was her turn next. On our makeshift scales – without feathers, head and feet – what used to be Arthur, and now resembled an obscenely plump naked baby, weighed in at thirty pounds.

Come Christmas Day, with Dad and Connie able to join us for the holiday, we drooled all morning as a heavenly aroma from the roasting bird wafted through the house. We were positively giddy with anticipation. Who needed presents when we had such a feast? One by one our loaded plates were ferried from the kitchen to front room, where every chair and bench had been put into use so we could sit together around the extended table.

When all the meals were delivered we were joined by Mum, flushed from the oven's warmth and the success of having produced such an incredible meal. But then, home-made paper hats on our heads, and paper chains made from magazine pages strung from the ceilings, implied a festive air we no longer felt. We sat in silence. Nobody wanted to take the first bite out of Arthur. It simply couldn't be done. We toyed with the veggies and the stuffing, and that was it. Not one of us ate a single morsel of that soft white meat.

I couldn't understand it. It wasn't as if he was our pet. The Hardys at the end of the garden ate their home-raised bunnies all the time. Arthur was not soft and furry; his vicious beak didn't compare with a cute twitchy nose. He was a ferocious bully, out to peck anyone brave enough to get close to him. Still, we couldn't bring ourselves to eat such a familiar bird.

Next day we buried his remains in the back garden. I thought Mum was going to dig him up a few hours later when she realised she could have given the meaty carcass to Mrs Hardy, who had hungry sons to feed. Even a swap for one of their rabbits would have been in order, since they didn't have names and nobody was sentimental about eating them.

Putting meals on the table was getting to be a full-time occupation. We still had a choice of food available within the framework of a points system. Each person had a ration book containing 16 points a month, and it was up to Mum, who kept the books, to spend those points as she thought best. Usually she bought what was available, eking out the points on tinned and other foods. If she knew Connie was coming home she might splurge on a tin of salmon; if not we could all have pilchards. These large sardine-like fish weren't particularly palatable with potatoes and carrots, but preferable to fatty meat.

Wartime propaganda machines urged us

to buy American dried eggs. We were glad enough to use them in baked goods, but when fried the rubbery substance they became made them unrecognisable.

Posters and pamphlets effectively told us how to make the most of our food supplies, how to cook them, store them and share them. 'Why not make baked cod with parsnip balls?' read the storyline of an advertisement for salted cod at nine pence a pound. 'It's not fair to have more than your share,' posters cried out, referring to the growing black-market.

Lord Woolton even had a pie named for him. And since we were lucky if we saw two eggs per person per week, women's magazines adapted pre-war recipes that called for two dozen in a single dish.

A lot of the editorial advice went over our heads. When Vi brought magazines home from the factory we'd laugh ourselves silly at the self-help articles. One I recall told us that compromises must be made. As an example it was suggested how we could save the parlour maid from undue fetching and carrying, by having buffet meals. Another urged us to serve dishes that were unpretentious, inexpensive, filling and popular, such as spaghetti, gnocchi and risotto. I'm afraid the Hobbses could only guess as to what the last two dishes were, and considered spaghetti a meal for Italians. The fact that 'one cannot tell the difference between crème brûlée made from dried egg custard and real eggs' didn't fizz on us either. Nor did the tip that 'if invited for the weekend, it is acceptable to slip the butler a little butter and sugar'.

Another upmarket magazine ran articles on how to dress. We shouldn't worry, their scribes wrote, if we had no more than pre-war evening clothes, or the so-called utility clothing to wear at dinner. Our host would understand. In fact, we might even be considered patriotic. This became a joke at 19 Kent. 'I'm just being patriotic,' we would say of our tatty jumpers and socks darned with the wrong-coloured wool.

Bread rationing wasn't introduced until after the war. Instead we had wheatmeal loaves, more commonly known as Hitler's Secret Weapon. Since we had always eaten tons of potatoes, we had no need of the Ministry of Food's 'Potato Pete', who encouraged us to consume more spuds. Ignoring 'Pete', Mum continued mashing ours with a noisy thump, thump, before slinging them on to our cracked white plates to mingle with the bread-filled sausages, Spam, or mock chicken – whose origin I forget but which we all likened to eating an eraser. Understandably, she had no time for suggested experiments, such as mixing potato with margarine to make it go further, or substituting grated potato for dried fruit in cakes. Better still, we were never subjected to Portable Potato Piglets, or Inspiration Pie, which was runner-up in Lord Woolton's potato cookery competition.

Cousin to Potato Pete was Doctor Carrot, a character promising schoolgirl complexions and better eyesight. He told us how ace night-fighter pilots such as Cat's Eyes Cunningham attributed their success to a diet containing lots of carrots. Since I had just been fitted with my first reading glasses, I ate carrots at every opportunity. All they did for me was to turn my rosy cheeks yellow.

All of us fell for some of the catchy slogans and cheeky characters staring down at us from wall posters, or featured in leaflets handed out at shops and food halls. Not all of them reflected well on us. Coal miners, for example, were leaving their dreary jobs for fatter pay packets to be had at city factories or the excitement of travel in the armed forces. In consequence, coal supplies were so low, we were reduced to buying mock coal (known as Coalite) to go with our mock cream, mock chicken, mock eggs and the rest.

Restaurants managed to survive the war years, but compromises were many. I don't recall ever having more than a cup of watery tea and perhaps a small cake (appropriately named Rock Cake) in Southend's Lyons teashop during the war years. Since we weren't used to eating out, now didn't seem the best time to start. For one thing, we chose not to hang around far from home in case there was an air raid.

In London, where office workers crowded the cafés at lunchtime, government-subsidised British Restaurants were opened in church basements, museums and other public places. The city's more exclusive restaurants still provided fancy menus, though I am told that had I ordered 'Ballontine de jambon Valentinoise', it would have arrived as hot Spam.

Pastry, made from wholemeal flour, tasted better than it looked. Vegetable pie topped by mashed potatoes was far more appealing when we talked Mum into leaving out the gristle and fat she felt compelled to include.

Only once did she return from a shopping expedition with a slab of tripe, quivering as if it was still alive. Rose stared at it dolefully and asked if we had boiled her knitting. Iris said that whatever it was had been struck by lightning and we shouldn't touch it while wearing wet boots. With her 'waste not, want not' attitude Mum fried the tripe, and forced herself to eat one or two bites. Then even she decided it was inedible.

We balked too at nettle soup, and although several butchers started selling horsemeat, we decided it was not for us. It would be too much like eating pigeons from the park or pets or Ernie the milkman's horse.

By 1943, with merchant ships being sunk at a reported rate of three a day, food became scarcer than ever before, and even legal rations weren't always available. Heaven knows they were precious little. Tea was down to two ounces a person, per week. This was worse than the air raids for poor old Mum, who would keep the tea leaves in her strainer and use them over and over. By the time Iris came home for her tea, it looked as if she was drinking wee-wee.

Our cooking was hampered, not only by a shortage of ingredients, but also the lack of decent pots and pans. Following the call for metal, my mother was as keen as housewives everywhere, who zealously donated saucepans and baking tins to the war effort. Most regretted it later when they didn't have the means to repair worn-out saucepans.

At this time, public and private buildings lost their iron fences and gates. Citizens were extremely generous in giving up just about everything that could be melted down, even jewellery, for the building of aircraft After a shortage was made known, Mum donated Dad's prized naval binoculars. It caused a row, as she knew it would, but she said she hated to see him using them to watch overhead dog fights, and cheering when one of

241

the Germans came spiralling down into the sea. The pilot, Jerry or no, was some mother's son.

By the spring of 1943, Buffy was laying fewer and fewer eggs, yet she still gobbled up our egg allowance in chicken food. Once again, we called on Mr Beardsley, who took one look at her all puffed up on her nest and declared her broody. He suggested we put half a dozen fertilised eggs under her.

True to his promise he brought over such eggs, deposited them into a ready-made nest and plonked Buffy back on to them. Glaring indignantly at him, she hopped off. Did she need privacy? After all, she was going to give birth. We pinned up a make-shift curtain shielding her from the rest of the world. Buffy would have none of it. She preferred her perch, from which she could view our comings and goings.

When it became apparent that Buffy was not going to supply us with baby chicks, Mr B suggested we skip a stage in the procedure and try her with ready-made babies. We told him we'd have six, and some days later he brought us half a dozen little balls of yellow fluff, saying they were younger and less strong than he would have liked but we could give them a go. On his further instructions we kept them indoors, in a netted box in the hearth beside the fire by day, and in the adjoining oven which – even with the door open – kept cosy at night.

For some weeks we had them cheeping about the kitchen, sending Clarabelle out of her mind. Eventually, with the warm weather of summer upon us, we put them outside. By this time they were a part of our family and kept returning to sit in the hearth.

One of the chicks died during its first week with us, four grew to be laying hens and the fifth was a cockerel, smaller and friendlier than Arthur. In view of past experience we decided not to give him a name, but he soon had one anyway when we began calling him Nameless. For the rest of the war, the odour of rotten vegetables permeated our house, as we cooked potato peelings daily to mix with the grain allowance. Once we started adding cockleshells to produce eggs with firmer shells, the kitchen smelled like a rubbish dump.

CHAPTER EIGHTEEN

Loving Friends
Who Enriched Our Lives

An unexpected source of food came from an American soldier friend of Connie's. Jackson's southern drawl and easy-going manner endeared him to all of us. Even better, when Connie was away he still came visiting, bringing with him ham sandwiches the size of bricks. Whether these were from his own lunch, or if he asked the army chef for extras, we didn't know. 'Never look a gift horse in the mouth' and 'Let sleeping dogs lie' had become Mum's favourite answers when we asked about Jackson's little food parcels, and black-market tins of goodies hidden in the rear of our air-raid shelter.

Once or twice a week we would answer a rap on the door and find our new friend standing there, all six foot two of him, cap in hand, parcel under his arm. Coming through to the kitchen he would simply plonk a wrapped sandwich, sometimes two, on to the table, saying something like, 'There you go, Ma. I figured you might be able to use this with your tea.'

Mum would eye the package briefly and, pride being her biggest fault, say primly, 'Ta, son. I can't say as I'm hungry now, after the big dinner I had earlier. If it's still nice tomorrow, I'll have it then.'

As soon as he was settled in the front room with whoever was there listening to the wireless, she would remove the ham, almost an inch thick, then the butter slathered on it as thick as cement between two bricks. Served with boiled potatoes and garden tomatoes, the now thinly sliced ham provided a dinner for the family. The bread, when spread with carrot jam, wasn't half bad either, even though to us it tasted more like cake.

Sometimes he brought fruit cake, the likes of which we hadn't seen in years. And a few weeks into our friendship, he introduced us to tea bags. The first time she saw these, Mum stared suspiciously at them, then carefully slit each one to fill her caddy. The leaves were so fine they slipped through her chrome strainer, until she lined it with the toe of a laddered silk stocking. I have to say, you know there's a war on when you come home to find your mum using her stockings to make a decent cuppa.

If my father was home when Jackson dropped by, the pair of them would go to the pub, or sit in the back garden discussing the latest war news and ports in America visited by Dad during his time in the navy. Just as we couldn't always understand Jackson's southern drawl, Dad – if he was in a teasing mood – would flummox our guest by slipping into bewildering cockney rhyming slang. Making comprehension virtually impossible to the uninitiated, custom has it that the second half of the rhyme is left off. 'Get your titfa [short for tit for tat, meaning hat] old son,' Dad would say as they prepared to leave for the pub or 'I just 'afta go up the apples [apples and pears for stairs] to tell me trouble [trouble and strife = wife] as 'ow we're off.' If we were in hearing we would interpret, knowing Jackson was thoroughly confused.

One day he came through the kitchen to the back garden, where Dad was sitting on the bench. Pausing long enough to study a small piece of paper taken from his pocket, and wearing the biggest of grins on his sunny face, our friend announced his 'plates' (plates of meat, i.e. feet) hurt because he'd taken the wrong 'frog' (frog and toad = road) on his way to buy a new 'whistle' (whistle and flute = suit). Looking only a little surprised, Dad raised his hands. 'Okay, son, I surrender. But I 'afta say I reckon that's a really big porky you just told me. [Porky = pork pie – lie.] But you win, mate. No more cockney. It ain't right with that funny accent of yours anyway.' We never learned who had taught Jackson his new slang words. Maybe he'd taken a butcher's (butcher's hook = look) at one of his pamphlets telling him how to act and how to converse with the English while living in our country.

It took our soldier friend a while to appreciate the severity of our food shortages. Once he did, there were larger portions of ham, sometimes a few eggs, even a carton of butter that Mum shared with Good Alf at the fish shop and Mrs Hardy, who returned the favour with a rabbit or two.

Jackson touched our lives on and off for about eight months before disappearing. With victory in Europe, we assumed he had gone home to his family. Then one day, in the autumn of '45, we received a letter in a pink perfumed envelope bearing an American stamp. It was from his sister, thanking us for befriending Jackson, who was killed in France at the Battle of the Bulge. Mum sat rocking Clarabelle that day, her tears soaking the pink paper. 'The bloody war. That lovely boy. Those bloody Huns...' was her constant lament, before she carefully propped the letter on the mantelpiece for the rest of the family to read.

Our brief relationship with the young American left an impression on all of us. A few years after the war, when Connie had a small refrigerator installed in our pantry, Mum said it would make her think of Jackson, and his dislike of our warm milk. (We continued to drink warm milk, because she plugged in the fridge only on hot days and, vowing it didn't work, reverted to her old habit of standing the milk bottles in a bowl of cold water on the stone pantry shelf.)

Years later, while touring the southern United States, Jackson would spring to my mind unbidden. In Florida, I found myself smiling whenever I came across grapefruits offered for sale by the highways. Lusciously pink inside, and dripping juice, those Indian River grapefruits are a far cry from Jackson's somewhat withered yellow fruit that had caused Mum such concern.

Occasionally, if he had missed the last bus back to his barracks, our young friend would stay over at 19 Kent. His feet hung over the end of the settee, and there wasn't a blanket big enough to cover his spare frame. Still, he enjoyed his sleep-overs. Said it made him feel he belonged to a real family, and that he would always remember the preserved tomatoes on fried bread we had for Sunday breakfast.

On one memorable Saturday night he brought a grapefruit, tossing it at Mum with a request that she put it in her ice box. Eyeing it as if she expected it to explode, she placed the unfamiliar fruit gingerly in the larder, the closest we came to having an ice box. This was early December and the weather was particularly harsh. In our house, keeping warm was more difficult than keeping cold, but – just to be sure – Mum decided to put the grapefruit in the backyard overnight. Not a good idea considering the hungry wildlife out there. In addition to which, it snowed.

Around dawn, when I thought everyone was asleep, I opened the back door to go to the toilet, and was startled to see my mother doubled over, scratching around in the snow with her gardening trowel. My dear old mum, her thick laddered stockings held above her knees with knotted elastic garters. Veined legs, visible in the space between stocking tops and faded fleecy bloomers, were turning blue. The shiny seat of her skirt was darned in several places with mismatched wool. On her feet she wore Dad's gardening boots.

She turned and saw me, despair written on her purple face.

'I can't remember what the bleedin' thing looks like,' she gasped, having uncovered a scrubby old ball and a rock collected from somewhere else to add to our rockery. I told her to come on inside and give me the boots, saying it looked like a big yellow orange. I would find it, while she made us some tea. When the grapefruit was located, cut and sampled, we decided it needed a week's sugar ration to render it edible.

'If you could get hold of a few bananas, though...' Mum told Jackson, who said he would see what he could do.

Our rockery was one of the few patches of colour brightening the back garden in those days. Since it wasn't practical to slip onions or carrots or Brussels sprouts between the stones, they continued to provide a haven for dark blue lobelia and white 'wedding cake' flowers that spread like weeds in beautiful contrast to the grey background. Recent additions to our pet cemetery beyond the rockery included a field mouse, Arthur, and a large black cat.

Did I mention the remarkable Clarabelle, who came with us from our old house on Church Hill, was a celebrity of sorts on that terrace? One Sunday morning my mother woke up to find Dad beside her covered in blood. Since the last she had seen of him was when he left for the pub the night before, she took one look at the carnage and decided he had been murdered.

Her screams alerted the neighbours – and my father, who jumped about a foot in the air (or so the story goes). Beneath him was a rat, a gift from Clarabelle wanting to show off her hunting prowess.

On Kent Avenue the largest hunting trophy she brought home was a stunned field mouse, which she deposited on the coconut matting inside our kitchen door. The poor little creature would wobble a few unsteady steps before Clarabelle pounced again, to playfully toss it into the air.

Four grown Hobbses jumped on to the table hollering. Each time the mouse was tossed, they squealed louder. Dad, digging up potatoes at the time, thought the Huns had invaded. Or worse. 'Never seen so many silly buggers in me life,' he complained, slinging the offending rodent into the potato patch from where it had come.

There was no cat to match Clarabelle for cunning, intelligence, dexterity and giver of emotional support. When the air-raid siren sounded she was first in line for the cupboard under the stairs, and later would trot with us to the Anderson shelter at the end of the garden. To come indoors she simply flicked up a window latch, pawed open the window enough to raise the inside bar, and hopped in. When she wanted to go out, the opening of a window was simple enough, but first she had to navigate a ledge crowded with small bottles and jars. To my knowledge, never once did she knock anything over with her paws or a flick of her tail.

Not everyone likes black cats. Her eyes, brilliant green, could stare right through you. So much so that strangers sometimes found her menacing. She was my mother's eighth child. Sitting beside her as she dug weeds and planted new life, they would talk.

'What do you think, Clara? Here or here?' Or, 'Look at these poor things, will you. Let's move them. Remember I told you they might not like it in this much shade...'

By way of response, Clarabelle might make a little noise that could be interpreted as an agreement. Or she'd shift her front paws slightly, while staring straight ahead, as if an answer was too undignified. She purred louder than a diesel engine as she sat on Mum's inadequately small lap. And knew better than to make a play for the chickens in their various stages of growth.

Clarabelle's most uncanny feat was that she knew when Mum was returning from the shops, and would sit at the bus stop waiting to walk her home. Since schedules were erratic, and we had a choice of three stops where my mother could conveniently leave the bus, it always surprised strangers to see our cat sitting at the right one. Closest stop for buses from Southend was a good fifteen minutes from home; the other two from Leigh Broadway were five and ten minutes away.

How Clarabelle broke her tail in the winter of 1943, nobody knew. We had never before seen a cat with a broken tail so couldn't be sure what was wrong. When she walked, it seemed normal. When she sat on the window ledge watching passers-by, it hung straight down the wall. She was carted off to a vet, who put the tail in white plaster, showing Mum how she could remove it on a certain date, because he would be off at war.

The plastered tail pointing skywards became a familiar sight around our estate. After dark, with blackout curtains in place and street lights out, no other part of Clarabelle was visible except for her shiny green eyes.

Violet, walking home from work one moonless night, turned down by the high school to Kent Avenue, and spotted this white tail walking towards her, preceded by a pair of green jewels. A few steps ahead, two American soldiers were peering at house numbers in search of an address.

'Holy shee-eet,' one of them yelled as Clarabelle ran towards Vi. They turned and fled before she could explain that her cat was attached to the white stick and shiny green gems.

What we thought was Clarabelle's worst ordeal was so bad, Dad was at a loss to know how to cope with the tears threatening to flood 19 Kent. My father, home from Coventry for three days, had just commented how nice it was to eat his dinner in peace for once, without the cat pawing his leg for titbits.

A neighbour's lad knocked heavily on the front door around seven one foggy evening to say that Clarabelle had been hit by a car on Manchester Drive. With the plaster removed weeks before, she was virtually invisible in the blackout. Leaving his meal, Dad took the nearest coat from several on the hall pegs, and went with the lad who had delivered the devastating news.

He returned, clutching the still figure wrapped in my gaberdine school coat. Mum went to stroke the body, recoiling at its stiffness, and crushed head with one dull green eye lying obscenely on the flattened mouth. In the back garden she sat with the wrapped bundle on her lap as Dad dug a shallow grave.

Fingering the tip of Clarabelle's tail for one last time, she wondered out loud what her beloved cat was doing on Manchester Drive at night. We sat huddled on the back step recalling our pet's full and eventful life. A simple prayer was said over the grave. I promised to mark it with a cross next day.

More tea was poured when our shocked little group returned to the kitchen. Iris came in, then Violet, neither of whom could believe the news. Around nine o'clock Mum re-heated Vi's dinner, which was horribly dried out. Iris began an anecdote about Clarabelle, when all eyes turned to the window. The latch went up, the window opened, and our cat walked through. Thudding to the floor, she pawed optimistically at Violet's dungarees in hopes of getting a tasty morsel.

In our stampede to the rockery with

torches flashing, we showed little regard for wartime precautions. Clarabelle watched with us as Dad dug up the cat, black with a small white patch inside its back leg. There was no way a stranger was being buried in my good coat. It was replaced by the *News of the World,* and Clarabelle was almost hugged to death. But not quite. She lived happily for some years after the war, and eventually died at the ripe old age of twenty-three.

CHAPTER NINETEEN

My Life at School

Even though wartime restrictions and school uniforms proved a great leveller, following our return to Westcliff I wasn't always comfortable at school. The bond with Monica and friends from Chapel was broken. The special loyalty to our school, so ingrained while we were evacuated, was gone too. For reasons I couldn't figure at the time, all too often I felt awkwardly out of step there. It wasn't that I was unhappy. Just that the sense of belonging, at home and at school, was foggy at best.

Probably I could have had closer friends if

I'd stayed for out-of-class activities. Solid friendships were formed in school during the lunch hour, but with Kent Avenue no more than a stone's throw away I was expected at home for a meal Mum had spent a good part of her morning preparing. For most students this was a time for piano lessons and extra sports tuition, or participation in knitting groups to make socks and balaclavas for soldiers. For me, piano was out of the question, tennis was torture and no soldier in his right mind would wear anything I created with knitting needles and wool. This was also a time for socialising and doing homework together – in short, becoming good mates.

Again at the end of the afternoon, I was home and dry when other pupils stayed behind. Persuading myself I had more important stuff to get on with, I was also keen to get indoors before my classmates saw where I lived. Looking back, I have to wonder if anyone cared a fig about this. Was it all in my head? Not entirely. Probably a case of being once bitten twice shy, and I didn't want to risk running into the likes of Mrs Granger.

Perversely, soon after the autumn term started I made two new friends *because* of where I lived. They were close mates, Ethel and Enid, commonly lumped together as 'the two Es' because they were seldom seen apart around the school. Both lived in flats above the same block of shops on the London Road, and walked along Kent Avenue on their way to and from school. A month or two after we were back at school they were passing by as I came through the front door and, since all three of us were in the same form, we walked together. After that they would wait for me by our gate, and by winter they were knocking at the door to see if I had already left.

Mum thought they were lovely, greeting them as if we were long-lost sisters, asking after their mothers, whom she knew slightly, and their brothers fighting at the front. Sometimes, for one reason or another, they would come in after school and stayed just long enough to share a pot of weak tea.

Enid's father managed a pub across from their flat; Ethel's parents owned the small newsagent's in which she helped out some weekends. Both girls had been at Chapel, but I never thought of them as possible pals. Not when I could be with Monica, who had a take-charge attitude and dared to be disrespectful to adults.

Ethel was a gifted artist, sketching anything from portraits to country scenes. She especially enjoyed coming home with me after school if Rose – who couldn't have drawn a sausage if her life depended on it – was there to admire her latest work. With great flair,

Ethel sketched my sister's portrait on the back of a large photograph, and was thrilled when Rose put it face up in the original frame so that it, instead of the photo, stared down from the mantelpiece.

If I met either of the 'two Es' outside of school it was by accident rather than design. Like me, they had chores to do at home. They were conscientious about their homework, and had little free time. Were they happy? Was I? I can't say. It wasn't an era in which we examined our emotions. Priority in our thoughts was given to the war. Would we win it? When? How could we help? Even so, I was grateful to have these two unassuming girls as friends.

Following matriculation from the high school in 1947 Ethel attended a London art college, and from there became an assistant to a prominent dress designer on Bond Street before moving to New York. Enid went into teaching, until she married and started a family. Long after I had left home, Mum would write that she had met 'one of the two Es' - couldn't remember which one, and didn't like to ask – but had to say she looked well, had three lovely kiddies, and motherhood agreed with her.

It was Ethel who one day shared a detention with me, standing to attention before a grandfather clock in the school's main hall, prominently situated near the headmistress's office and teachers' staffroom. I forget the nature of her crime, but remember mine had been to absent myself from school halfway through an afternoon.

I was made aware of this handsome timepiece, or one very similar, at our school in Chapel-en-le-Frith, and remember smiling when told of its secondary purpose. It was a means of punishment, with the errant pupil standing before it for half an hour or longer after school. Recalling Charbury's Gaffer Farrow with his bamboo cane, brought down relentlessly on Edward and his brother for no apparent reason, I felt this clock business was a bit of a laugh. Until I found myself standing in front of it.

My troubles started on the day before an exam when, with no teacher to control our class during a spare hour, the atmosphere was not conducive to serious studying. Rolled-up balls of blotting paper were tossed about, jokes passed down the rows, whispers so loud I could hear them three or four desks away.

It was the last session of the afternoon and, knowing there was nobody at 19 Kent, I gathered up my belongings and went home. Stealthily, across the hockey field and through a hole in the fence, in five minutes flat I was on to Middlesex Drive separating the school from my house.

Next day, towards the end of our exam, a

first-former tip-toed into our classroom to tell the teacher Pamela Hobbs was required to report to the headmistress as soon as possible. My studious intent of the day before vanished, as I tried to concentrate on the papers before me.

Seated poker-straight on her chair, an unsmiling Miss Wilkinson told me I had been seen leaving the school yesterday at mid-afternoon. I made no attempt to deny it. Miss White, I learned, had come on to the hockey field in time to see me sneaking through the fence. I tried to explain how it was too noisy to study in the classroom, but our headmistress wasn't having any of it. I was, according to her, simply taking advantage of my teacher's absence to get home and do heaven knows what. My punishment was to stand in front of the clock for half an hour after school for the next two days.

The first five minutes were fun. I exchanged whispers with Ethel, who was anxious to show Rose her latest sketch. Then a prefect came by, eyed us scathingly and continued with me where the head's lecture had left off. (What a privilege it was to be at this school ... what if everyone came and went at their pleasure...) I had hardly recovered when the head girl came by, looked aghast at me and said she really couldn't believe her eyes. Goody Two Shoes, no less. Truly, I was the last person she expected to see there. I hung my head in shame.

Next my lovely Miss White paused in front of me, widening her eyes in feigned disbelief but saying nothing. Staring above her head, I tried to show disdain rather than the disappointment I felt over her turning me in. After serving my time in front of the clock, I concluded there was no need for a bamboo cane here. What's more, I reckon our ancestors knew a thing or two when they erected stocks in town squares. It's all about humiliation.

Given the choice, I would have elected for an hour's detention every Wednesday had it meant missing gym class. Why I was such a dummy at gym, I could never fathom. It wasn't as if I was overweight or sedentary, but still I couldn't catch a ball, do a decent handstand, leapfrog without clipping my partner in the head, or jump the bar without sending it flying. I couldn't run after a field hockey puck, or across a tennis court to lob a ball, without panting like a dog in heat. Nobody wanted me on their sports teams.

During our evacuation, the lack of gymnasium equipment necessitated improvisation. All that changed now, with a revitalised Miss White – all gung-ho and jolly hockey sticks about the gymnasium apparatus. Here we had slippery ropes to climb and an enormous wooden horse to vault over and a bar whose lowest level seemed to be higher than Ben Nevis.

Gym class was so worrying I spent some of my limited spare time practising at home. Leap-frogging over a footstool topped by cushions resulted in a broken Doulton fig-urine, and even mild-mannered Rose ob-jected to my attempted handstands, which called for reorganisation of the furniture in the front room.

On weekends, I rehearsed my high jumps for hours on end with a rope tied across the yard between the lavatory and coal shed doors. This ended when my sisters protested loudly about their denied access to the toilet, by which time I had managed to clear an impressive two feet six. Not that it did me a lot of good, since the next round was at three feet and my aspirations didn't reach such dizzying heights.

Even though I approached her gym classes with unreasonable fear and loathing Miss White continued to have a soft spot for me. Inevitably I was chosen to raise the bar for the high jump, which meant sometimes I escaped having to make an attempt to clear it. Golden words to my ears were 'We're out of time, Pamela. I'm afraid you'll have to give it a miss today.' Perhaps noting my relief, she would smile as she said it.

Humiliating though it was to fail almost everything expected of me in the gymnasium, I continued to try my hardest. Completing my first full handstand one day (after ump-teen attempts), Miss White, and then the whole class, clapped. But this was not my most embarrassing moment. It came at the end of term when the gym prize was to be awarded.. Nothing more sensational than a ribbon such as Uncle Fred's horses won in county fairs, but still the long-legged athletes among us were mustard-keen to receive it. So, as the obvious contenders straightened their pigtails and socks and sat a little taller, I allowed my mind to wander to more import-ant things – like the promise of dumplings for dinner made with a little bit of suet, thanks to the generosity of Mum's butcher.

When my subconscious started hearing phrases like 'it isn't whether you win or lose, but how hard you try...' and 'because each of us is unique, not everyone can hope to excel...' I snapped back to attention. Oh, please God, no. I broke out into a sweat to beat any experienced by Mum when she had to run for her bus. My palms were wet, my face probably the colour of a plum. Other girls began looking my way as I stared straight ahead, glassy-eyed.

If God wouldn't help, perhaps Miss White would. I willed her to change direction, but it didn't work. Her grin stretched from one ear to the other, her cornflower-blue eyes sparkled, as she wound up: 'So because, con-sistently, she has tried harder than anyone here, I have decided to give this year's award to Pamela Hobbs.' Stunned silence was replaced by desultory clapping. Lacking the grace of a born winner, I snatched the ribbon, mumbled my thanks and fled the gymnasium.

Miss White's choice was not a popular decision. In the changing room, Enid's congratulations were sincere and effusive. Other girls around me remained sullen. Obviously they were waiting for my departure before they exploded with catty remarks and indignation and the consoling of more deserving candidates.

In academic subjects it was only hard work that kept my marks at the A and B levels. Learning did not come easily, and circumstances at home seldom contributed to quiet study. When both wirelesses were screeching, and my sisters calling from one room to the next, Mum carefully removed the jug and basin from her marble-topped washstand so I could work in her bedroom. I loved it there. If weather warranted an open window I could hear no more than the birds chirruping from our elderberry tree. On cold damp days, with rain pattering off our slate roof, I had to wear my blazer and fingerless mittens, but still enjoyed the silence, the faint smell of lavender permeating the room, and the challenge of solving maths problems, writing a long essay, studying maps of far-off lands.

Although I was interested in Modern History, I seldom felt confident enough to speak up in this class. Most of my peers lived in homes where *The Times* or the *Telegraph* were practically required reading. In my house the *Daily Mirror* was a family favourite. One of my sisters might bring in the left-wing *Daily Herald* if they found a copy abandoned on a bus or bench, and it wasn't untoward for Dad to have the *Daily Worker* poking out of his dungarees pocket. In consequence I learned to keep quiet if class discussions were on recent events. After the war it was worse, when dissertations turned to the stock market and importance of oil prices and I had no idea why. On the other hand I was the only girl who knew when the hod carriers went on strike.

CHAPTER TWENTY

Entertainment Time

As the war dragged itself into the winter of 1943, shortages became more than an inconvenience. We were fed up with substitutes, tired of being told to 'Make Do and Mend'.

When Dad tried to repair a hole in our only large saucepan, he found himself danger-ously close to swallowing a sharp triangle of tin with his dinner next day. Coats made into jackets earlier were now being patched; jumpers were unravelled so their wool could be reused.

It was my job to cut newspaper linings for shoes that should have been discarded years before. Also newspaper squares threaded on to a loop of string, to be hung on a nail in the lavatory. Shiny magazine pages were out. The *News of the World* was more acceptable, although Iris swore that newsprint from its juiciest stories came off on her bottom. But then, to cheer us up, we did have lots of entertainment.

Violet's workmate, Gladys, was a frequent visitor to our home that winter. On most Saturdays, she and Vi went dancing. Often it would be at the American base, where they first met Jackson and his pals. Local fac-tories also organised dances, with live bands and singers. If she was on leave, Connie went with them. Iris too, on promise that her sisters would bring her safely home. While I had no interest in going to these Saturday-night hops, I loved the merriment that preceded them in our kitchen.

One of Gladys's assets was that she was an only child, whose mother had been rather glamorous in pre-war days. Now her daughter had access to left-over lipsticks and dried-out rouge brought to life with drops of water. She even had half-decent blouses and skirts, which were generously shared with my sisters. Still, certain cosmetics had to be replaced by whatever we had on hand – such as soot from inside the chimney to substitute for shop-bought mascara.

Where these girls found their energy I don't know. Iris always worked until six on Saturdays; Violet and Gladys were home earlier only if they started at seven in the morning. Twelve hours later, they had their hair in rag curlers and pipe cleaners, and little tin clips if they could find Rose's hidden stash. Stale lipsticks became usable when melted in front of the fire. A gravy mix painted on their legs was an acceptable replacement for silk stockings. When it dried I was called upon to crayon a straight black or brown seam down the back, keeping one eye on Clarabelle, who liked the taste of gravy enough to lick their legs if given half a chance.

Lots of laughter, vocal accompaniment to songs on the wireless, and the telling of the latest Adolf jokes, served to make our kitchen a warm and happy place on Saturday evenings.

But for all this frivolity, they were serious times for Violet and Gladys. Barely out of their teen years they, and thousands of

youngsters like them, had taken on grave responsibilities. Their small factory, which
made rubber houseware before the war, now
produced inflatable dinghies and parachutes
to save the lives of our boys.

They also made barrage balloons, those
massive silvery blimps designed to deter
enemy pilots from reaching their targets. If
aircraft flew above them they were too high
for accuracy in dropping their bombs. Were
they to dive underneath they would tangle
in fine cables to which the balloons were
attached. Operated by ground crews in
open fields and parks, there were close to
500 balloons in the London area in 1940,
and double this number by 1944.

The smell of rubber was so strong in the
factory, at first it made most of Violet's
fellow workers ill. My sister reckoned she
actually liked the odour, and her work. She
enjoyed knowing she was helping the war
effort, relished the challenge of meeting
deadlines and quotas, and was friends with
most of her co-workers.

Her workmates were a real mix. Univer-
sity-educated girls who could have been
officers in the forces, but chose not to leave
their homes and families. Youngsters like
Violet and Gladys. Mothers, whose children
were evacuated. Happiest, apparently, were
women whose husbands were in the forces.
For many of them a regular pay packet

brought an independence they hadn't known before. Loyalty and teamwork prevailed in these factories, where few workers booked off sick unless they were seriously ill or injured.

Violet and Gladys were cutters, a skill learned only after weeks of practice. They earned two pounds ten a week, plus overtime, from which Vi gave Mum a pound for her keep. Ironically there was little to spend their money on, and even less time to shop. In any case, they wore dungarees at work, and improvised on Saturday nights with borrowed blouses and skirts. Once in a while, when Mrs Hardy happened upon fabric 'fallen off the back of a lorry', she would run them up attractive pleated skirts so perfect for jitterbugging.

Also clothes had become expensive. Handbags and hats could cost as much as six times more than in pre-war years; a nightdress that would have been a pound in 1939 was now ten. And even if you had the money, you might not have sufficient coupons. Week after week Mum looked longingly at a winter coat in Dixon's windows, but couldn't bring herself to part with the required eighteen points – more than a quarter of her annual clothing allowance.

Long after the war, Vi talked fondly of her war work at Skyborne Industries. Unlike some of the larger munitions factories up north, all of its ninety-five employees were local, which meant they weren't necessarily strangers to start with. Occasionally a young girl would leave for something more glamorous, or because she couldn't stand the stink of rubber. For Violet it was the coarse language and sexual innuendoes from certain co-workers that took getting used to.

By war's end she had made it to inspector, partly because few of the older employees could cope with the claustrophobia they experienced while crawling around inside an inflated 45,000-cubic-foot balloon. Vi loved it – enjoying the prospect of searching for a leak, almost as much as the triumph she experienced when her sixth sense directed her to the pinprick of a hole.

Contrary to company rules, some of her mates slipped their names and addresses into finished parachutes, and were contacted after the war by grateful airmen. Vi never did that, but she wasn't above sneaking parachute silk out of the factory by wrapping it around her thin body beneath her trousers. Mrs Hardy made it into camiknickers, slips and nighties, which became the mainstay of Violet's wedding trousseau. Coarse jokes about underwear made from parachute silk went the rounds, since it was said to shrivel to practically nothing when ignited.

When Vi switched from parachutes to balloons we all had new silver cases, made from balloon fabric, for our gas mask boxes. They were water-repellent, and looked so smart we were stopped by strangers on the street who wanted to buy them.

Everything was done to keep factory employees interested and alert and producing to their fullest potential. Visiting entertainers crossed the country, performing for them during lunch and dinner breaks. Some of the shows were broadcast on a radio programme called *Workers' Playtime,* which was even more stimulating for the host factories. Skyborne wasn't big enough to attract Vera Lynn or Anne Shelton, but they did have Ted and Barbara Andrews, step-father and mother of Julie, who was soon to make her appearance on stage with them.

Beauty contests created their own brand of glamour, as factory pin-ups competed at various levels, with the final winner representing England. Newspapers featured scantily dressed American movie queens as pin-ups, the most famous being Betty Grable – star of lavish musicals, whose likeness even appeared on the side of American bombers. One particular photograph of her wearing a one-piece bathing suit, saucily posed to show off her long shapely legs, was said to be pinned up in canteens and mess halls, as well as personal lockers of ships and submarines and in army camps around the world.

Most home entertainment during the war

years was provided by our wireless. On her programme called *Forces' Favourites,* hostess Jean Metcalfe played requests for and from people in the forces. Mum sent hers for 'Connie who hails from Leigh, now serving in the ATS' but we never did hear it on air.

One of the most popular radio shows was *ITMA (It's That Man Again)* starring Tommy Handley as the Minister of Aggravation. Nobody I knew would miss it on purpose. And yet, a few years ago when I heard a recording, it sounded so banal I found it hard to believe we once found it hilarious.

We loved to mimic the show's characters. When offered something, for example, we would imitate the boozy Colonel Chinstrap, with a cheery 'Don't mind if I do.' Mrs Mopp, *ITMA*'s dour cleaning woman's 'Can I do you now, sir?' was said with a chuckle by shop assistants all over Britain. A spy called Funf, ('Diss iss Funf spikking ...') and Signor Soso were imitated everywhere, while 'I'm going down now, sir', the signature phrase of the show's diver, was invariably repeated by lift passengers. TTFN (ta ta for now) has endured to this day as the cheerful replacement for 'goodbye'. Silly as they seem, these simple phrases brought laughter bordering on hysterics at a time when we most needed it.

After a couple of pints, Dad could do a fair imitation of his favourite music hall entertainer, Stanley Holloway, whose repertoire included well-loved cockney songs and lengthy monologues. A favourite for all of us at Christmas was my father's *Albert and the Lion* in which Albert brandishes a 'stick with an 'orse's 'ead 'andle, the finest that Woolworth's could sell'. When Dad came into the front room waving a brolly, we settled down to hear the entire monologue.

Songwriters weren't exactly idle either, turning out tunes we would hum endlessly when going about our business. Sentimental? Patriotic? Laced with propaganda? Absolutely, unashamedly. I can hardly believe now that I would walk home from the cinema singing 'There'll Always be an England', after witnessing distressing war scenes. But I did, because such songs gave us a tremendous lift.

Vera Lynn, known as The Forces' Sweetheart, always received foot-stamping ovations when visiting our troops and factory workers. Even hearing her on the wireless, we would stop what we were doing to listen, or sing along. Who doesn't remember the words to 'I'll be Seeing You' or 'The White Cliffs of Dover'? Nobody who lived during the war years, I'm sure. 'When the Lights Go on Again' I can hear her now as clearly as I did then, when I leaned out of our bedroom window on pitch-black nights, wondering if that time would ever come.

Even during the worst of the bombing,

cinemas were well attended by a public hungry for escapism. If the siren sounded during a film, it was interrupted by an announcement telling us a raid was in progress. The movie continued, with a few patrons leaving for the shelters and others to man command posts. Most of us went to 'the flicks' at least once a week. On Saturdays, I would go often with Rose and Mum to Southend's Odeon. On a weekday, if Violet could get time off, we would walk to the Corona or Gaumont cinemas in Leigh. Later I might learn that Enid or Ethel had seen the same film with their parents on that day, but I never did run into them at a cinema.

We recognised the propaganda films for what they were, but enjoyed them anyway. *In Which We Serve* starring Noel Coward as a naval captain and *Millions Like Us* about women in munitions factories, certainly wore their patriotism on their sleeves. We never missed a new Margaret Lockwood/ James Mason movie. Usually they were cast as villains, with newcomer Pat Roc as their victim and a suave Stewart Granger coming to the rescue.

In those days, cinemas played two films and a newsreel as one complete programme, then repeated the whole thing after a short organ recital. When the words of our favourite songs flashed on to the screen we were invited to sing along to the music. Iris and

Violet did so at the tops of their voices; I chose that time to go to the cloakroom. People would come and go during the film. If we arrived halfway through the programme, no matter. We simply saw the entire film next time around, even though it meant staying in the cinema for three or four hours.

We all had our favourite leading men. Mum fell for Clark Gable in a big way, I rather fancied James Mason, Rose liked the quiet John Mills. And everyone in our house – except Dad and Clarabelle – cried upon hearing that Leslie Howard had been killed when his aircraft was shot down on the way home from Lisbon. These actors, you see, were immortal to us. For those few hours each week they blocked out the dreariness, the horrors, the soul-destroying shortages of every day. We never thought of them as being ordinary vulnerable people, doing anything outside of a script.

Leslie Howard came to our attention in *Gone with the Wind*, that three and a half hours' epic of 1939. The first time I saw it was with Mum and Rose. We sat in the front row of the Odeon, munching our sandwiches in the dark, longing to exchange places with Vivien Leigh.

Highlight of this winter of 1943 for the family, and Vi in particular, was her wedding at Leigh's St Clement's Church on a chilly Saturday in mid-January. Connie had first met the groom, Lionel, at one of the Saturday dances. When he came calling two days later Connie wasn't home, but Violet was, and they saw each other every evening for the rest of his leave.

Lionel was in the submarine service, teaching new recruits the rules for living in a large metal tube beneath the sea. Based in Scotland on the Clyde, he managed to visit once a month or so. His honest face with its square jaw and wide-set eyes appealed greatly to my mother – whose first thought was that he was consumptive due to his pallor. Dad loved him on sight. They could sit for hours discussing the navy, the sea, the war. Lionel was the son he'd always wanted.

It was no surprise when the young couple became engaged, with wedding plans for Lionel's next long leave. Considering wartime restrictions it was a beautiful wedding, with a traditional church ceremony. There was a big turnout, from former neighbours on Church Hill just below St Clement's, along with some of the Broadway's shopkeepers and Dad's mates from the Old Town pubs. Lionel, who had grown up in the area, chose a local friend for his best man, while his parents came from north London with his sister Marge.

Vi's co-workers chipped in, with one providing a wedding dress, while another lent a headdress and veil. Her friend's uncle made a lovely bouquet of deep red roses from his greenhouses, where a little space was reserved for flowers grown to accommodate weddings and funerals.

This was a truly happy affair. Edie and Sam came with five-year-old Billy and Jean. Connie, home on a forty-eight-hour pass, was sporting her brand-new sergeant's stripes. Kath, the only one of my sisters alive as I write this, says she doesn't remember being there. I expect she was, since Wally wasn't called up until later that year, and wouldn't have missed the chance at seeing us all together.

Gladys and another friend from work were bridesmaids in borrowed outfits. The reception was held in a function hall above Dowsett's cake shop, a five-minute walk from the church. The only thing missing was the sound of church bells, which before the war would have brought shoppers and neighbours running to ooh and ahh over the bride whether they knew her or not. The bells would peal again one day, to tell us this awful war was over. We were pleasantly surprised, then, to see how many old neighbours and friends, girls from Vi's work, shopkeepers and even a couple of Rose's ARP pals were in the historic church to wish the couple well.

The reception brought expected ribald wartime jokes, mock shrimp paste sandwiches and dubious-looking soup. After sitting like statues, Billy and Jean vomited into their soup, and their parents took them home after explaining they had never eaten in a restaurant with other people before. They missed the best part of the dinner – the cutting of the wedding cake. The traditional three-tiered cake, sporting a fluffy dove of peace on top, photographed well. Rented from Dowsett's, it was actually plastered cardboard mounted over a tiny sponge cake provided by Mum. She had spent precious coupons, and hoarded ingredients for weeks, in order to make four of these sponges so we could all have a slice. They looked so tired and flat, we were tempted to giggle, but nobody did. It brought home the fact that, in spite of the joyous afternoon, we were a nation at war.

Within a week Lionel was shipped out to destinations unknown. Mum had urged the couple to take a few days' honeymoon in Wales, where she'd heard the scenery was lovely. Instead they opted to accept use of a friend's flat in London, and reckoned they had a marvellous time before he went back to his submarine, and Vi returned home to live with us.

CHAPTER TWENTY-ONE

Sergeant Connie

Even at the tricky age of sixteen, Connie and the army were a perfect fit. Had she been required to stand demurely at the grocer's cheese counter much longer I think she would have burst, but when given the opportunity to live up to her potential she quickly showed her true worth. After the war, eighteen-year-old men in Britain were conscripted for two years, an experience often described by parents as being 'the making' of their sons. The same could be said of Connie. In the forces she found her niche.

No route march was too long, no weather too rough, no task too onerous for my sister. She was big and strong and energetic, and made no bones about roughing it in accommodation as uncomfortable as an unheated Nissen hut shared with twenty other girls. While some of its occupants complained of the assorted snores and snorts, even the stifled sobs from homesick recruits, Connie slept like the dead and then cheerfully jumped out of bed at the first sound of the wake-up bell. She cleaned her buttons with vigour, made her bed to pass even the strictest inspection, did the more menial tasks assigned her without complaint, and aced her aptitude tests.

I know all this because her friend Mavis told me. Mavis, from Liverpool, lived and worked with Connie for her first eighteen months in the ATS, during which time they were stationed in towns along the south-east coast. On a weekend pass it was hardly worthwhile – if possible – for Mavis to get home, so Connie brought her to 19 Kent.

Unfazed by our already crowded house, Mavis would bunk down on the settee or a folding army cot in the front bedroom. They slept late, scoffed down enough fried bread and tomatoes to feed their battalion, and spent Saturday evenings with my other sisters getting ready to go dancing. More sleep, more food next day and they were off to their barracks, with clean laundry in their kitbags thanks to Mum and me.

Sometimes Connie and Mavis spent their overnight passes in London, where they slept in hostels provided for members of the forces, had free admission to theatres and enjoyed cinema discounts. On her visits home, Connie would have us in stitches recalling the antics of men who were embarrassed by duties that took them into the women's quarters. But while she made light of her army experience, we knew too well it wasn't all fun.

Connie was what Mum termed 'well developed'. Sometimes her voice I swear could be heard a mile away. With her at home, there was no peace. When she wasn't talking or banging cupboard doors or pawing her way through cluttered drawers for something that wasn't there in the first place, she was fiddling with the wireless, causing it to squawk and squeal like a prodded pig.

On the other hand, her comedic antics saw us laughing till our sides ached. One that never failed to have us doubled over was her preparation for the Saturday-night hops. Wearing no more than her enormous khaki bloomers (passion killers) and one of the voluminous bras known as hammocks, she would stand in front of the mirror, writhing to the music and oblivious to the fact that Dad might walk in at any time. Spitting noisily on the iron to make sure it hadn't overheated in the fire, she pressed her uniform to perfection. And if all the hair curlers were taken, she would poke a pair of tongs into the fire or gas stove flames, then test them on the newspaper before creating dozens of little curls. During Connie's visits, my father's biggest frustration was that he couldn't read his newspaper where its pages were ruined by scorched stripes.

Her standard dress at home would be

khaki trousers (if it was wet outdoors, these were tucked into Dad's wellies) and a V-necked khaki jumper, so loose she fastened the neck together with a giant pin from my old tartan kilt. There was nothing remotely feminine about her dung-coloured uniform, and yet when she wore it with her buttons shined and a little forage cap snug between her naturally blond curls, she turned the heads of almost every man and woman she passed.

Something else I remember about Connie: when it suited her purposes she was known to tell the odd porky. Always with an endearing smile destined to melt your heart. While others queued outside the telephone box, she pleaded an emergency and smartly leapt to the front of the line. In pubs and restaurants she commanded instant service. Men hurried over to light her cigarette or open a door for her before she even reached it, and women seemed only too pleased to run her errands. 'You do it so much better than I can,' she'd say, asking me to fry her egg and chips or wrap a present for her pal's birthday. Sometimes, as she packed to return to her barracks I would even shine her shoes – with a Kotex she tossed in my direction from a supply for which she found multiple purposes.

Connie craved company. Whereas I liked to be left alone with my schoolwork, on evenings she didn't have Mavis with her Connie would inveigle me into walking to the red box by the Albany Laundry, and from there she would call her current boyfriend and coo sweet nothings into the chipped telephone. A beau I remember best was Roly, an officer stationed in Oxford. Conversations with him were educational at the very least.

It would seem Roly was missing our Con so badly, he wanted to know what she had done that day, what she was wearing, what she would be having for dinner. How he fell for her side of the conversation I'll never know. Fact is we would have eaten dinner – probably Spam and spuds – at midday, as is customary in working-class homes, but for these little talks Constance (as he knew her) was strictly Upper Crust.

First, I had to squeeze into the phone box with her, ready to hand her the right coins while pressing the door shut to keep out the noise from the traffic and people walking past. It was all I could do to keep quiet, as she described what she was wearing. One night it would be her little black dress, with the silk stockings he had given her on their last date. And let's not forget her gold bracelet and amethyst pendant, heirlooms from our fictitious Grandma Elizabeth. Another time it would be her red blouse with matching velvet jacket and flared skirt with high heels that he would simply love if only he could see them.

On the day of the little black dress she could smell the lamb and mint sauce Agnes was preparing for dinner about to be served in the dining room. After that she may take her kid sister to the cinema, or settle for a quiet evening by a roaring fire in the lounge. If clinking coins brought realisation that his beloved Constance was in a phone box and not snug at home, her explanation was that an uncle was visiting from London and expecting an urgent call. Yes, he was the chap she'd told him about – the one with the hush-hush job at Whitehall. So far as I knew, the only uncle we had in London was my mother's brother Ted. Before the war he was a tic-tac man at the racetrack and part-time racketeer. God only knew what he was up to these days, but Connie was right about one thing: more than likely it was very hush-hush. In all her conversations with Roly, I should add that my sister's accent would have done Princess Elizabeth proud.

Leaving the cramped telephone box we would tramp home – me in my gaberdine raincoat and voluminous school scarf, Connie in Dad's wellies, her ratty jumper and army trousers topped by her greatcoat. There, I would likely fry her a plate of chips which she would eat huddled by our miserable little coke fire in the kitchen, all the time rattling on about the latest love of her life. Why did she make it all up? I asked her once. 'Gawd knows,' she replied airily. 'It's who he wants me to be.' I thought it sad that she felt the real Connie wasn't good enough.

Roly's parents lived, or so I was told, in London's Montpelier Square handily close to Harrods, but his mother spent most of the war in Cornwall, where part of the family home had been taken over by evacuees. I sometimes thought what a lark it would be if it turned out that Roly too lived in a little council house with numerous siblings, and sat around wearing his dad's gardening attire.

There were many reasons for wartime romances to end abruptly. He couldn't get leave when she did. She was posted far away. He was sent on a secret assignment... I suspect Constance ducked out of this one when Roly wanted to visit her delightful family in their Tudor house, and sample our housekeeper's lovely Welsh lamb.

Connie was bright and she was adaptable. Within months of joining the ATS she came home wearing the single stripe of a lance corporal. Soon after, she was promoted to corporal and eventually sergeant. Results of an aptitude test showed her to be suited for work on predictors, those precise instruments made to measure distances and angles at which the guns were to be fired at approaching enemy aircraft. It was serious, demanding work, performed under fire, and a tremendous responsibility for one so young. Mum was horrified when she learned of her daughter's new skills. Her understanding had been that all ATS girls were cooks, cleaners and orderlies, or office workers far from the action. She had hoped Daughter Number Five would come home with a nice sensible trade to keep her going until she settled down as a wife and mother. Obviously she didn't know Our Con.

Officially the Auxiliary Territorial Service was the women's branch of the British Army, formed in 1938 as a women's voluntary service. The first recruits were given civilian-type jobs in kitchens, storerooms and offices, but as their numbers expanded – 65,000 in the first two years of the war – the ATS was given full military status and its members were no longer simply volunteers.

Although women were not allowed in battle, their support tasks were all-important. The fact that she could be fired on but couldn't fire back was a source of heated discussion between Connie and Dad, who refused to believe any young woman capable of the more responsible work performed by men. As Mavis politely pointed out one day, she had to be brave enough and smart enough to load guns, which Connie had directed to aircraft, but neither girl was allowed to fire on the enemy.

We liked Mavis, a short dark-haired girl with a big grin, forever telling us about her two brothers in the navy and a third, Reggie, at home with his mam. According to his sister, young Reggie loved the war. Evacuated to the country when the bombing started, he was so miserable that after a fortnight he was brought home to Liverpool. Both parents worked in munitions factories, leaving the twelve-year-old on his own. Although their part of the city was spared from the ruthless bombing, other areas were so demolished they provided young Reggie and his mates with plenty of scope to scavenge for souvenirs. Pieces of shrapnel and bomb parts, even chunks of downed German aircraft, were important to little boys all over England, so this was not a worry to his mother. Nor was the lad's smoking while she was out. Her main complaint was that on most days he had his friends in for a fry-up, depleting her precious rations and filling the house with cooking odours.

During a particularly warm spell, the familiar smell of burned chips was overpowered by the stench of something distinctly rotten. A dead animal perhaps? Reggie said he couldn't help his mam on this one: had no idea where the stink was from, did he? The last dead animal he'd seen was a dog, being hauled away by its distressed owner. When his mother's nose led her to the cupboard where he kept a gym bag containing his souvenirs, she expected to find some small creature that had been killed in a blast. Instead she found a human head, a bloody head, severed at the neck, with black hair matted to its face, which had an eye missing.

Her screams brought the neighbours running with brooms and rakes, in the belief she had discovered a German under the stairs. Reggie and his bloody sports bag were marched to the police station, where he admitted he had been charging a ha'penny a look and had so far collected fourpence ha'penny. Of course, he planned to donate it to the Widows and Orphans Fund.

CHAPTER TWENTY-TWO

The Bombing Gets Personal

Believing that his missing lung would keep him out of the forces, towards the end of 1941 Wally had joined a building crew at an aerodrome in Norfolk, and was there when news reached him that he had become a father. It was in early February 1942, a cold wet morning in east London, when my brave sister rode on a bus to Epping with her bag of baby clothes soaked from a long wait at the bus stop. By the time she checked into High Beach, a large country house converted to a maternity unit for Londoners, Kath too was soaked. Her waters had broken and she was in labour. Four hours later she gave birth to a beautiful baby girl they called Valerie, who was a week old before her dad could get away from work to meet her – and eighteen months when he received his call-up papers. Mum told him not to worry. He'd never pass his medical would he? Well, we all knew that. I mean, here's a man whose voice sounded hollow and his breathing laboured, and when the medic saw that dent in his back where a lung had been removed years before, he'd recognise this one as an army reject.

Next we heard, Wally was in the Royal Engineers stationed at Sandbanks for training before being shipped to India. From there he went to Burma, and that's where we caught up with him via a film presentation in Kensington.

We had known little about the war in the Far East, except that conditions in their prisoner-of-war camps were barbaric. Rumour had it that beatings were everyday occurrences, hard labour extracted under torturous conditions and sadistic guards dreamed up punishments that broke the strongest of men. By 1943 all of Burma was in enemy hands, and to imagine our gentle Wally captured by the Japanese was unbearable.

It was with some relief then that we received a note from Kath, inviting us to see him on film. More propaganda. Still, it would give us the unusual opportunity of seeing Kath, Wally and Valerie all in the same day. So Mum and I went to London and passing through it saw the dreadful bomb damage first hand.

The film wasn't much. With Kath and Valerie, and twenty or so other families, we assembled in a small theatre in one of the government offices. The first soldier appearing on screen was an officer who sounded uncannily like *ITMA*'s Colonel Chinstrap. He thanked us for coming, and the government for arranging this brief reunion with loved ones. One by one, his men stepped forward to say a few words. Wally's turn came and went within two minutes. He stood there stiffly, looking thin but tanned.

'Hello, Kath. Hello, Valerie,' he said in his familiar husky voice. 'I miss you both, but look forward to being home soon.' Then he stepped smartly back in line. Kath dried her eyes, and the next chap came forward to say something similar. Valerie was a schoolgirl of five and a half when she saw her father again.

From Kensington our journey back to East Ham required two buses, the first being re-routed because of an unexploded bomb. The scenes we passed were so shocking neither Mum nor I could bring ourselves to speak. Some buildings looked as if they had been sliced through with a giant knife to reveal flowered wallpaper, doors, baths and toilets hanging through floors and ceilings. Reflections of the personal lives of former inhabitants, exposed for everyone to see. It was sad, it was obscene, it was this bloody awful war.

On the second bus destined to leave us near Kath's home, Mum asked for tickets to the White Horse. The conductor looked startled for only a moment before asking, 'You 'aven't 'eard luv? It's a gonna. I thought everyone knew it got a direct hit.' Rolling off our tickets, with typical cockney humour he added grimly, 'More like the bleedin' Black 'orse now.'

The Londoners' humour is legendary. Every day newspapers showed photos of victims beside their bombed homes and stores, giving the V for victory sign, sitting on a broken chair amid the rubble with a sign reading 'Adolf won't get the better of us' or 'We'll never give in'. Now we were seeing it for ourselves: a barber's shop with no windows, and the door propped against what remained of a wall. A chalked message on it read: 'We've had a close shave. Come on in and get one yourself.' Other damaged buildings displayed signs promising, 'Business as Usual' when there was nothing at all usual about the windowless premises. A child's blackboard on what used to be a house had a message for Hitler. 'You can smash our windows,' it read, 'but not our spirit.' Where, I wondered, was the child who once owned that little blackboard.

It was as heartening as it was depressing. When we passed what remained of Wally's local, and turned on to Kath's street, we were dismayed to find several houses demolished. Incendiaries had rained down some months before, and Kath hadn't told us. 'No point in worrying you,' she said now. 'It was a day raid. Remember when Rose came back with me from Leigh, just for the day to get my rations? Well, it was then. We spent most of our time under the stairs.' Mum was appalled to learn that two of her daughters had come so close to death. Worse still, she hadn't known of it.

'That's Londoners for you,' she said, sounding more cheery than we knew she felt. 'Grin and bear it.' She was right, of course. And the bosses in Whitehall were wrong when they planned the evacuation of London's 'lower classes', in the belief that they would panic and 'behave badly' in times of disaster.

After tea Kath, with Valerie in her push-chair, walked us to East Ham station. Along the way she pointed out public shelters she could duck into when the siren sounded. Only once, she said, they had gone into a Tube station for the night, but the noise and repulsive smells proved more awful than the raids. Her next-door neighbour had a Morrison in their front room. An ugly, useless thing is how she described it. A man had come and offered to install one for Kath, but she refused. I can't say I blame her.

Named for Herbert Morrison, the Minister of Defence, these were full-sized iron tables bolted to the floor. Had Kath agreed to such an installation, it would have practically filled her living room. The idea was to put blankets or sleeping bags underneath to convert it to a bed. Now Kath told us she didn't fancy the house falling on top of her, trapping her inside an iron cage. She heard of this happening some streets away, and the people weren't reached until the next day – by which time two of its three occupants were dead. She did have an Anderson like ours in her back garden, and went into it at night when the siren sounded. By arrangement, a young girl from next door joined her there for safety and to give Kath and Valerie a bit of company.

In reality, nowhere was safe, unless perhaps it was Churchill's War Rooms beneath Whitehall. A high explosive bomb could tunnel fifty feet into the ground, and when Marble Arch Underground station received a direct hit, tiles flying off its walls became deadly missiles. At other stations, smashed water mains caused platform sleepers to drown.

Although it is otherwise illegal to sleep in Tube stations, during the Blitz close to 200,000 people in Greater London did so, simply by purchasing a platform ticket and staking out their space. Some bombed-out families set up makeshift homes there, using this as a base from which to go about their everyday business. Special trains would stop off with snacks and drinks; sing-songs added to the noise. Thieves, prostitutes and criminals on the run had a fine old time in those Tube shelters.

We didn't have underground trains in our home town, but we did have public shelters, usually in converted basements of commercial buildings. We were told to memorise the location of shelters close to our homes, or on our regular routes. You couldn't miss them, marked as they were with a large white 'S' on a black background, and surrounded by sandbags. I don't recall ever going into one; they looked so dank and smelly, and totally forbidding. Not that I had much need of them, since I didn't go further than the shops or cinemas from where it always seemed simplest to run home if Moaning Minnie started up.

Perhaps because I had spent the earlier part of the war in safety, once I returned to Leigh I was scared silly of the bombs. I hated myself for being a coward, when everyone else was either foolhardy or brave. I still do, because of what I put my mother through. I guess I had always been a worrier. Now there was something real to fret about.

Other girls would mark their menstrual cycle on a calendar, but I circled nights when the moon was full. At such times the raids were at their worst. I remember one morning just before dawn, when a big round moon lit the sky. From my bedroom window I watched a lone aircraft fly overhead, so low I could clearly see the black and white German cross on its wings, and the pilot in his leather helmet.

My sisters took little notice of the sirens. Iris would cover her head with her pillow to shut out the noise. Rose wearily put on her ARP gear and headed for the streets. Violet seldom heard anything. After working long hours at the factory, she was dead to the world. That left Mum, who longed to sleep in her own bed but couldn't because I insisted on going to our Anderson shelter at the bottom of the garden.

If I could be persuaded to start the night upstairs, I would lie there waiting for the siren. When it sounded, its first wail had barely gone into the second, before I had my wellies on and was off to the garden shelter. One night my mother tripped over Clarabelle on the stairs, falling on to a bicycle propped in the hall. Its brake handle went through her cheek, causing a scar she had for the rest of her life, as witness to my self-centred timidity.

Most nights around nine o'clock, the two of us trooped down the garden path with our eiderdowns and pillows, and tried to sleep on the Anderson's narrow wooden bunks. Mum never complained. She even silenced my sisters who told her I was old enough to go to the shelter on my own. Every morning, without comment, she trotted back to the house at first light, to put the kettle on for her morning tea with Clarabelle.

It was horrible in that shelter. Beetles, mice, moles, all manner of small creatures crept through the sacking over the doorway. It was cold and it was damp, yet we continued this routine night after night. Eventually, after two or three weeks without raids, I was convinced the Luftwaffe was down to a handful of broken aircraft so wouldn't be bothering us again.

In my defence I have to say that during London's night-time raids, it was as if we in Leigh lived on a battlefield. Mobile ack-ack guns fired from our street and others nearby, aiming to destroy enemy aircraft before they reached the capital. I used to pray the guns would miss, allowing the planes to go on their merry way. Then, next morning, when I heard of the damage inflicted on their targets I felt horribly guilty.

Long after the London Blitz in which enemy aircraft passed over us in droves, we would still come under attack by pilots unable to reach a planned destination. Some deliberately dropped their deadly cargo on the sea or mud; others hit towns such as ours in Essex and Kent. Seen from the air, our council estate resembled an army barracks, which made it an acceptable secondary target.

It was almost a relief when we did get hit – something like hearing the other shoe drop, I suppose. It came on one of the few nights I shared a double bed with Violet in our front bedroom. There was no warning. We didn't even hear the whoosh of an approaching bomb. We simply woke to flying debris, breaking glass and screams. And a choking, plaster-smelling dust so dense we could barely breathe. All our windows were gone; the front door was blown halfway up the stairs. The Beardsleys, and their neighbours, had a direct hit, which virtually demolished their three houses.

Several minutes passed before Violet and I realised what had happened. Had we put up the blackout screens there would have been less damage, but we rarely did in our bedroom. As a result, the glass had blown inwards, cutting our bedding to ribbons, covering the floor. In the darkness we didn't know where to put our feet. Wardrobe and dresser mirrors were in shards and slivers on the linoleum. Strangely though, neither of us had so much as a nick or scratch on our faces. Looking in wonder at our pillows, we saw two round spaces where our heads had been; glass all around, yet nothing had touched us.

Dad, who was home for the weekend, rushed out to help. At dawn he returned, with a borrowed helmet on his head, his face caked with grey dust. A tear streaked through the grime as he said in a voice, quiet with controlled anger, 'The buggers got Mrs Beardsley, Ede. The old chap was in the lav. Escaped with a broken arm.'

All day rescuers searched the rubble for a young woman, recently moved here from Plaistow. When they found her broken body, it was melded to that of her small son. Her other boy, Willie, was discovered dazed but unharmed on Manchester Drive, the next street from ours. In one of those quirks of war that nobody quite believes, his mattress had been blown over the roof tops, with him still on it.

Replacing our windows was not a priority with the council. Cadging frames and glass from derelict houses, Dad repaired the damage bit by bit, but for some weeks our home was darker than usual because of cardboard and newspapers filling the holes. It took even longer to get up every last piece of glass from the floor, and soon every one of us had cuts of varying sizes on our feet.

CHAPTER TWENTY-THREE

One of Our Own is Injured

Everyone said what a pity it was Rose didn't have children of her own, seeing as how she was so good with everyone else's. But, as Mum was quick to remind her, first she had to get a fella and that wasn't likely to happen so long as she was so fussy. In pre-war years, friends and relatives had tried to 'fix her up' by introducing an available nephew or cousin or someone's brother. All, according to Rose, were lacking. One young man's eyes were too close together, another's nails weren't clean. And she couldn't abide a man who didn't laugh at things she thought funny. During the war years I didn't see her with anyone of the opposite sex, other than her ARP pal who would walk with her to 19 Kent on his way to his mother's place two streets away.

Before the war I found Rose something of a mystery, a person slightly aloof from the rest of us. Perhaps because she was the eldest sister at home, she had our third bedroom to herself, so missed the giggles and whispers of the rest of us cuddling up for warmth. Not that her room could have accommodated a second body, being what real estate agents describe as a 'box room' with space for no more than a single bed, a dresser and a small chair.

In her spare time Rose read romance novels that Mum picked up for her at the library just off Leigh Broadway. Or she would get comfortable in one of the armchairs in the front room, listening to the wireless with a bag of toffees in her lap and a pot of tea on the side table. Often I would sit with her, more for the toffees than the wireless programmes.

Rose liked to dress well. Her one good suit – grey patterned with a light blue check – looked expensive. It hung on the back of her bedroom door, along with a perfectly ironed blue crepe blouse. Shoes and slippers were kept under her bed, which, unlike the rest of the beds at 19 Kent, was always perfectly made. Nobody was allowed into her room, unless invited.

In the late 1930s Rose worked at a dental office located on the ground floor of a house across from Chalkwell Park. She enjoyed the patients and the environment. Often she stayed longer than required to straighten out the office, or to give the dentist's wife a break by taking her baby into the park. Even at weekends, sometimes she could be seen walking along the seafront with young Philip in his high bassinet. Strangers admiring the tot could be forgiven for assuming that Rose was his mother. Certainly she looked the part in her nice suit and fawn suede court shoes with matching handbag.

Then the dentist went off to war, his office was closed and his little family moved to Somerset. At twenty-four years of age, single and fighting fit, when it came to military service Rose was quite obviously one of Britain's most eligible women. But it wasn't to be. Without her day job, she simply signed on for more hours as a warden.

As they had tried with their matchmaking before the war, now acquaintances urged her to join up. Rose wasn't buying any of it. She was not about to make bullets, she said, or guns, bombs or anything else designed to kill. Asked why she refused to work in a factory like Vi's where they made parachutes and dinghies that saved lives, her answer was a quiet smile and a 'No, thanks. I'm all right where I am.' Second call-up papers arrived in the post, and like the first were banished to the dustbin.

In the summer of 1943 Janet from across the road came to see us, wearing smart breeches and a khaki sweater of the Land Army. Did she really think her enthusiasm for picking apples and mucking out stables would be contagious? If so, she didn't know my sister. The formerly shy homebody went on to say how she loved living with other girls, and couldn't wait for Saturday nights when they went to the flicks or dances at a nearby army base. Patiently Rose said she was glad to hear it, then went on to enquire about Janet's mother, who she noticed was limping last time she'd seen her.

The thing was, she liked being with the ARP, and was considered an important part of a team. If neighbours decided other war work was more important – too bad.

Close to one and a half million Britons served as wardens during the war. Some were paid, others were volunteers, and all were dedicated to helping distressed civilians. For some this was a full-time job, while many came on duty after putting in a full shift at a factory. Usually, young wardens in Rose's age bracket were men and women who were physically unfit for the forces.

For Rose, being a warden was right up her alley. Even in pre-war years she enjoyed her chats with neighbours of all ages, introduced herself to strangers who moved on to the street, and carried sweets in her pockets for local children. Now she made a point of knowing them more intimately, so her knowledge could be put to good use if required.

Unlike London's wardens, Rose didn't have many bomb victims to deal with. Mostly she did routine patrolling, looking for blackout flaws, helping pedestrians in the dark, directing them to the nearest shelter when necessary. During a raid she knew immediately if old Mrs So-and-so would have been in the kitchen having a cup of tea before going to bed, or if her soldier son was home. She was aware of who slept in their shelters, and who went to bed as usual. Even knowing the interior layout of a house, and how many people lived there, was information she could pass on to rescuers.

My sister was never to know about the white feather, delivered through our letterbox one night to eloquently label her a coward. At least that's what Mum said, when I found her in the kitchen with the offensive feather. Grim-faced, in quiet control of her fury, she said it had been lying on the hall's doormat when she came down for her morning tea. Sitting alongside her on the table, and doubtless sensing her anger, Clarabelle too stared unblinkingly at the feather as if expecting it to attack. Four or five inches long, it was from one of the area's seagulls. 'Some turd sent it for Rose.

You know what it means, don't you?' she spat out. I nodded. 'Means she's a coward,' Mum continued through clenched teeth. I was horrified. Rose was the brave one. I was the coward. Had someone seen me creeping into the shelter each night, raids or no raids, and sent it to me?

My mother shook her head. No, this was for Rose. Some filthy toe-rag meant it for her. Probably the new people in the corner house. Their cheeky sod of a boy called her a 'conchi' just last week. Thinking for a moment, she added that it could have been 'that cow over the road'. She'd have her guts for garters if she found out it was her. Miserable to the core, I struck the flint to light the stove and put on the kettle for our tea. My mother continued speculating on who could have sent the horrid feather, and about the injustice of her daughter being considered a coward.

'Who was it who fetched the old widow woman's shopping twice a week?' she wanted to know. 'Who carried a kiddie with a broken leg all the way to the hospital, and then waited with him for hours because he cried for her to stay?' Mum sipped on her scalding tea, deep in thought. 'Salt of the earth, she is,' she continued harshly, directing her wrath at the unknown feather sender. 'Give you the shirt off 'er back, she would. You know what she did once?' I shook my head miserably, understanding that she didn't expect an answer. 'Gave her last penny to a young woman with a baby so they could get a tram home, then walked all the way from Southend because she didn't have any more money on her.' I listened wide-eyed. Eventually, sounds of someone moving about upstairs caused Mum to jump into action. Unable to snap the awful feather in two, she poked it between the litter in the hearth and made me promise not to tell a soul.

After the war I ran into one of Rose's ARP friends, who told me how good it had been to work with her. People loved her, he said. They told her their life's stories when they wouldn't give him so much as the time of day. She was offered enough tea to sink a battleship, in those days when rations were puny. Never too busy for a pleasant word, always had a smile.

He wondered often, he said, whether she had followed her heart and got into social work of some kind. Rose? Social work? The idea was so remote, I wanted to laugh. Instead I told him I had to run for my bus. I couldn't bring myself to explain how our lovely Rose was in a mental hospital, unable to look after herself, let alone anyone else.

I will never forget the time Rose was hit by shrapnel. It was the summer before war's end, an unusually warm day following a night of skies lit by a full moon. With the exception of pilots, I suppose just about everyone living in a war zone hates the full moon. I know I dreaded it even more than gym days, because it guided the way for German bombers.

Sometime after midnight, a lone enemy aircraft emptied its bomb load on a residential area behind the laundry. Rose had left home the evening before, carrying her snack and thermos flask in her helmet, because that's what she did often on the walk to a little shed packed with sandbags which served as an ARP post. Because of the full moon, she may have expected more trouble than a chink of light shining through some home owner's blackout curtains, but I can't say we were concerned when we didn't see her first thing next morning. It wasn't unusual for her to stay out so long, and in any case, she could have been in her room. Sometimes after a rough night, she'd go straight upstairs to bed without coming into the kitchen.

In consequence we didn't know anything was amiss until the front door opened, and she walked into the kitchen around mid-morning. Mum and I were the only ones home. Deathly pale, but for hideous black bruises under her eyes, Rose looked for all the world like an Egyptian mummy such as I'd seen in our tattered *National Geographic* magazines at school. All of her head and part of her face were bound in bandages. A white plaster covered a secondary wound on her neck. Her cheeks resembled two over-ripe plums, her swollen nose had been bleeding. Mum's hand flew to her mouth. 'My God, Rose, what happened?'

Instinctively I lit the flame of the gas stove, filled the kettle and put it on to boil. 'No tea, Pam. Thanks,' Rose said, as polite as ever. 'I'm beat. I'll go right to bed.' By way of explanation she told us in a few words how she had been hit by shrapnel from a Jerry plane or bomb or something. She had no recall of where or when she was hit, or even how she got home.

All she knew was that she'd found herself in hospital, lying on a bed, and a nice old doctor had said all the bleeding was from a four-inch piece of steel imbedded in her skull. Opening her hand now, she showed us two white pills to be taken for pain. And that was it. No instructions for follow-up treatment. No indication of the severity or after-effects of a piece of steel wedged in one's skull. I poured her a glass of water and we helped her up the stairs to her room, where she slept on and off for the next twenty-four hours. Weeks later she told us she had been advised to stay in hospital, but chose to walk out. Lots of people there were far worse off than her, so she didn't want to take up more of the doctor's time. Anyway, she just wanted to be home in her own bed.

And that was the extent of our knowledge on the accident which I believe changed my sister's life. Next morning, forgoing her usual trip to the Broadway, Mum went to the hospital where Rose thought she had been treated. She learned nothing, except that because her daughter was of age, this was Rose's business and not ours. In any case, according to the weary woman at the front desk, things were so chaotic that night Rose could have come and gone without having her injuries recorded. Within a month she was back at work, her helmet on her head, her lunch and flask in a leather satchel.

CHAPTER TWENTY-FOUR

The Beginning of the End

As I write this in the summer of 2008, a government campaign is underway urging us to conserve energy. Every form of media is encouraging me to turn off lights when I go out, not to leave my computer on over-night or keep the television on solely as company for the dog. Such entreaties are unnecessary for anyone who lived through the Second World War, when shortages compelled us to be frugal, to waste nothing, to recycle.

All these decades later, it is simply not in me to leave a light on in an empty room or turn up the heat indoors when a sweater will do the job of keeping me warm. Water, electricity, clothes, food – I, and others like me, can't stand waste in any form.

During that winter of 1943-4 shortages on the home front were grave. Early on, our merchant ships' priorities were to carry planes, tanks and munitions to us in Britain and our Soviet allies, causing food imports to dwindle. Now also, factories built to manufacture consumer goods were converted to produce war materials, while salvage drives had us parting with things we later regretted not keeping.

To feed the nation's pigs, kitchen waste and grass cuttings were collected – though not from 19 Kent, because ours were boiled down to a mush for the chickens. Jars were picked up, or taken to a salvage depot. Paper was a big item for the salvage trucks. Books by the ton were donated for recycling into new paper. And even the classiest among us considered it their patriotic duty to shop at second-hand stores.

At 19 Kent we knew all the tricks. When sheets wore thin in the middle, we cut them in half and sewed them back together with the outsides in the centre. Threadbare collars on shirts and blouses were painstakingly unpicked and turned. All mail was carefully slit open, with a view to reusing the envelope. (Right through the 1950s my letters from Mum were in used envelopes with tape sealing the opened end, and a small label covering an old address.)

We made our own slippers from woven scraps of material or padded cloth, using felt or string for their soles. Laddered stockings and strips of worn fabric were plaited into small rugs. I remember one Saturday when I ran into Thelma, a girl from school. Barely recognisable out of her school uniform, she was dressed in her brother's shirt and corduroy trousers and a really bizarre cardigan she had knitted herself. We agreed it could win a Make Do and Mend competition, with its multi-coloured knitted sleeves and a hodgepodge of patches for the body. She called it her Memory Jacket, reminding her as it did that sleeves were from her Aunty Em's shrunken jumpers, the sides cut from her mother's tweed skirt, and the back was part of her father's plus-fours from his pre-war golfing days. For someone who used to enjoy twice-a-year shopping trips to London, followed by sumptuous afternoon tea at a posh hotel, the war had become something of a challenge.

Actually Thelma's errand that morning had been more serious than to show off her jacket. She was on her way to a government office with pre-war photos and postcards from her family's holidays in France and Germany. A request had gone out for such pictures, from which the military could possibly identify enemy-occupied sites.

Some of our wartime habits made us thrifty for the rest of our lives. Just as I can't waste electricity or petrol, neither can I throw out brown paper wrapping, no matter how creased it is. For years I kept a ball of string to which I added any lengths that came my way.

During the war, my mother's tin foil ball was impressive. She was like a dung beetle rolling its mud into a bigger and bigger ball, except that hers was made of shiny purples and kelly greens and brilliant blues. Since we had so few sweets and chocolate bars at that time, I can't understand where the foil came from. In any event, when the ball was about six inches across, she gave it to the scrap collectors.

Schools were hard hit by shortages. Notebooks had to be used sparingly, atlases and textbooks shared, and an exchange post was set up for uniforms. Our art teacher had us gather wild flowers from which to make our own dyes and paints, and when all the drawing paper was gone, we were asked to bring blank pages from books at home.

On weekdays our school provided an oasis of normalcy. Nobody was allowed to slack off. Unless a raid was underway, excuses about tardy buses were not accepted from late-corners. Homework had to be finished neatly, raids or no raids. If we were on the playing fields when a siren sounded, we formed an orderly double line and walked to the basement shelter.

Exams were tricky during the raids. At the siren's wail we trooped into the school's basement to sit on long benches against the wall. Although instructed to leave everything in our classrooms, some students managed to whisper hurried answers to friends. If nothing else, such interruption during an exam gave us extra time to think.

Outside of school we were encouraged to help the war effort by collecting salvage, assisting in the local hospital, shopping for elderly people living on their own, and volunteering to help at ARP posts. Here, young people delivered messages during raids. Dangerous though it could be, when phone lines were down they dodged bombs and ack-ack shells to get help from hospitals, police and fire stations.

Despite such shortages, the queues, the weariness of it all, there was a definite air of optimism that spring. Obviously something was up. It had to be an allied invasion, and every indication told us it would be soon. Messages to resistance organisations, especially in France, were sometimes given at the end of the BBC News. For instance, 'Brother Jacques is going to church on Friday' might tell of a parachute drop in some part of France. Troops were gathering, leaves cancelled. Jackson came to say goodbye. Even at 19 Kent there was an air of secrecy, though we didn't know why at the time.

Only after the June invasion did Violet tell us the reason she had been working virtually around the clock. We figured there was a sudden need for extra parachutes, and that much was true. More importantly though, her factory was producing hundreds of inflatable rubber tanks. They were assembled at a phoney departure point, to indicate a landing at Calais (France) by invading allies. Also, as part of this gigantic hoax, dummy gliders made from plywood were lined up in unused airfields. Meanwhile genuine equipment was hidden from aerial view beneath a canopy of trees in the New Forest.

During these weeks, on the rare occasions he came home, Dad tucked into his sawdust sausages or Spam fried in week-old grease as if they were tender slices of Welsh lamb. There was a new air of confidence about him as, with a wink and a nod, he suggested he was finally doing something constructive for the war effort.

He was too, working on the so-called Mulberry Project at Wivenhoe, some thirty-five miles from Southend. Following the Normandy invasion, we learned that this was one of several locations across Britain where thousands of workers assembled pre-fabricated concrete units for towing across the channel to form a temporary harbour at the landing site.

In the weeks leading up to D-Day (6 June 1944) military activity around us gathered momentum. Trains were commandeered, roads blocked off, and leaves cancelled as troops assembled for the massive invasion of France.

I don't recall how many times we went to the Odeon to watch the extraordinary drama unfold, but it was a lot. Sometimes we queued for hours to get in, considering it worth the wait to see those thousands of parachutes (some perhaps made by Violet) falling from the sky like giant mushrooms. And that great armada crossing the channel to German-occupied France. In the darkened cinema men and women wept unashamedly, searching the screen for their sons, and their sons' friends, knowing full well that many would pay with lives or limbs.

The battle for Normandy continued during our school's 1944 summer holidays.

Returning in September, we were brought up to date daily with the war news, including the liberation of Paris by General de Gaulle and his troops, which had our French mistress skipping in the halls.

Welcome as this latest event was, it was hard to be joyful for long when food shortages went from bad to worse. Even more so when Hitler revealed his secret weapons.

A week after D-Day we were still rejoicing at the allies' offensive when the first pilotless aircraft crossed the English coast, heading for London. They were given names: buzz-bombs, doodlebugs, flying bombs and V1s. Many landed short of their targets, ending up in Kent across the estuary. Others fell directly on us.

Three days after the first buzz-bomb produced its powerful explosion, they rained down on London day and night. In the next few months 8,000 fell on London; 2,500 more in Kent and our home county of Essex.

At school, following morning prayers one day, Miss Wilkinson described the new enemy weapon to us. Although she rarely used this time to talk about the war, now she instructed us to look up at the sky when we heard the throbbing, distinctive sound of the stubby pilot-less aircraft with a flame streaming from its tail. Once its engine cut out and the fire extinguished, the bomb would fly downwards, carried forward by its momentum.

At that time, we were told, we must lie on the ground, in a nearby ditch or under cover. Better still, we should run in the opposite direction. They may have had silly names, and cartoons of the day made them appear comical, but these V1s were deadly enough to cause 10,000 casualties in the first month.

Anti-aircraft gunners found them difficult to hit. Barrage balloons were no better because these 'tricky little buggers', as Dad called them, were fitted with blades to cut balloon cables. Fighter aircraft were usually too slow to intercept, and anyway their machine gun bullets had little effect on the bomb's steel structure. So, until September, when allied forces reached the launch sites, we were pretty well stuck with Adolf's doodlebugs.

Often we were unaware of the noise until it stopped, and only then looked skyward to see the menace overhead. For most of us it became second nature to run in the opposite direction. Not so my mother. She was thoroughly fed up with the war, anxious to get back to growing flowers instead of carrots, weary of the queueing and of our grumbling about meals. So now, she wasn't about to waste time back-tracking if a buzz-bomb crossed overhead while she was walking home carrying two baskets of shopping.

Half the time she didn't seem to hear them, and certainly failed to look up to see if she was on a deadly route. One close shave had her telling us breathlessly how a perfect stranger, whom she was about to wallop for being a 'dirty old man', pulled her into a ditch and lay on top of her. She escaped, outraged, covered in mud, and with a nasty cut on her knee. The bomb landed on some allotments, causing minimum damage. Had she kept on walking, she may well have been severely injured or worse.

In spite of this, Mum refused to leave the queues when a flying bomb appeared overhead. Instead she moved up the line, into vacant spaces left by fleeing shoppers. Since the V1s couldn't be aimed at specific targets they tended to hit civilians, and did nothing to win the war. On the other hand, if the enemy's intent was to reduce our morale, I suppose he could claim success.

Even more sinister was the V2 rocket which, unlike the V1, could follow its trajectory perfectly. The allies first learned about its existence from Polish resistance workers who passed this startling information to British intelligence. Bombing raids on the German factory manufacturing the rockets at Peenemünde on the Baltic coast slowed production. Even so, in September of 1944, they came calling.

The monstrous V2s were more destructive than any weapon aimed at England to date. Flying so fast they could arrive at their target undetected, they gave no warning prior to their huge explosion. By this time, anyone in the vicinity had nothing more to worry about.

Some time between the arrival of V1s and V2s, we received the welcome news that blackout regulations were rescinded. Since Germany's latest weapons needed no lights from the ground to guide them, and the threat from piloted planes was destroyed along with Germany's airfields, our blackout curtains and screens could be taken down. Never again would a warden come hammering on our door because of light escaping through our windows.

Now this longed-for day had arrived. My mother, Iris and I set fire to our dilapidated screens in the back garden. Most were ripped, patched and sagging from warped frames. Those from the bedrooms were already stacked by the fence, because we hadn't bothered to use them for weeks.

It should have been a joyous exercise, with the three of us singing patriotic songs. But it wasn't. Mum momentarily looked across to the Beardsleys' house, still little more than a pile of rubble. Our next-door neighbours were off somewhere in the forces. And across the road Mrs Heelis hadn't opened her curtains since her eldest son had been reported Missing in Action.

Vera Lynn's 'When the Lights Go on Again All Over the World' was one of the war's most popular songs. Throughout the war years we hung on the singer's every word, longing for that day to come. The truth is that when it did, our little corner of the world was still rather bleak.

I became very close to my mother during these final months of the war. Together we worked the queues, shared household chores, saw current movies at the Odeon and jawed over endless cups of weak tea. I particularly liked our early mornings together at the large wooden kitchen table: me at one end doing my homework and Mum at the other as she pored over her household account book, or wrote to Connie and sometimes Kath or Edie. Between us, in the middle of the table, an assortment of bottles and jars stood like palace guards around the teapot snug beneath its thatch-roof cosy. Also on the table, Clarabelle, my mother's personal guard, sat watching her pen move across her paper.

Mum was a clever woman. Over the years I have thought how different her life would have been had she and Dad emigrated to Canada or Australia, where opportunities abounded for someone with little education, but excellent business skills and wily ways, and who was no stranger to hard work.

Her interest in my schoolwork was genuine. She especially liked my atlas. 'Hard to believe your dad has been there,' she commented one day, looking at the Asian continent.

'Mmm. He loved it didn't he? Well, we'll go there together one day, Mum,' I promised. 'Can't you just smell it, feel the heat...' But she wasn't curious enough about a far-off continent to continue the conversation.

Had things been different, she confided, she'd have that Bed and Breakfast along the seafront, or maybe a café down there by the station to catch workers on their way to and from London. 'Wasn't in the cards though, was it? So here I am.' She shrugged her shoulders, with just a hint of sadness. All she wanted now, she said, was to get back to growing her roses. 'But you'll see all those places, Pam,' she predicted. 'And I'll wait on the postman to bring me your postcards from the countries on those maps.'

During such unpredictable times I couldn't even imagine where I would end up. My love for writing had blossomed into a passion when I started sending long descriptive letters home from Derbyshire. Now, with nobody to write to, I honed my creative skills on school essays far more detailed than asked for, and always too long to earn approval from my English teacher. Did people really make a living from writing? Since the adults in my life worked in factories and on building sites, I had no way of knowing. As for the idea of travelling to exotic lands, well how barmy was that? I might as well aspire to visiting the moon I hated so much – and we all know how daft a notion that is.

On Friday mornings, before anyone but the two of us were up, Mum would count out her money into little piles for the collectors who would come calling each week. If they didn't materialise, one of us had to queue for hours at the requisite office to pay our few shillings because – as my mother would have been quick to tell you – she couldn't abide being in debt. Not for her a bill stamped 'overdue'. No little girls were sent to answer an authoritative rat-tat-tat to inform the caller 'Mum says to tell you she's out.' I said she reminded me of Shylock from *The Merchant of Venice*. 'Yeah, well,' she responded without taking her eyes off the piles of coins, 'I just hope 'e's got more than me to play with.'

Banks were foreign territory to Mum. She neither trusted them, nor understood their reason for being. Even her Post Office savings book was a thing of the past. On rare occasions when she received a cheque she would hand it over, carefully signed, to the fishmonger Good Alf, who replaced it with cash. She always seemed surprised that it could be worth real money.

Anything left over from Mum's accounting sessions was kept in a brown striped teapot on the top shelf of the kitchen's china cupboard. The rest was set out on the sideboard with appropriate cards or folders to be marked 'paid' by the old men who called for them during the week.

One collector was short-changed regularly, and when he arrived everyone in the house except for Mum would rush through the back door as he knocked on the front. The gas man. Located under the stairs, our gas meter's appetite for pennies was so voracious sometimes we had to improvise by using substitutes. After all, if we could get by on mock eggs and mock coal, then it could make do with mock coins – such as medallions, metal buttons, a brass name tag from some dog's collar. But every now and again the fake coin jammed, and if none of us could ease it out of the slot, then – Gawd help us – we had to face the wrath of the meter man.

On the occasion I chose to stay indoors and finish my dinner in spite of his imminent arrival, I was amazed at my mother's acting skills. Even the wide-eyed Bette Davis couldn't have looked more surprised when shown the dog tag. 'So, that's where it went,' she said, straight-faced. 'I've been looking everywhere for that, ever since Fido lost it.

Ta very much.' She slipped the tag into her pinny pocket for future use.

'It reads Rick, not Fido,' the man sighed, unaware that he couldn't win this battle.

'Yes well 'im too. He lost 'is too, didn't he?' she responded without missing a beat. 'I'll not 'arf give 'im wot for when he gets 'ome.'

With that, she ushered the bewildered man through the front door, called out 'all clear' to Rose and Iris sitting in the back garden, and sat down to finish her meal.

CHAPTER TWENTY-FIVE

Victory is Ours

After a gloriously hot summer, invoking thoughts of sunny days to be spent on the beach when this abysmal war was over, the winter of 1944-5 was one of the most frigid on record. To alleviate severe coal shortages, former miners were released from the army for return to the collieries, and some of the new male conscripts were diverted to coal mining as 'Bevin Boys' (named for the Labour Minister). It didn't seem to help a lot.

This time it was Mum who came with me

to the yards for whatever small pieces of coal we could scrounge. Whereas it had-always been the custom for summer deliveries to fill our coal shed, it was now empty. Evacuated families returning from the country to damaged homes fared even worse. What heat they were able to generate flew straight out of broken doors and windows.

There was an uneasiness too about the war news. Were we celebrating an anticipated victory too soon? First there was Arnhem in Holland. In September 1944, Operation Market Garden, designed to capture an important bridge there, had been so badly bungled that British airborne units parachuted into an area heavily occupied by German troops. As a result of this cock-up, casualties were high and our lads never did reach their objective.

Connie's boyfriend at the time was a young parachutist from the Airborne Division who returned safely from Holland. Recognised by his distinctive maroon beret, Laurie was stopped by well-wishers in the street, and it was weeks before he was allowed to pay for his own beer in the pubs. With anger shadowing his grief, he described landing far from the bridge they were supposed to capture and into stiff resistance from the Germans stationed in and around the city. Now, at the kitchen table, our cups of tea in hand, a great sadness descended on us as he talked of two of his friends – their hopes for a bright future now buried with them at Arnhem.

More bad news reached us from the front in December when Jerry launched a surprise offensive in the Belgian Ardennes. The month-long 'Battle of the Bulge', so-called because of the bulge German troops drove into the region's allied lines, claimed high casualties, which made for a dismal Christmas across Britain.

After that, events moved swiftly. Every evening, those of us at home in 19 Kent huddled by our kitchen wireless for the six o'clock news. Even Mum paused in her task of counting her ration book coupons, and making notes of how they would be spent next day. She rarely commented on the war. I don't think she followed it really, other than wondering where our local boys were. And about Connie who, last we heard, was in Belgium.

Put simply, in January the Russians turned the war around with their own offensive in Eastern Europe, advancing to within forty miles of Berlin. March saw the Americans crossing the Rhine, followed by General Montgomery's men on their way to the Ruhr. Our south coast received its last doodlebug on 27 March 1945, with the final V2 of the war arriving two days later. Moaning Minnie, Wailing Willie – whatever we chose to call the siren announcing a raid – had sung its mournful tune for the last time.

President Roosevelt's death in April 1945 caused great sorrow in Britain, for the loss of a friend, a man gifted with the common touch. 'Well, we still have Our Winnie,' Mum sighed with the resignation of someone who had lost one close mate, but still had another. She remained Churchill's biggest fan. We saw him often, of course, on the Odeon's screen – touring bombed areas, giving us a pep talk, praising the little people, raising two fingers in the famed V for Victory sign. I think Mum would have laid down her life for him had it been asked of her. Instead, she shushed anyone who dared to whisper when his cherubic face smiled down on us. 'Good old Winnie', was the inevitable muttered comment, when the rotund little man grinned back at her from her *Daily Mirror.*

On 7 May 1945, victory was ours. The end of our war in Europe was heralded by the now unfamiliar sound of church bells pealing across Britain. The following day was declared a public holiday for the nation to rejoice and give thanks. From all accounts Londoners had the best of times, cramming the parks and squares, surging down The Mall to Buckingham Palace for a distant glimpse of our royal family on their famous balcony.

In residential areas throughout the land, joyous VE parties were held at schools, in clubs and on blocked-off roads. Kent Avenue had a street party, but I can't say it was as successful as those we saw on the news. Later we agreed it would have been different had we lived in London.

Ours was organised by Mrs Jones, the woman across the road who raced Mum for the horse manure. We brought out chairs and makeshift tables, which were stretched end to end along the road. To encourage singing and dancing, Dad lugged his gramophone and a few records to the front porch. For me, it all seemed a bit false. Several of our neighbours had lost loved ones. Many were new to the area, and came with children whose names we didn't know.

Mum valiantly brought out a plate of Spam sandwiches and a red jelly on the verge of collapse. I joined her, because she insisted, but as a shy fifteen-year-old, and a bit of a snob, I was uncomfortable eating sandwiches in the street with people I barely knew.

Rose was noticeably absent from the party, choosing instead to sit on the old green seat in our back garden. Mum was probably relieved, not knowing who had sent her the white feather.

Iris had wanted to go to Trafalgar Square with Lilah for London's VE Day celebrations, but didn't get further than Southend, where bunting stretched across the high street and there were enough young soldiers around for them to dance away the night.

Violet joined us briefly, until Gladys came and took her to the home of their workmate Carol, whose husband had died in Europe. Three other girls from the factory went to her tiny bungalow, and together they managed a little cheer. Tears were shed, too, for her twin boys who would never know their father.

I knew about Carol. There had still been hope, when the official notice said her husband was Missing in Action. But then, a few weeks ago, she received a letter from a gentleman in Lille who told her the sad news. It was written in French, which nobody in her family could read. Vi brought it home to me for translation. My fourth-form French was too sketchy for such an important task, and when the word *mort* leapt out at me, I took it to my French teacher for an accurate interpretation.

Sitting at her worn desk, fighting back tears, she carefully wrote a translation, word for word, telling us the writer had brought this young soldier to his house, nursed him for several days, and had promised to write to his wife if he didn't make it.

Our street party started in late afternoon, and a couple of hours later neighbours began drifting away. Dad and his brother George did a rousing 'Knees Up', before wandering off to look for some of their mates in Old Leigh's pubs. When Mum nudged me to pick up the remaining Spam sandwiches and our chairs, we joined Rose for a fresh pot of tea.

We didn't want more. We didn't say much. We thought about the long, long six years behind us, and now and again voiced our hopes for those ahead.

A certain peace did settle about us, though it took years for things to be anywhere near normal again. Bread rationing was introduced only after the war; shortages continued through the early 1950s. Wally was still fighting in Burma, from where news of Japanese atrocities to prisoners continued to reach us. Worst of all, we had seen the horror of a Nazi concentration camp in Germany close to the Belgium border.

Some time after the Normandy invasion we had received a card from Connie telling us she was in Belgium. Mum and I even saw her on the news during one of our Odeon visits. There she was, ankle deep in mud, carrying a huge duck board on her back as she helped to lay a path to the latrines. Considering her task, she looked surprisingly happy, and even managed to give a thumbs-up into the camera.

We heard little from her in the next few

months – a card from Paris, a photo from Brussels. And then one day she came home, unannounced, looking more subdued than we had ever seen her. Unbuttoning her tunic, she removed a small blue album from her pocket and placed it on the kitchen table. Inside, its photographs, taken by an American news photographer, introduced us to the atrocity that was Bergen-Belsen concentration camp.

Women guards stood in line to smile into the camera. One, according to Connie, had ordered lampshades made from human skin. Other photos showed dead bodies piled high, like so much rubbish ready for the dump. Crouched against a wall, dazed skeleton-like figures in tattered prison stripes looked as if they neither knew nor cared what was going on. The camp commandant, Joseph Kramer, smiled benignly at us with all the confidence of someone who has done no wrong. 'Keep this for ever, kid,' the photographer had told Connie, 'so you and yours never forget this hell hole.'

When the concentration camp in Lower Saxony was liberated by the British 11th Armoured Division in April 1945, Connie's unit was asked for volunteers to help care for its victims. Anyone accepting the challenge, they were warned, would see things so terrible they could be seared into their minds for ever, and nobody would be thought less of if they chose not to go.

Connie was one of the first to sign up. Now, at home, she showed us the three- by four-inch photo album, stared at each of the damning photographs and said it was hell, but offered little more on her experience at the camp.

We dared to hope the pictures lied, that they were bizarre fakes. But of course they weren't. Next day similar images were splashed across our copy of the *Daily Mirror*, and other papers at newsstands all over the country. At the Odeon we saw the walking corpses, the sickening piles of bodies, the gas chambers.

We learned that approximately 50,000 inmates died at Bergen-Belsen, 35,000 of them during this 1945 spring alone. Among these was Anne Frank, the little Jewish girl taken by typhus here in March of that year, and whose diary later earned her a place in history. Unlike Auschwitz-Birkenau, Bergen-Belsen did not have gas chambers to annihilate its prisoners. These were victims of hunger, cold, disease and brutality. Originally designed to hold 10,000 inmates, the camp population had swelled to 60,000. Most were Jews, others whose only crime was to be homosexuals or gypsies.

Because of Connie's first-hand knowledge of Belsen, we followed news stories about it more closely than those of other camps. And so we learned that forty-eight members of its staff were tried. Eleven of them – including the despicable commandant, Kramer, also known as the Beast of Belsen – were hanged.

In the 1950s, on a picture-perfect autumn day at a lakeside cottage in central Ontario, Connie opened up just a little to me. 'I never thought I'd ever see anything this beautiful, ever again,' she whispered, staring at a shoreline ablaze with orange and gold maple trees. I knew she was back in the dark place to which she sometimes retreated, her eyes glazed, her beautiful face blank.

She told me her job, and that of the other ATS girls, was to bathe the blistered faces of hideously emaciated and scarred victims suffering from a skin disease. Like so many of the prisoners, they may have had typhus. She didn't say. 'They thought I was an angel,' Connie whispered on that day by the lake. 'Can you believe that? When I washed them and fed them, not knowing whether they would live or die, some of them looked at me and asked if I was an angel.'

Forty years later, in Connie's possessions, I came across a small brown box containing three medals. Had every soldier received similar citations or were they awarded for bravery? I will never know. I like to think one was for her special work at Bergen-Belsen, which called on the courage of a young girl barely out of her teens.

CHAPTER TWENTY-SIX

Off to Grandmother's House We Go

Between the two world wars, most of my father's family left London, and although several came to Leigh-on-Sea we didn't know them well. Right here on our estate we had his brother George at 39 Kent, and their sister Mag living with her family up on Suffolk, while a third brother, Harry, had a house just below Leigh Broadway. Harry was a conductor, which meant a free ride for any of us boarding his tram into Southend. I seldom saw Uncle George who worked on the railway, but if we met his wife (Aunt Mill) in one of the queues, Mum would stop and chat. Dad was more up-to-date with their news, because he ran into one or another in local pubs, but as families we didn't socialise.

We had already moved to Church Hill when one of Dad's numerous stepbrothers brought their mother, Topsy, to live in the Old Town. With her sight failing, they wanted her out of London traffic, before she met the fate of her last husband, who was killed by a double-decker during one of the city's infamous pea-souper fogs.

Despite her rapidly declining vision, Topsy commanded her grandchildren to Sunday tea, instructing each one to bring a darning needle. And so Sunday afternoons saw several of the little Hobbs girls – without their mother, who stayed home with the latest baby – hand in hand, walking through Old Leigh with needles threaded through the yokes of their dresses. A sewing bee? Darning instruction? Not on your nelly! They were to be served brown bread and butter with fresh winkles, and required the needles to extricate flesh from the shells. Always the girls re-turned home with beauty spots on their faces created from the little caps removed from their winkles.

I don't remember the winkle teas, but one of my earliest memories is of Sunday morn-ings when Dad was supposed to be taking Iris and me for a healthy walk along the seafront. Instead we stopped by one of the Old Town's several pubs where, along with other happy youngsters, we sat on the kerb eating plate-sized water biscuits while our father downed a pint or two inside with his mates. It was some years before my mother tumbled as to why we were never hungry for her cooked lunch on Sundays.

Up-to-date news of Mum's family in Camberwell Green was scant. Her mother was always a little frightening to me. A diminutive figure dressed in black, she would sit hunched in her worn armchair by the window from where she could keep an eye on passers-by. By her side was a large trumpet, which she held to her ear if she was interested in what was being said.

On pre-war visits Mum took me to Camberwell, and Iris too if there was nobody at home to keep an eye on her. If our transportation was on time – a rare occasion even then – it was at least a two hours' journey door to door. And yet when we arrived, exhausted, the parrot was more chatty than Gran.

I suspect our visit, though, was mainly to see Mum's older sister. Grace, bless her, smothered us in hugs and kisses, provided enormous teas (even though it was lunchtime) and cried when we left. A puzzlement to me was that Grace looked old enough to be Mum's mother, while my Gran could well have been hers. There was a third sibling, Ted, an elusive man, older than Grace and purportedly a resident of the same house although I never saw him. He was their provider, a smart dresser, unless the photo on Gran's sideboard lied, and apparently into some slightly shady dealings in addition to his day job at a racetrack.

As a seven- or eight-year-old I never questioned their circumstances. The family member I enjoyed most was Sinbad, a red, gold and blue parrot rescued from a pub whose owner planned on having him put down when his verbal abuse to patrons became too much. Sinbad's main quest in life was to sit on a pole in Gran's doorway issuing profanities to everyone who passed by. Aunt Grace's threat to wash his mouth out with carbolic soap always caused me to smile. One look at his huge beak and I knew he'd never let her do that.

During the war we were out of touch with Gran and Grace for months on end. Uncle Ted's cards saying all was well were sporadic at best, while Kath's visits ceased a couple of years back. Now the time had come for us to see if all was still well with them.

I agreed to accompany my mother to Camberwell at the first opportunity, which turned out to be a hot July day. By now you'll understand that we had to wear our best outfits, which for me meant my school clothes. (I don't think there was another girl in Britain who wore her school uniform during the summer holidays.) Mum was dressed in one of her floral print frocks, a navy straw hat and crippling shoes that made no concession to her ever-tender bunion. In her basket she carried assorted foods from her secret cache at the back of the pantry, including some precious tea in a tin caddy.

Our journey was more than tiring; fraught

with anxiety, it was debilitating. London was hot and dusty, and the bomb damage proved heartbreaking. Repeatedly Mum wiped her face with a tiny white handkerchief, one of several she owned with forget-me-nots embroidered in the corner. Whether she was simply perspiring, or also crying, I couldn't tell.

Whatever the level of her distress, it was amplified by a wailing 'Oh my Gawwwd' when we reached Gran's street to find some houses were no more than piles of bricks. Others looked habitable, until we came close enough to see unhinged doors and missing windows and walls at angles indicating severe structural damage.

Perched on a mound of bricks and jagged concrete slabs beside a still-standing pub, two workmen sat eating their lunch. Replicas of Dad, dressed in cement-dusted dungarees with heavy boots on their feet and chequered flat caps planted on their heads, they stared at us as we stared back. 'Looking for some-one, muvver?' the smaller man enquired amiably. Mum dropped herself on a pile of blocks beside them, and wiped her plum-red face yet again.

''Ere, me luv, 'ave a drop of tea. Okay, missus?'

They looked concerned. I stood there like a dummy, clutching the heavy basket as the man called Will poured strong brown tea from his flask into its bakelite cup. My mother gratefully gulped it down.

'What 'appened? she finally managed.

In their cockney accents, far too rich for me to fully understand, they told us everyone was gone. Some copped it. Some were 're'oused by the govinmint'.

On the verge of total collapse, Mum moaned into her hanky. I crouched beside her, clutching her ice-cold hand. Will added that he didn't know where the survivors had been relocated, poor bleeders. 'Most of 'em caught it some time gone. Incendiaries. Fire spread through 'em like they was matchboxes...' By now Mum had turned ashen.

A few moments' silence ensued before Wilf's mate spoke up for the first time. Gulping down the last of his tea, he suddenly remembered. 'All gorn 'cept the 'Oly Terror. Lives with 'er daugh'er.' Mum stared in disbelief. I asked if this ''Oly Terror' ever used an ear trumpet. Wilf nodded excitedly. 'Not to be disrespectful, missus, but we call 'er that cos she won't let nobody move 'er for love nor money. Looks 'alf asleep till you get close, then she'll clout you one with the trumpet as soon as look at yer.'

As if shot from a cannon, Mum was on her feet and straightening her dress. 'Thanks, mate,' she said hoarsely, handing Wilf her empty cup. Picking up our basket, I followed as she set off at a trot along the war-ravaged street. Had Miss White been there, she would definitely have told her to straighten her hat.

It was eerily like an abandoned film set. Before the war this street was alive with people. Women chatting in their doorways, a baby on one hip and a basket of washing on the other. Little girls skipping rope, boys shooting marbles in the gutter. Laughter emanated from the communal backyard where women gathered to do their washing in large stone sinks, rubbing their knuckles bare on corrugated washboards, having a laugh. Now it was deserted, but for the two labourers at the far end. And us.

There was no response to our knock on the door of Gran's house, and we couldn't see clearly through lace curtains covering the windows. Thinking she saw a shadow of movement inside, Mum rapped harder. 'All right, all right ... keep your 'air on. 'Old your 'orses will you...' was accompanied by shuffling and bumping, as a piece of furniture was moved from behind the door.

Slowly the crooked green door opened a crack to reveal a very thin, very old-looking Grace. Her stringy grey hair was pulled tightly into a bun at the back of her head, her face was pale and worn. Visibly relieved that we weren't from the authorities, she perked up considerably. 'Sorry about the knocker, luv. Someone went and nicked it, didn't they?' Then, looking from Mum to me, the penny dropped. 'Gawd love us, if it isn't young Ede,' she gasped, both hands flying to her mouth.

Happily Grace tugged Mum into the semi-dark room, hugging her close. My mother introduced me, in my stupid uniform, and I too was hugged. Grace turned to the tiny woman by the window, wrapped in a black shawl so voluminous only her lace-up boots were visible below it. 'Look, Mother. It's our Ede and her youngest,' she bellowed. Gran nodded in recognition. She had no teeth; wisps of white hair poked from the all-enveloping shawl. Eyes like two currants showed no more than a flicker of interest as they stared from her daughter to me.

Their home, or what was left of it, consisted of a front room with a large iron bed in the middle, surrounded by pieces of damaged furniture. I can't think that they had electricity, yet somewhere in the dimness Grace put the kettle on for tea. Their water source was a rusting iron bucket by the back door. I sat on the edge of a backless chair watching Mum and Grace eagerly catching up.

There was a similarity to their faces I hadn't noticed before. Now, a glowing animation took over, brushing out the worry lines, the care-worn set of their mouths, anxiety in the eyes so commonplace these days. They could have been two young girls gabbling on about a party the night before, or a summer holiday. Not that teen parties and holidays were ever on the slate for these two women. But at least here and now they knew love and joy.

Excitedly, Grace told me I was so smart in my posh uniform, and so big, she'd never have recognised me. And how was Jack? Still in the navy? She thought of him often, so handsome in his sailor suit, and young Ede with all them little girls.

Mum explained that Dad was in the first war, not the second. But yes, thanks, he was well. 'Of course he is. Like our Ted,' Grace carried on, not pausing to think. 'Moved out he has. Lives with his fancy piece in Upton. Comes round now and agin though, brings a bit of food and a few bob. Does well by us, our Ted.'

Momentarily lost in thought, she then wrenched open the dresser's stubborn drawer and lifted out a snowy damask cloth, which she spread on the bed's tattered quilt. Next, from under the bed she retrieved two large biscuit tins containing – if you can believe – miniature sausage rolls, salmon sandwiches and tiny iced cakes. We were handed dainty plates with scalloped edges, and told to dig in. I felt sure I had stepped into Alice's Wonderland.

Gran was passed a selection of food,

which she broke into crumbs and put in her mouth with claw-like hands. Noisily sucking on her food, she nodded her thanks to Grace. Mum and I were handed cups of tea. Before either of us could speculate on the incongruity of our sitting here in a bombed-out house, enjoying an elegant tea, Grace told us how she profited from cleaning the pub at the end of the road. Just a couple of hours each morning, she explained. Hardly worth turning out for really, but the people were lovely. They let her use the bathroom and gave her left-overs if there was a wedding or something.

Saturday's groom had done a bunk to goodness knows where, so there was no reception. The bride's dad got on the blower to explain the situation, and invited everyone at the pub to share the spoils. 'A real bit of luck you came today to share them with Mother and me,' she added generously.

All animation was gone, as a sobered Aunt Grace told Mum about life-long mates who were her former neighbours. The few survivors of two attacks that destroyed their street were now relocated. Only she and Gran remained. 'They're coming for us any day now,' she offered in hushed tones as if her mother could hear. 'Tried before but Mother wouldn't 'ave it. I think they'll just pick her up and put 'er in an ambulance or something when they're ready...' Ted did find them a place in the country a month or so back, she added, but Gran had refused to budge. Nobody could talk any sense into her these days.

'Remember how fly she used to be?' she suddenly grinned. 'Remember, luv? If the milkman left an 'alf-pint instead of a pint, she'd run after 'im blowing 'er whistle.' Mum nodded and smiled, although she was probably long gone by the time Gran relied on a whistle to get the milkman's attention.

Plucking up the courage to finally say something, I enquired about Sinbad. 'Oh 'im.' Grace rolled her eyes dramatically. 'Left us 'igh and dry, that one. Joined the army I'm told, or was it the navy? Ask your dad. He's sure to have run into 'im somewhere on the seas.' She stared thoughtfully through the curtained window. 'Well good riddance to bad rubbish I say. Always thought 'e was too good for us. Had a sea-faring background you see...'

I looked away. This was a parrot she was talking about. Embarrassed, Mum dusted the crumbs from her dress into her hand, studied her little Rolex and said we'd best be going.

The biggest shock of the day for me was when I opened the back door, which I thought led upstairs to a toilet, and found it blocked by rubble held in place by wire mesh. 'Oh no, darlin',' Grace said apologetically, 'you 'afta go to the pub for their lav. Tell 'em Gracie sent you.' We kissed Gran's papery face, ice-cold in spite of the hot little room, and hugged my aunt. I asked her to send us her new address so we could visit. She nodded absently. 'It'll be difficult getting used to a new place, not knowing streets and all. But I'll 'ave to won't I? Ted will send you our address. I'll make sure of it.'

In the train to Leigh my mother told me she would always be grateful to Grace, who had insisted she stayed at school till she was fourteen, while others in the neighbourhood left much earlier. Ted was twelve when he finished his formal education and began supporting the family. Grace, she was pretty sure, had never gone to school. Couldn't read or write, so yes it would be rough for her living somewhere new.

Towards the end of summer Mum and I met Uncle Ted in a Southend café. He wore a long loose camel-haired coat over a check suit, and a saucy pork pie hat instead of the traditional cap favoured by working men. He gave us a slip of paper with an address on it, saying Gran and Grace were doing well in Barking, in a nice ground-floor flat he had been instrumental in getting for them.

Other than that he had little to say. It was hard to believe he and Mum were brother and sister. Perhaps thinking of Dad's thread-bare herringbone coat, she commented on Ted's nice clothes, and he agreed he was doing well even if he did say so 'imself. On leaving, he gave me a five-pound note with which to buy 'some sweeties'. It was the first fiver I had ever seen. I never asked what was in the bulging envelope he gave my mother, but can guess it held many more. Ted was a spiv, a wide boy, a new breed of businessman who grew out of the war to deal in the black-market.

CHAPTER TWENTY-SEVEN

Our Winnie Gets the Old Heave-ho

Mum was beside herself. Here her Winnie had brought us through this war as she always knew he would, and now it was over there was talk of giving him the old heave-ho. Tossing him aside like a used rag. And here was Dad, acting as if he'd won the Irish Sweepstakes – sitting on the back porch, clucking like some old hen with his head buried in the newspaper. 'Our time has come, Ede' or 'The man of the hour is Our Clem now, not Our Winnie' were his favourite phrases. We just wished he would shut up about the approaching election, and go back to saying he had almost, but not quite won the pools.

As I've said before, my mother thought the world of Churchill. Sitting there in the darkened Odeon she admitted to fancying Clark Gable and Humphrey Bogart. But really it was the rotund Winston with his winning smile and V for Victory sign whom she idolised. Beaming back up at his puckish face on the silver screen, her faith in him never wavered. She wasn't alone, of course. When he toured the bombed areas, victims who had lost everything managed to exude good cheer in response to his two-finger salute.

On VE Day, when Churchill shouted to the masses gathered in Whitehall that this was their victory, they responded with a heartfelt 'No. It's yours,' then followed him in an emotional rendition of 'Land of Hope and Glory'. Mum would have given the world, she said, to have been there.

Although he had been in and out of politics for decades, Churchill came to our notice in May 1940 when King George VI asked him to be Prime Minister and to form an all-party government. His first wartime speech booming from our kitchen wireless informed us he had nothing to offer but 'blood, toil, tears and sweat'. This was confident and inspired, but the one that really got Mum – the oratory she liked to repeat to herself and anyone else who would listen – included those most famous lines: 'We shall fight on the beaches, we shall fight on the landing grounds, we shall fight in the fields and in the streets, we shall fight in the hills: we shall never surrender.' It caused Mum to stand tall, and straighten her corset under her dress as if preparing to face the Hun. 'Nevah surrendah' she repeated with perfect mimicry. Yes, those were the words she had needed to hear.

All these years later there are few who could be anything but impressed by his rhetoric, his rumbling voice, his determined scowl that earned him the 'bulldog' caricatures in newspapers and magazines. As for my mother, I don't know that she could have kept going through the war without Churchill's encouragement. His evangelistic zeal lifted her up in the darkest of times.

Although Mum didn't follow the war battle by battle as my father did, back in 1940 all of us were only too aware that the fall of France had propelled the enemy to practically within spitting distance. This news brought a quiver to her lips, there in the kitchen as our Prime Minister told us to brace ourselves to our duties, and so bear ourselves that if the British Empire and its Commonwealth last for a thousand years men will still say, 'This was their finest hour.'

Even Dad didn't sneer at that one.

It was his common touch that endeared Winnie to the British public in general, and women in particular. Propaganda pictures reflected an ordinary bloke in his dressing gown and slippers, or eating in the mess hall with troops at the front. They even captured him trowel in hand, as if doing a bit of bomb repair work. He was, after all, a competent bricklayer who had personally constructed outbuildings on his Chartwell estate in Kent.

So my mother had a right to be incensed that summer, when everything indicated her hero would be tossed aside after returning the country to peace.

Actually, this newfound peace took some getting used to. Sitting on the garden seat one Sunday morning, scraping carrots with unwarranted concentration, I was joined by Rose carrying two cups of tea. 'Listen, Pam,' she instructed.

'What?'

'Nothing. No buzz-bombs. No cries for help. No need to look up if a plane goes by.' She blew on her scalding drink before sipping it gingerly. 'Doesn't seem real does it?'

I knew what she meant. I continued to stare fearfully at the full moon, while an aircraft flying overhead caused my stomach to turn over. I still had to run to Woolworth's or the Co-Op when tipped off that something edible was to be put on sale; Mum kept on queueing endlessly for shopping and services. But, the fight was gone from us. Those brave – keep your pecker up, luv – faces, worn for the past six years, had now slipped. We wanted to eat decent meals off unchipped plates. We needed new clothes and curtains and a hall mat we didn't trip over regularly. And, according to my father and his mates, we needed a new government.

The man to lift us up now, people were saying, was not that war-monger Churchill. It was Clement Attlee, deputy prime minister in the wartime coalition government, who was about to become prime minister of a Labour government with fifty per cent of the total votes in the 5 July 1945 general election.

Politics were earnestly debated at school, where I'd say some ninety per cent of students and staff members were Conservative. While I couldn't bring myself to speak up in class, I had no problem parroting what I heard to Dad, who for his part took pleasure in taunting me about the preachings of my uppity teachers.

Oh the arrogance and ignorance of youth! My repetitive theme was that if you chose to educate yourself, better your life through hard work and dedication, you should be allowed to enjoy your riches. Take my father. Had he followed his wife's urgings he would have his own building business by now and a nice house on the seafront. Never once did it occur to me that he wanted neither.

As a young teenager, I angered him as much as he frustrated me. What I saw was an intelligent, hard-working and honest man – humbled by authority into believing that neither he nor his children should 'rise above their station'.

Now it's too late to tell him, I fully understand his subservient manner, his contempt for anyone who used his head instead of hands to earn a living. And his lowly ambitions that were limited to merely making ends meet. It took me years to realise he had simply been hammered into the ground once too often. Given half a chance, he always left his wife to talk to the few professionals who ventured into our lives. His Ede had no problem with this. The 'yes sir, no sir, three bags full sir' attitude was not for Mum, who could argue the hind leg off a donkey when she thought she was right. And even if she didn't.

So of course my father was thrilled at the prospects of a Labour government, which promised full employment and a tax-funded National Health Service. Their slogans and messages were applauded by many whose memories of the aftermath of the First

World War remained fresh. In 1918, young men who survived the trenches returned home to gloomy prospects. Affordable housing was unattainable and jobs scarce, while medical attention often became a nightmare involving hospital charity wards, excruciatingly long waits for treatment and an uncaring staff.

Heaven knows I heard the stories often enough to show my father a little compassion. Especially the tale about my birth in that tiny house on Church Hill. Born prematurely, and thought to weigh no more than two pounds (no scales at home, and it was considered too risky to take me to the greengrocer's to be weighed, as would happen with a larger infant), I resembled a small doll wrapped in a blanket and placed in an open dresser drawer beside my parents' bed.

The midwife in attendance had rushed up the hill to fetch a doctor. When he arrived, he asked sarcastically if my mother had a cold. 'Yes,' she is said to have replied, 'my cold is there in the drawer.' Glancing into the makeshift cot, the doctor decided there was no way he could help 'that'. His business here was to save the mother of all these children sitting wide-eyed around the room. Mum had a monstrously high fever, for which a neighbour was pressing cold flannels on her face. Medication was prescribed, and she recovered in time. On his way home from the chemist, Dad scrounged two orange crates from the greengrocer with which to make my coffin.

Enter the neighbour's son, who had recently nursed a motherless baby rabbit with milk in an eye dropper. Illustrating a patience seldom attributed to a twelve-year-old boy, young Lennie cradled this little scrap of humanity for hours, singing softly and feeding me with that same dropper. At six months I was a fat and happy infant, spoiled by everyone on the terrace. I would love to say Lennie went on to be an asset to the medical profession, but we moved away from the hill when I was five, and our families lost touch.

Then there was the matter of Edie's arm. While the doctor who dismissed me as a gonner was callous, another was downright negligent. As a little girl, my eldest sister Edie broke her arm when she fell on the wickedly steep Church Hill. Dad took her on the crossbar of his bicycle to a Southend hospital, where she was treated and sent home. When they went back to have the plaster removed, he was dismayed to see the arm hanging at an awkward angle, and blurted out as much. The doctor replied that it was good enough for scrubbing floors, and 'Ha ha ha, it's not as if she will ever be a concert pianist wearing evening dresses, is it now?'

Seething all the way home, my father's humiliation was nothing compared to Mum's fury as she sent him straight back to get the arm reset. Decades later, she told us she had never been so relieved as when Dad came home with a small brown velvet coat on his handlebars, but no Edie. It meant the hospital had kept their daughter overnight to put her arm right.

Dentistry had its own horror stories. Like the one about my mother waking from a full anaesthetic in the hospital's dental clinic to find she had no teeth, even though she had been sent there to have only two extracted. She was a young woman, in her early thirties, when the obnoxious dentist told her he had taken all her teeth to save her having to make return visits.

Before Britain's national health programme brought satisfactory care to everyone, school nurses were usually the first to detect health problems in children. Regularly a nurse and her assistant would arrive to set up a small clinic in our school hall. Row by row pupils would have their ears, eyes, teeth and hair inspected. If a child had head fleas, a letter was sent home with instructions for treatment. Anything more serious was dealt with at a public clinic, divided into sections. My few appointments there were in the dental section, where a local anaesthetic was given only if it was considered really necessary.

On my last visit at about age seven, I remember the dentist and his assistant arguing heatedly about an issue unrelated to my teeth. I began to cry. In an unwarranted display of temper he slapped my leg and told me not to be a baby. I screamed for the one person I knew would help me. Rushing in from the waiting room, Mum pushed the startled dentist out of the way and yanked me from the chair, sending a tray of instruments flying across the floor. Later, we heard that the dental clinic was closed for the rest of the day. As for my decayed tooth, it was treated by Rose's employer when my mother could spare some of her hard-earned cleaning money to pay for his services.

So yes, had I recalled these stories in 1945 I may have been more sympathetic to Dad's reaction, when he and his friend Bill stayed up all night listening to election news with noisy jubilation. By morning the results were crystal-clear, although in a computer-free age it took three more weeks for confirmation of the official tally.

CHAPTER TWENTY-EIGHT

What's It All Been For?

A hundred days separated the German surrender from that of the Japanese, and there wasn't one went by without we thought of Wally, still fighting in Burma. His letters to Kath were irregular, heavily censored and so old when they arrived they did nothing to alleviate fears for her husband's safety. Her biggest dread was that he had been captured.

Towards the end of the war, one of the first questions asked when learning of a son's or brother's imprisonment by the enemy was 'Jap or Jerry?' If the answer was 'Jerry' there'd be a loud sigh of relief, on the understanding that the Germans treated their prisoners fairly well.

Captives in the hands of the Japanese lived in appalling conditions, and as stories of those camps' atrocities filtered down to us they added to our anxiety. Kath and Valerie made frequent though still short visits to Leigh during the weeks between VE and VJ Day. Train services were as erratic as ever, but since ours was no longer a restricted area my sister didn't require a pass to get in.

One of the few bright lights for us was four-year-old Valerie, as golden-haired as the rest of us at that age. Kath even ventured out to the cinema with Rose, leaving her daughter with Mum and me.

Not that the newsreels offered any joy. Gone was the excitement of war heroes such as Monty and Winnie and even Ike boasting another victory. Instead we saw the devastation in Germany, where women and children scavenged in rubbish dumps for food. One scene showed a mother peeling bark from a tree to feed to her little girl. We were told that close to two million civilians died in Germany following the end of hostilities. Most were very old or very young, or already weakened by hunger. Even so there was more anger than sympathy in Britain when we learned our ships were delivering food and supplies to the Germans instead of to us.

Although we didn't expect a quick fix from our new government, we hadn't anticipated additional hardships. And although we weren't down to eating bark, still our rations had diminished to skimpy portions. Two ounces of butter and three ounces of margarine could be used up in a couple of sandwiches, yet in those victorious postwar years this was our weekly allowance. Bread was rationed for the first time, meat limited to a shilling's worth each week.

Rose, now out of a job, was disinclined to find another. And following her demob Connie couldn't settle. We never knew where she was until she came back, usually from Paris or Brussels with silk stockings, and canvas shoes sporting high wedge heels, which were readily sold to girls in Vi's factory.

Horrors more damning than we believed possible in our lifetime brought about the end of the war in the Far East. On 6 August 1945, an American aircraft – named Enola Gay for the pilot's mother – released an atomic bomb on the Japanese city of Hiroshima. In stunned disbelief, Mum, Rose and I sat in the High Street's Odeon, watching that giant mushroom cloud and its effects on a terrified population. Screaming children with skin hanging from their arms and legs ran through the streets, stark terror on their faces, their bodies disintegrating before us.

Three days later a second atomic bomb was dropped on Nagasaki. In Hiroshima an estimated 80,000 people died, and a further 60,000 expired over the following months. According to statistics, Nagasaki's dead totalled 73,884, with close to 100,000 more injured or diseased from the nuclear attack. Almost all the victims were civilians, innocent of any war crimes.

We left the Odeon in silence. Ahead of me,

Mum limped up the aisle to an exit, leaning heavily on every seat she passed. Her rheumatism, she said, was troublesome today. The war had aged her so, she looked far older than her fifty years. Her cheap dress had rucked up at the back, showing her gartered stockings. The bulging black leather bag she held on her arm had its handle repaired with green cotton. Her hair, the colour of liquid honey before the war, was now liberally laced with white.

Past a line of people waiting to witness the horrendous spectacle that had left us numb, we continued to the bus stop. No tea at Lyons today, as was the custom. We needed to get home. Easing a bunioned foot painfully out of her over-sized Joyce shoe, Mum turned to me as our double-decker came into view, and asked, 'So, what do they say at that posh school of yours, Pam? You tell me now. What's all this been for?'

Truthfully I told her I didn't know.

Postscript

Mum and dad lived out their years at 19 Kent. The building boom kept my father steadily employed. He even won a few pounds on the pools now and then. Mum went back to nurturing her roses with Clarabelle at her side, and until she was well into her eighties continued her daily treks to the shops on Leigh Broadway. My parents chose not to own a car or a telephone, or even a house, but did enjoy a small television set bought in 1953 so they could watch the coronation of Elizabeth II.

Edie and her little family, virtually untouched by the war, continued to live quietly in the Essex countryside.

Rose's mental condition deteriorated, so in the post-war years she was hospitalised from time to time. Nobody could say for sure whether her condition resulted from the war injury. In 1952 my parents were persuaded she should have a frontal lobotomy. We were told it would make her happy but docile, and I suppose it did, although the Rose we knew was gone long before she died in the 1960s.

Kath is my only sister alive as I write this.

Following Wally's safe return from Burma a year after the war's end, he became a successful building contractor in London. Eventually they retired to Chelmsford, where Kath lives still, enjoying good health, the closeness of her family, lunches in country pubs and her prolific garden.

Violet lived in Leigh all her life. Lionel continued to be a submariner after the war, while Vi worked at Skyborne on and off for more than fifty years. Until her health failed, they loved to travel and visited us several times in Canada.

Connie, too restless to settle in Leigh, emigrated to Canada in 1947. There, she became a successful businesswoman, eventually marrying a former Royal Air Force flyer who had spent much of the war in a German prisoner-of-war camp. They retired to Bournemouth in the early 1980s, returning often to Canada.

Iris and Lilah remained friends, working together for several seasons at Butlin's Holiday Camp in Clacton. Iris's wedding in 1952 was a happy occasion, accompanied by the pealing of bells at St Clement's church atop the hill where we were born. The entire family attended, as did Aunty Min and Uncle Fred, who drove from Derbyshire with Sylvie and stayed for a week.

I joined Connie in Toronto in 1950. For nineteen years from the early seventies I wrote travel articles exclusively for the *Globe and Mail*. When my assignments took me to England, or to destinations I could reach via London, I always managed to meet some of my sisters for a pub lunch in Leigh Old Town. Inevitably, as talk turned to the war, I was given additional titbits to include in my book. When I last saw Iris she said she wanted two things: to read my account of our war years and to visit Disney World. Sadly, she didn't live long enough to see this book, but she loved Disney World.

Acknowledgements

For me this is the end of an almost continuous journey which began seventy years ago. A journey of love and generosity but also one of sadness, as together with family and friends I have dredged up some memories we would have preferred to forget. And so it is a real pleasure, finally, to be able to thank the most important players in my story. My late parents and sisters, who so often recalled for me their parts in our war. My sister Kath, now in her ninetieth year and clearly not wanting to remember, but doing so anyway – with the help of her daughter Valerie Browne. Jill Berry, for her support and encouragement ever since she read an early draft of this manuscript five years ago. In Australia, Eileen Pennycott, a good friend for more than sixty years, who lived through the war and called frequently (usually in the middle of the night) with suggestions and ideas to be included. In California, my daughter Liza and her husband Paul, for their continued support and encouragement. My agent Ian Drury for introducing me to editor Charlotte Cole of Ebury Press, who had me dig just a little deeper for memories I didn't know were there. Her understanding of the subject, and enthusiasm for it, have been intoxicating.

In Canada too I have had overwhelming support from people who were evacuated, or know somebody who was. My two daughters here in Toronto, Sarah and Susan, have been hearing this story for decades, yet still found time in their busy lives to read the evolving manuscript and give insightful comments. Above all, there's my husband Michael, to thank publicly for his research and for being there always to cheer me on.

The publishers hope that this book has given you enjoyable reading. Large Print Books are especially designed to be as easy to see and hold as possible. If you wish a complete list of our books please ask at your local library or write directly to:

Magna Large Print Books
Magna House, Long Preston,
Skipton, North Yorkshire.
BD23 4ND

This Large Print Book, for people
who cannot read normal print,
is published under the auspices of

THE ULVERSCROFT FOUNDATION